We Shall Not Be Moved

The University of Georgia Press

Athens and London

We Shall Not

Robert A. Pratt

Be Moved

The Desegregation of the
University of Georgia

© 2002 by the University of Georgia Press
Athens, Georgia 30602
All rights reserved
Designed by Louise OFarrell
Set in 10/14 New Caledonia by Bookcomp, Inc.
Printed and bound by Thomson-Shore
The paper in this book meets the guidelines for
permanence and durability of the Committee on
Production Guidelines for Book Longevity of the
Council on Library Resources.

Printed in the United States of America
06 05 04 03 02 C 5 4 3 2

Library of Congress Cataloging-in-Publication Data

Pratt, Robert A., 1958–
    We shall not be moved : the desegregation of the University of Georgia
/ Robert A. Pratt.
        p. cm.
    Includes bibliographical references and index.
    ISBN 0-8203-2399-3 (alk. paper)
    1. University of Georgia—Students—History. 2. College
integration—Georgia—Athens—History. 3. African Americans—Civil rights.
I. Title.
    LD1986 .P73 2002
    378.758'18—dc21   2001054841

British Library Cataloging-in-Publication Data available

For my wife, Anita, and our
children, Raven Naomi and
Steven Robert Armstead, and
for my mother, Barbara E. Pratt
(1938–2001), whose eternal
presence continues to order my
steps.

And to the memory of my "other"
mother, Doris D. Lavender
(1929–1999), and my mentor and
friend, Armstead L. Robinson
(1947–1995).

Contents

Preface

Except for the *Dred Scott* decision of 1857, the most devastating judicial decision ever rendered against African Americans in the United States was perhaps the Supreme Court's 1896 ruling in *Plessy v. Ferguson.* As a consequence of the Court's legalization of "separate but equal," constructions of blackness and whiteness—already ingrained in the American psyche—now had the imprimatur of the law, and perceived racial differences soon became the defining feature of virtually every aspect of political, social, and economic life in American society. The defense of white privilege and the sanctity of the white race became rallying cries for those whites who stubbornly refused to acknowledge that the South had indeed lost the Civil War and that the descendants of African slaves were fully entitled to all the privileges associated with citizenship. But the fight for racial equality would be a long and difficult one, and many lives, black and white, would be lost in the process.

For most of the twentieth century, legalized segregation was enforced by law and by custom. The separation of black and white children in the classroom was one terrible aspect of segregation. Separate was not, and never had been, equal. Led by Charles Hamilton Houston in the 1930s, the National Association for the Advancement of Colored People mounted a legal assault on Jim Crow education. The NAACP focused many of its early efforts on the nation's white colleges and universities, believing that white resistance to desegregation in higher education would be less protracted than at the lower levels, where the number of blacks coming into contact with whites would be far greater. Further, since many states simply did not have graduate or professional schools for blacks, the separate but equal argument could hardly be sustained. Fairness would seem to dictate that African Americans would have to be admitted into educational institutions for whites if no institutions existed for blacks.

After rulings in *Pearson v. Murray* (1936), *Gaines v. Canada* (1938), *Sweatt v. Painter* (1950), and *McLaurin v. Oklahoma State Regents* (1950), in which the courts had ordered admittance of black plaintiffs into white universities to pursue degree programs that did not exist in black colleges, NAACP attorneys had reason to be optimistic. But many white universities, especially those in the states of the former Confederacy, refused to go one step beyond what the courts had ordered. The Supreme Court's eventual repudiation of *Plessy* with the 1954 *Brown v. Board of Education* decision did not signal societal acceptance of integration, but rather a declaration of war in defense of segregation, and many of the battles would be fought on the nation's school grounds and college campuses. Emboldened by their political leaders who had staked their careers on continued defiance of integration and by the vast number of southern whites who were determined to resist any and all federal government encroachment for as long as possible, officials at white southern universities adamantly refused to desegregate. As the nation moved into the second half of the century, the color line separating black from white appeared to be deeply entrenched and enduring.

What follows is the story of a dedicated group of black lawyers and plaintiffs who shared a commitment to equal justice and who, along with their white allies, were determined to break down racial barriers at the University of Georgia. This study not only chronicles the achievements of those early freedom fighters but also reveals the various ruses and subterfuge that state lawmakers and university officials were willing to use in order to keep blacks out, including outright deception. Knowing that race could no longer be used as a legal means of excluding blacks from the all-white campus, Georgia lawmakers and university officials, including the university chancellor and the president, one after another took the witness stand and swore under oath, as late as 1961, that race had never been used to disqualify black applicants, despite the fact that none had ever been admitted. In their determination to maintain segregation, they subverted the legal process. When the state's lies were finally exposed, and when the federal courts decided that justice had been delayed long enough, two black students, Hamilton Earl Holmes and Charlayne Alberta Hunter, were admitted to the University of Georgia, ending 175 years of de jure and de facto segregation at the state's flagship university.

But there are two stories here. While the desegregation of the University of Georgia is the primary focus and white southern resistance and subterfuge the overriding themes, at times the life of Horace T. Ward will take center stage. In 1950, Ward applied to the University of Georgia's School of Law. He subsequently refused the state's offer of out-of-state aid and insisted that his application be evaluated on its merit, becoming the first African American to do so. After being denied admission on the grounds that he was unqualified, Ward sued. In 1957, six and a half years after he first applied, Ward's suit was dismissed on several technicalities, and he went on to earn a law degree from Northwestern University. But with law degree in hand, he returned to Athens, Georgia, in 1960 and became part of the legal team that would claim victory with the admission of Hamilton Holmes and Charlayne Hunter, who had filed suit for admission to the University of Georgia the year after Ward's lawsuit ended in defeat. After serving five terms in the state legislature, Ward was nominated for a federal judgeship by President Jimmy Carter, and he joined the district court bench in 1979, becoming the first black federal judge in Georgia's history. His is a story of remarkable achievements in the face of overwhelming odds and serves as a lasting tribute to the civil rights pioneers who came before him and paved the way.

The desegregation of the University of Georgia has never gotten the level of attention, or the scholarly treatment, that the desegregation of the University of Mississippi and the University of Alabama has received, despite the fact that the University of Georgia was the first of the three to desegregate. Part of the reason is that, although Georgia certainly had its share of racial violence in the 1960s, the bloody campaigns in Mississippi and Alabama became flashpoints for the civil rights movement, and those have been the images—etched indelibly into our consciousness—that have been the most enduring. Another reason is that most of the previous accounts of UGA's desegregation have downplayed, perhaps unintentionally, the seriousness of the violence on the campus, creating the impression that Georgia's response to the integration of its flagship institution was more subdued, and thereby less confrontational, than what took place on the campuses of its neighbors. While it is true that the University of Georgia managed to avoid the terrible violence that occurred at Ole Miss in 1962 when James Meredith enrolled as its first black student and that there was none of the George Wallace–type political grandstanding that preceded James Hood's and Vivian Malone's admission into the University of Alabama in 1963, the evidence clearly shows that the resistance that did occur at the University of Georgia was deliberately calculated to force Holmes and Hunter from campus permanently, and that the

Autherine Lucy episode was fresh in the minds of many of the protestors. After being admitted to the University of Alabama in 1956, Lucy was greeted by mob activity that lasted for several days, prompting university officials to suspend her "for her own safety." During her suspension, her attorneys charged that University of Alabama officials had conspired with the rioters to create a moblike atmosphere, an accusation that prompted the Board of Trustees to expel Autherine Lucy permanently. It would be seven years before the University of Alabama would finally desegregate. Indeed, a good number of white Georgians were hoping that their defiance of federal law would win them a similar reprieve. While some denounced the campus violence, and some—including more than a few of the state's prominent politicians—applauded it, many others dismissed it as being akin to a harmless fraternity prank. But because no one was killed, the notion has persisted that the University of Georgia desegregated peaceably. Such was not the case.

While the desegregation of the University of Georgia has been discussed in several essays, articles, and book chapters, this is the first full-length scholarly treatment of the subject. Calvin Trillin's *An Education in Georgia* (1963) is a journalistic account of UGA's desegregation based largely on oral interviews. Charlayne Hunter-Gault's *In My Place* (1992) is a personal narrative that focuses only partly on her experiences as one of the first two blacks to attend the University of Georgia. *We Shall Not Be Moved*, coming thirty-nine years after Trillin's study, relies on oral history and archival materials and is a more thorough and critical examination of the events leading up to UGA's desegregation.

The University of Georgia has long been an institution of academic excellence, honor, and tradition; until very recently, however, it has also been an institution of white privilege and racial exclusion. In January 1961, Hamilton Holmes and Charlayne Hunter began the process of changing all that. But the process is far from complete. Despite the racial problems that remain (and there are many, to be sure), this society has undergone a remarkable transformation in the forty years since Holmes and Hunter entered the University of Georgia and in the fifty years since Horace Ward applied to the university's law school. Whatever racial progress has been achieved in these United States has been because of their efforts and the efforts of so many others who shared their commitment to equal justice under the law. This is largely a story of triumph, and a testament to those who made it happen.

Acknowledgments

This book has been several years in the making, and I am indebted to many people for helping to bring it to fruition. Many of my colleagues at the University of Georgia read the manuscript in its entirety and offered suggestions for revisions, and I hope the book reflects our collective wisdom. For their insightful criticisms, I am especially grateful to Bud Bartley, Jim Cobb, Robby Cohen, Tom Dyer, Peter Hoffer, Will Holmes, John Inscoe, John Morrow, and Emory Thomas. Thanks also to our departmental word processing specialist, Bonnie Cary, for her valuable technical assistance, and to Travis Rose and Robert Smith, my able research assistants. I am grateful to the University of Georgia's Boyd Graduate School for its support of this project by awarding me a Senior Faculty Research Grant in 1998. I also wish to thank UGA photographer Peter Frey for helping me to locate photographs.

I reserve a special note of thanks for my editor, Malcolm Call, whom I have known personally since I joined the faculty at the University of Georgia in 1987. Malcolm expressed great enthusiasm for this project from its inception and I benefited immensely from his support and encouragement at every stage in the process. He meticulously read each individual chapter as I wrote it, long before anything resembling a monograph emerged. His professionalism is evident from beginning to finish, and I am delighted that this is one of the last books he edited before he began his retirement. He will be sorely missed at this place.

My greatest debt is to the many people who took the time to share with me their recollections and impressions of this important episode in Georgia's history. While this book relies heavily on archival sources, it required a human element that simply cannot be found in libraries and archives, and I am grateful to the following, who helped bring the story to life: Milner Ball, Leslie K. Bates, J. Ralph Beaird, Robert Benham, Harold Black, William A. Bootle, Thomas Brahana, Gene Britton, Chester C. Davenport Jr., Ken Dious, Thomas Dyer, Mary Frances Early, T. David Fletcher, Thurmon Garner,

Hugh Gloster, Richard Graham, Donald Hollowell, Gary Holmes, Hamilton Holmes Jr., Herbert Holmes, Isabella Holmes, Marilyn Holmes, Charlayne Hunter-Gault, Randall Johnson, Giles Kennedy, Alfred Killian, Archibald Killian, Charles B. Knapp, Earl T. Leonard Jr., Calvin Logue, Walter A. Lundy, Betty Mapp, Pete McCommons, Adrienne McFall, Horace Montgomery, Ray Moore, John H. Morrow Jr., Constance Baker Motley, Rubye Potts, Caroline Ridlehuber, Gregory Roseboro, Bill Shipp, Edward D. Spurgeon, S. Ernest Vandiver, Horace T. Ward, Homer Wilson, and Joan Zitzelman.

The one name that is noticeably absent from the above list is that of Hamilton Holmes. Unfortunately, I was unable to schedule an interview with him before his untimely death in October 1995. His words and image have been preserved in various other formats, but I would have loved to have talked to him about his turbulent years as a student on UGA's campus, as well as the later years in which he began his reconciliation with the university. Fortunately, I did have the opportunity to gain some of those insights from more formal settings. I first met Holmes in 1989 when he was invited to give a lecture to a history class. Later, he and I served as panelists in a discussion of race relations at the University of Georgia. The things that struck me most about him were his warm and congenial personality, his broad smile and hearty laugh, the uneasiness he felt about his celebrity status, and the fact that he seemed to harbor no resentment toward those who had made his life intolerably difficult for two and a half years—all in stark contrast to the image that many had of him as a student. I understand now, as he did then, that his reserved demeanor during his college days at UGA was a necessary part of his protective armor, which he was able to shed when he felt it was no longer needed. He was a remarkable man and I feel honored to have known him. I hope that this book will be a fitting tribute to his legacy.

We Shall Not Be Moved

CHAPTER ONE

More than a Matter of Segregation

I like the nigger, but I like him in
his place, and his place is at the back
door with his hat in his hand.
—Eugene Talmadge, governor of
Georgia, 1933–1937, 1941–1943

As long as I am your governor,
Negroes will not be admitted to
white schools in Georgia.
—Herman Talmadge, governor
of Georgia, 1948–1955

Black Americans had reason to be hopeful about the prospects of their being accepted as equal citizens as the nation approached the beginning of the
second half of the twentieth century. Although race prejudice and discrimination remained deeply embedded in American society as the United States
entered World War II, blacks clearly understood, perhaps better than other
Americans, that the defeat of Hitler and Mussolini would have an impact
that reached far beyond the battlefields of Europe. Indeed, blacks pursued a
"Double V" strategy: victory at home as well as abroad. Blacks had expressed a
similar optimism in the period following World War I, a war in which they had
fought and died in order to make the world safe for democracy, but their gal-
lant service and personal sacrifice was not enough to halt the proliferation of
brutal racist violence, which reached epidemic proportions in the 1920s. The
worldwide distress brought on by the Great Depression shifted the nation's

1

concerns to more pressing economic matters, and the election of Franklin Delano Roosevelt as president held the promise of a more liberal society on both social and economic issues. First Lady Eleanor Roosevelt, whose racial sensitivity far exceeded that of her husband, embraced the cause of civil rights as no other president's wife had, and her concern for minorities and the poor helped bring about an increased awareness from the nation as a whole, even if these issues were not yet a national priority.[1]

One of President Roosevelt's most enduring legacies was his role in helping to create a more liberal federal judiciary, which was reflected in a series of Supreme Court decisions. In 1944, the Court struck a major blow against racial discrimination in *Smith v. Allwright,* in which the justices ruled 8–1 that Texas's all-white primary was unconstitutional.[2] In 1946, in *Morgan v. Virginia,* the first transportation case to be brought to the Court by the NAACP (National Association for the Advancement of Colored People), the Court ruled 7–1 that it was unlawful to subject interstate passengers to state laws requiring segregated seating.[3] And in 1948, in *Shelley v. Kraemer,* the Court's six sitting justices ruled unanimously against restrictive covenants, which were private contractual agreements between whites to prevent the sale of property to blacks.[4] While all of these Court decisions represented victories for blacks, they were all limited in their scope, due in part to the precise wording of the decisions and in part to the difficulty in enforcing laws that were usually at odds with local custom. The Supreme Court could rule against state-sanctioned efforts to restrict black voting, but such rulings would be meaningless as long as the poll tax remained in effect and as long as whites were free to terrorize, with impunity, any blacks who dared to exercise their constitutional rights. The Court had sent the right message in *Morgan,* but actual enforcement was another matter. In fact, most bus lines continued to allow Jim Crow seating on all their interstate trips throughout the South, and intrastate segregated seating was not affected at all. And while *Shelley* was a step in the right direction, the Court had phrased its language carefully, and, in effect, had stopped short of actually nullifying restrictive covenants. The Court had merely said that restrictive covenants were "unenforceable" by resort to the courts. In other words, these covenants would have to be challenged on an individual basis.[5]

The legal battles that lay ahead would be fought by some of the most brilliant black attorneys the country had ever known, many of whom were trained by Charles Hamilton Houston. A 1922 graduate of Harvard Law School, Houston became the first black to be chosen as a member of the prestigious Law Review, and his academic excellence attracted the attention of Harvard law professor and future Supreme Court justice Felix Frankfurter, who sponsored Houston for an overseas fellowship and supervised his postgraduate work at Harvard. Houston joined Howard University's faculty in 1924 and was appointed academic dean in 1929 and began immediately to redesign the law school curriculum. Howard's law school had been a typical city law school, operating in the evening so that working students could study law. But beginning in 1930, Houston phased out the evening division and secured accreditation of the law school from the Association of American Law Schools. Houston possessed a serious work ethic and was described as "a very hard man" and a "perfectionist" who demanded that his students become "highly skilled professionals." He believed in using the law to promote social change, and he often said that a lawyer was either a social engineer or a parasite on society. Houston's academic rigor and vision enabled him to train a cadre of young black lawyers who would not only provide basic legal services to the black community but also force the nation to deliver on its promise of fair and equal treatment for all its citizens. Over the next several decades, Houston's students—those who could withstand his demanding requirements—worked tirelessly to reshape the Constitution and to make civil rights law.[6]

In 1935, Houston stepped down as dean of Howard Law School to become special counsel for the NAACP. One of the organization's top priorities was to address the issue of unequal education for black children in the South. Although black and white children had been receiving segregated education in the South and in some places in the North well before *Plessy v. Ferguson*, the Supreme Court's 1896 ruling gave legal sanction to "separate but equal," which became the governing principle for race relations in the South for most of the twentieth century.[7] Houston would often travel throughout the South, taking pictures of black schools and white schools to document the inequities that existed between them. Part of the NAACP's legal strategy during this time was to pursue the equalization of black and white schools, thereby forcing whites to bear the financial burden of maintaining two separate school systems. The NAACP was determined to pressure white officials to comply with the *equal* as zealously as they had with the *separate*. Although some black schools were upgraded (though hardly equalized) over the next decade, segregation remained firmly intact. Regardless of the cost, white southerners were willing to pay the price.[8]

While continuing with their litigation to equalize black elementary and secondary schools, NAACP lawyers began to focus some of their attention on the area of graduate and professional training, which, in many respects, presented a slightly different set of issues. Though southern states provided undergraduate education for blacks, they did not have graduate and professional training programs for them. At the graduate level, "separate but equal" did not apply.

In several important cases between 1936 and 1950, the federal judiciary (the United States Supreme Court in particular) made it clear to the southern states that if there were no black graduate or professional schools in operation, black students would have to be admitted into white universities—or separate universities would have to be created for them. In December 1934, Donald Murray, a black man, applied for admission to the University of Maryland Law School. He was promptly rejected. The University of Maryland did not admit blacks to its law school, nor did it operate a separate law school for them; instead, it offered out-of-state tuition assistance for blacks who were accepted into law schools outside the state. Donald Murray's attorney, Thurgood Marshall, had been rejected years earlier by the University of Maryland and had gone on to study law at Howard under Charles Houston. During the trial, the state contended that its out-of-state tuition program fulfilled its obligation under the separate but equal doctrine. The issue here, though, was whether a state could satisfy its obligation to its citizens by forcing them to pursue their education in another state. As Marshall put it, "What's at stake here is more than the rights of my clients; it's the moral commitment stated in our country's creed." The crux of the matter, Marshall emphasized, was that the state had conflated segregation with *exclusion*. This was much more than just a matter of segregation. "Donald Murray was not sent to a separate school of the University of Maryland. . . . Donald Murray was excluded from the University of Maryland entirely." The Court of Appeals found Marshall's argument persuasive, and ordered the university to admit Murray.[9]

The NAACP followed up its victory in Maryland by bringing a similar suit in Missouri. When Lloyd Gaines applied to law school at the University of Missouri, school officials refused to consider his application and instructed him to apply either to Lincoln University or to an out-of-state law school. Gaines had graduated from Lincoln, which was Missouri's state-supported black college, but Lincoln had no law school. The state legislature, however, had authorized the creation of a black law school at Lincoln should the need ever arise.[10] If Gaines chose to attend law school out-of-state, then Missouri would pay any tuition fees that exceeded what he would have paid at Missouri's law school, though the state made no mention of paying for extra travel and living expenses necessitated by his attending an out-of-state school. Writing for the Supreme Court's 6–2 majority, Chief Justice Charles Evans Hughes reaffirmed the decision in the *Murray* case. The University of Missouri could admit Gaines to its law school, or the state could open a segregated law school at Lincoln—but Gaines was entitled to a legal education *within* the state of Missouri, and that educational opportunity had to be made available to him within a reasonable time frame.[11]

With victories in both *Murray* and *Gaines,* the NAACP had been successful in getting the high courts to acknowledge that blacks were entitled to educational opportunities at the graduate and professional level; however, the issue of equality still had not been addressed. Could a law school that had been created overnight be as good as an existing one with a well-established tradition? And, if in fact a black student were admitted into a white university, to what extent could a university practice segregation within the university? Two cases that were now winding their way toward the Supreme Court would strike at the heart of both issues.

In 1946, Heman Sweatt applied to law school at the University of Texas. After the university rejected his application, the NAACP sued on Sweatt's behalf. Although he ruled against Sweatt's admission into the University of Texas, the trial judge gave the state six months to create a "substantially equal" law school for Sweatt. The state legislature responded by setting up what was supposed to be a temporary law school in the basement of a building near the state capitol. There was to be a modest library, and three professors from the University of Texas were assigned to teach courses there. When the temporary law school opened on March 10, 1947, there were no students.[12]

Meanwhile, George McLaurin had sued for, and won, admission into graduate school at the University of Oklahoma. But when he showed up for his first day of classes, the sixty-eight-year-old discovered that he was to sit at a desk by himself in an anteroom outside the regular classrooms. In the library, he was assigned to a segregated desk in the mezzanine. In the cafeteria, he was required to eat at a segregated table and at different hours from the white students. To McLaurin's embarrassment and to the NAACP's dismay, Oklahoma's state legislature had revised its state laws to require that all such instruction of black students was to be given "on a segregated basis" within the university. As Richard Kluger put it, "it was surely Oklahoma's most inventive contribution to legalized bigotry since the adoption of the 'grandfather clause.'"[13]

The NAACP appealed both Sweatt's and McLaurin's cases to the Supreme Court, and the Court issued its decisions on the two cases on June 5, 1950. In *Sweatt v. Painter* a unanimous Supreme Court ordered that Heman Sweatt be admitted to the University of Texas Law School because it was clear that the makeshift black law school that Texas had created was inferior. In *McLaurin v. Oklahoma State Regents* the Court ruled that "the restrictions placed upon him [McLaurin] were such that he had been handicapped in his pursuit of effective graduate instruction" and such restrictions had to end. While both decisions were important milestones in the NAACP's legal battle for educational equality, the sweeping indictment of "separate but equal" that NAACP attorneys hoped for did not materialize. The Court had ruled in Sweatt's favor not because the state of Texas wanted to provide him with a separate education, but because the education it offered to blacks was not equal to that offered to whites. In McLaurin's case, the Court had chosen its words very carefully: it had referred to the inequities and indignities heaped upon McLaurin as "restrictions," not segregation. *Plessy* had been shaken, but not dismantled. "Separate but equal" was still the law.[14]

While the significance of these rulings should not be underestimated, it is important to note that up until now all of these court cases had taken place outside of what was traditionally considered the Deep South. States like Maryland, Missouri, Texas, and Oklahoma, it was believed, would offer less resistance due to their smaller black population. It was reasonably assumed that states in the Deep South, where the black population was much larger and where desegregation rulings would have a far greater impact, would offer greater resistance. And because the Supreme Court had not overturned *Plessy* in one fell swoop, those who opposed desegregation were emboldened by the Court's apparent reluctance to do so and were encouraged in their determination to resist change. State officials in Georgia would be prepared when their turn came.

By the end of World War II, Georgia's segregated social system had hardened into a rigid caste structure accepted by virtually all whites and a substantial number of blacks as an immutable fact of life. As historian Numan V. Bartley observes, "The ubiquitous words 'white' and 'colored' that adorned virtually every public facility from drinking fountains and restrooms to the Bibles used in Georgia courtrooms for administering oaths were an accepted part of the Georgia scene, like red clay and kudzu."[15] Whites viewed segregation not only as a device for maintaining social order and stability but also as an effective way of preserving economic and political opportunities for themselves and their posterity. Blacks viewed it the same way, except their perspective came from the bottom rather than the top.

The dominant features of Georgia politics in the mid–twentieth century were states' rights, rural domination, and white supremacy, and the political figure who best symbolized this era in the state's history was Eugene Talmadge. First elected governor in 1932, Talmadge dominated Georgia politics for more than a decade, being elected governor four times. Referred to as Ole Gene, and the Wild Man from Sugar Creek, Talmadge became one of the region's foremost race-baiters and demagogues. Although he professed a commitment to bringing about social and economic reforms badly needed by poverty-stricken Georgians, he never delivered. Instead, maintaining the South's racial status quo became the raison d'être of his administration. Eugene Talmadge was not the first southern politician to exploit racial prejudices for political gain, nor would he be the last, but his racist rhetoric clearly set the tone for Georgia politics for the next forty years, and few of Georgia's politicians during that period would be courageous enough to deviate from the segregationist norm.[16]

Herman Talmadge's election as Georgia's governor in 1948 signaled the reemergence of racial politics within the state and ushered in an era of virulent white supremacy and increased racial repression throughout the entire state. Following in his father's footsteps, Herman Talmadge was every bit the race-baiter that Eugene had been, and he went to great lengths to make it clear that white supremacy was the cornerstone of his 1948 campaign, proclaiming, "My platform has one plank which overshadows all the rest . . . my unalterable opposition to all forms of the 'civil rights program.' "[17] Despite the Supreme Court's 1944 ruling in *Smith v. Allwright,* which invalidated the white primary, many blacks were still afraid to assert their political rights, knowing that white violence against blacks was still all too frequent and that the state could not be counted on to protect them.[18] Furthermore, Georgia's archaic county-unit system effectively diluted the political strength of those blacks who did dare to vote. Under the county-unit system, the rural portion of the state—which was predominantly white—retained political dominance, despite its sparse population. More than half of Georgia's black voters were registered in the thirty-eight most populous counties, all of which were under-represented under county-unit apportionment. Hence, when raw terror and intimidation failed to check black ambitions, the system of laws itself could present insurmountable obstacles.[19]

Despite the *Sweatt* and *McLaurin* decisions of 1950 that appeared to be chipping away at separate but equal in public education, Herman Talmadge vowed to maintain segregation in Georgia at all costs.[20] Talmadge had run on a segregationist platform and was convinced that white Georgians had given him a mandate to do whatever was necessary to maintain racially separate schools. Totally committed to the sanctity of white supremacy, he believed that segregation was the only thing that prevented miscegenation. Skillful politician that he was, Talmadge understood that raising the specter of interracial sex was the surest way to stiffen white resistance to desegregation. During the 1950 gubernatorial campaign Talmadge promised that "As long as I am Governor, Negroes will not be admitted to white schools. . . . The good women of Georgia will never stand for the mixing of the races in our schools."[21] For the duration of his term as governor Talmadge kept to his pledge, and he instructed his subordinates to make sure that no integration took place while he was in office, even if it meant shutting down the public schools and creating a statewide white private school system.[22]

From kindergarten to graduate and professional study, the color line was rigidly maintained in Georgia. White and black children had attended separate schools since well before *Plessy,* and there was certainly no anticipated change looming on the horizon in 1950. Higher education was no different, with blacks and whites attending their own colleges and universities. State lawmakers were no doubt concerned about recent Supreme Court decisions that seemed to be threatening segregation, but so far none of these rulings had any impact on Georgia. But that was about to change. On September 29, 1950, Horace T. Ward, a twenty-three-year-old black native Georgian, formally applied for admission into law school at the University of Georgia.

Horace Taliaferro Ward was born in LaGrange, Georgia, on July 29, 1927. His mother, Minnie Ward, was unmarried and worked as a domestic. Ward never knew his father. Because his mother lived with the white people for whom she worked, Ward lived his first nine years with his mother's parents. When his stepfather got a job as a laundry worker, the family moved to a community near LaGrange College, this time taking Ward with them. Though he did not start school until he was nine, he was a bright and eager pupil. After completing the fourth grade, his teacher convinced the principal that Ward should be allowed to skip the fifth grade and go directly to the sixth. He graduated valedictorian of East Depot Street High School in 1946.[23]

Ward's high school principal had recommended that Ward enroll at Morehouse College in Atlanta after finishing the tenth grade, but Ward preferred to finish high school by completing the eleventh grade. (At the time, Georgia public schools had only eleven grades, not twelve.) After high school Ward enrolled at Morehouse, majoring in political science. While a student at Morehouse, Ward was greatly influenced by Robert E. Brisbane, a professor of political science, as well as Benjamin E. Mays, who served as Morehouse's president. Upon completion of his bachelor's degree in 1949, Ward enrolled in Atlanta University, another private black institution, where he earned his master's degree in political science in 1950. While there, Ward came under the tutelage of William Madison Boyd, chairman of the political science department and president of the Georgia state branch of the NAACP. Boyd would later become Ward's principal adviser and confidant.[24]

Ward's interest in studying law developed early and was motivated in part by a black lawyer named Austin Thomas Walden. Walden occasionally visited Ward's hometown of LaGrange, and Ward was immediately impressed with this black man who practiced law. Ward recalls that "during those days I was not even aware that there were any black lawyers. Once I learned about Walden, I knew that I wanted to study law."[25] Commonly referred to as Colonel, A. T. Walden (who would later become a member of Ward's legal team) was one of the first blacks to practice law in Georgia.

Born in 1885 in Fort Valley, Georgia, the son of former slaves, Walden was educated in Fort Valley's public schools, during which time he developed a zeal for learning and eventually decided to study law. After graduating from Atlanta University, Walden earned a law degree from the University of Michigan in 1911. He began his law practice in Macon, Georgia, in 1912, interrupting it in June 1917 to enter the army during World War I, there serving with distinction as a captain of infantry and as a trial judge advocate of the 92nd Division. When the war was over, Walden returned to his practice in Macon, and during the next forty years would become one of the state's best-known black attorneys, successfully tackling such issues as the all-white Democratic primary, racial disparities in teacher salaries, and segregation on Atlanta's city buses.[26] His civic involvement and political prominence throughout the state was such that he served as an adviser and confidant to the Reverend Martin Luther King Sr. and was widely perceived to be a major force in black Atlanta's political arena throughout the 1950s. Over the years he had served as president of the Atlanta University Alumni Association, president of the Atlanta chapter of the NAACP, and chairman of the Atlanta Urban League and had helped found the Atlanta Negro Voters League, a nonpartisan black political organization.[27]

Ward's admiration for Walden, combined with the persistent nudging of some of his professors who had been impressed with his academic record, helped convince him to pursue a career in law. Having no desire to attend an out-of-state law school, Ward wrestled with the possibility of applying to the University of Georgia in Athens. Knowing that the University of Georgia had never admitted a black student to any of its schools, graduate or undergraduate, Ward was reluctant to apply, but decided to send for an application nonetheless. Ward had known for some time that his former Atlanta University professor William M. Boyd had been searching for someone with solid academic credentials to break the color barrier at the University of Georgia; Boyd had initially approached another Morehouse student, Martin Luther King Jr., about the possibility of serving as a plaintiff in a test case against the university. But King declined, indicating that his real interest was in theology, not law. Ward, however, was interested in law, and though not eager to serve as a plaintiff, he understood that any attempt on his part to enroll at the University of Georgia would very likely be met with resistance from state and university officials; and he insists that it was he who approached Boyd, not the other way around. Boyd gave his assurance that he, as president of the Georgia NAACP, would do all he could to assist Ward with the application procedure and the litigation process, if it came to that. Ward agreed to apply.[28]

On September 29, 1950, Ward formally applied to law school at the University of Georgia. He sent his application to the university registrar, Walter N. Danner. Several days later, Ward received a reply from L. R. Seibert, executive secretary of the Board of Regents, to whom Ward's application had been forwarded. In an attempt to dissuade Ward from pursuing his application at Georgia, Seibert offered Ward financial assistance if he would attend an out-of-state law school. Ward wrote back to Seibert refusing the aid and insisted that his application be evaluated solely on its merits. On October 18 Seibert replied that a committee would review the matter.[29]

For three months, Seibert did not communicate with Ward. On January 5, 1951, Ward wrote to Seibert asking for a status report on his application. Seibert wrote back promptly, saying only that he hoped to complete the evaluation of the application "at an early date." Three more months passed, and still no word from Seibert. On April 26, Ward wrote Seibert another letter in which he pointed out that he met all of the qualifications for admission into law school as listed in the university's catalog and stressed that he wished to enter law school in the summer term, which was to begin on June 13. On May 1 Seibert wrote Ward, "I shall endeavor to place your request before the proper authorities at an early date." The decision finally came on June 7, 1951. In a letter from university registrar Walter N. Danner, Ward was informed that "Your application for admission to the University of Georgia Law School has been considered and is hereby denied." The rejection letter had come just six days before the beginning of the summer term and more than nine months after Ward had filed his application.[30]

Still hoping to be admitted before the beginning of the summer term, Ward appealed immediately to the university system chancellor, Harmon Caldwell, who claimed that he had not been in communication with Danner and that he did not know the reason for Ward's rejection. Caldwell further claimed that he had no jurisdiction over the matter and that Ward should take up the issue with Danner. With the help of his attorney A. T. Walden, Ward continued his correspondence with UGA officials throughout the summer. He wrote to Danner demanding an explanation for his rejection, and he wrote another letter to Chancellor Caldwell in which he pointed out that the Board of Regents, and not the university registrar, had maintained jurisdiction over his application, which was a clear violation of the rules and regulations of the university system. On July 5 Ward wrote to university president O. C. Aderhold, protesting that he had been rejected solely on the basis of race. Aderhold responded by promising Ward that he would create a "special commmittee" to study the matter (a procedure that had never been adopted for a white applicant). The committee did not meet for nearly two months, during which time Ward informed Aderhold that he would consider his appeal denied if he received no favorable response from the committee by August 9, 1951.[31]

On August 7 Aderhold informed Ward that the committee had met that morning and that the committee members requested information concerning Ward's military status, which Ward supplied immediately. Nine days later the committee requested a meeting with Ward, which he refused to grant, declaring that for a month he had continuously made himself available to appear before the committee, and that "in view of the circumstances I see no purpose to be served by my appearance other than further unreasonable delay in the matter."[32] Again Ward appealed directly to Chancellor Caldwell, but again Caldwell refused to take any action. Acting on the advice of his attorney, Ward agreed to meet with the special committee on September 8.

A. T. Walden accompanied Ward to Athens for the meeting with the special committee, consisting of law school dean J. Alton Hosch, law professor Robert L. McWhorter, and history professor E. Merton Coulter. Why President Aderhold chose these three faculty members to serve on this committee is unclear. What is known, however, is that all three were committed to preserving segregation at the University of Georgia. As law school dean, J. Alton Hosch toed the administration line on segregation, and his law school colleague Robert McWhorter was a dependable ally. As a history professor, E. Merton Coulter was well known for his racist views, as is clearly reflected in his writings, both professional and personal.[33]

One of the most surprising things about the meeting, Ward recalls, was that the three-person committee asked him virtually nothing about his academic credentials, but rather chose to focus on more personal aspects of his life. As Ward remembers, the interview began with questions about his fitness for military service. Ward had developed a hernia years earlier that he had never had surgically corrected. Because of the hernia, which the army considered a medical disability, Ward was classified as 4-F, meaning that he was physically unfit for military service. As Ward explains it, "The hernia had never bothered me, and I did not deem it a priority; hence, I had never bothered to have it corrected. I considered it totally irrelevant to my application to UGA, but it became a big deal for Dean Hosch."[34] Dean Hosch continued to press Ward about his failure to have surgery to correct the hernia, implying that because Ward was service age (he was twenty-four at the time) it was unpatriotic of him not to have corrective surgery that would qualify him for military duty, especially in light of the fact that the United States was at war with North Korea. Hosch reasoned that Ward was either shirking his military obligations or that his priorities were confused.[35]

After Hosch had finished grilling Ward about his fitness for military duty, Professors McWhorter and Coulter tried to determine whether Ward was really serious about attending law school or was a tool of the NAACP. They wanted to know, for example, why Ward had chosen the University of Georgia and whether he himself had written the letters pertaining to his appeal. Ward answered that he had written his own letters, but when asked more specifically later in the interview, he acknowledged that his advisers (mainly Walden and Boyd) had assisted him to some degree. As to why he had chosen Georgia, Ward remembers it this way:

> I told the committee that I chose the University of Georgia because I was a citizen of this state, that I planned to practice in this state, and that as far as I could tell, it was clearly advantageous to attend law school in the state where you intend to practice. Now, I did dance around the question of whether I applied to UGA for the purpose of desegregating it. That was not my primary goal, but it clearly had to be a factor. I was familiar with the ongoing cases before the United States Supreme Court, and those things were in the back of my mind. In light of some recent court rulings, I thought that I might have been admitted. I know that sounds a bit naive, given the climate of the times, but I really did think that Georgia might admit me.[36]

Upon learning that A. T. Walden and William M. Boyd both were graduates of the University of Michigan, the committee asked Ward why he himself had not selected Michigan and why neither Walden nor Boyd had suggested Michigan, given their interest in Ward's career. Sensing the hostile nature of the question (as well as the committee's hostility in general), Ward declined to answer. Dean Hosch then pointed out to Ward that one of the requirements for success in law was the ability to speak and write effectively and proceeded to have Ward write a paragraph explaining why he had chosen to attend law school at the University of Georgia. After Ward had written his statement, in which he reminded the committee that he had been a lifelong resident of the state, Dean Hosch read it aloud to the committee, but none of the members offered any assessment of Ward's writing ability. The committee members thanked Ward for his time and told him that the appropriate university officials would soon be in touch with him.[37]

A week after the meeting Ward received a letter from President Aderhold informing him that the special committee had recommended that Ward's application be denied and that the president concurred with the decision. Again Ward appealed to Chancellor Caldwell, saying that race was the sole reason for his denial. Caldwell disagreed and wrote Ward on October 18 that there was no legitimate reason for him to overturn the decision of university officials. In the final step to exhaust all administrative remedies, Ward appealed to the Board of Regents.[38]

In his letter of appeal, Ward listed all the reasons he believed compelled the regents to rule in his favor, including the unusual manner in which his application had been handled, repeated delays and administrative maneuvers, and the refusal of UGA's officials to give him a reason for their rejection of his application. Ward's complaints that university officials had been dragging their feet would get little sympathy from the regents, who were using the same tactics in the hope that Ward would eventually give up. The regents, through their executive secretary, L. R. Seibert, informed Ward on November 19, 1951, that the board's Committee on Education would study the matter, and on January 10, 1952, they informed Ward that the committee needed more time. A month later, the regents notified Ward that they had adopted several resolutions that had a direct effect on his application. Not surprisingly, all of the resolutions worked against Ward and had clearly been designed with his application in mind.

The Board of Regents had apparently decided that this was an ideal time to revamp the university's admissions requirements and restructure the curriculum. In the past, the law school at the University of Georgia had admitted most candidates solely on the basis of their having completed a minimum of two years of course work at an accredited institution. Now, the board noted, the nation's better law schools had begun to administer entrance examinations to applicants. Therefore, to make sure that the university's academic reputation would not be diminished, the regents would now require "the faculty of the School of Law of The University of Georgia to confer with and cooperate with the officials of the Georgia Bar Association and members of the judiciary in this State [to] work out an adequate program of examinations for all who apply for admission to the School of Law." In order to achieve their desired goal, the regents voted unanimously that "all applications now pending at any stage . . . be considered . . . under the aforesaid resolutions."[39] The only application pending at the time was Horace Ward's. The following month, the law school faculty unanimously passed a motion concurring with the regents' mandate and authorizing the law school dean to create a committee to oversee the new requirements. Both Dean Hosch and Professor McWhorter were members of the committee.[40]

The intent of this new rule was evident both to Ward and his attorneys. Ward complained that his application should be considered under the rules in effect when he first applied, a sentiment echoed by Thurgood Marshall, who argued, "Ward cannot be required to do anything that was not required when he applied—anything else is unreasonable."[41] The Board of Regents disagreed, and informed Ward that "Inasmuch as all persons having applications pending at any stage for admission to the University of Georgia School of Law are required to conform to the admission requirements, the Committee recommended that the Board require you to conform to these requirements also. The Committee was of the opinion that any other action by the Board would result in discrimination against other applicants." On June 11, 1952, the Board of Regents unanimously adopted the following resolution:

(1) Any resident of Georgia applying for admission to an institution of the University System of Georgia shall be required to submit certificates from two citizens of Georgia, alumni of the institution that he desires to attend, on prescribed forms, which shall certify that each of such alumni is personally acquainted with the applicant, that he is of good moral character, bears a good reputation in the community in which he resides, and, in the opinion of such alumnus, is a fit and suitable person for admission to the institution and able to pursue successfully the course of study offered by the institution he desires to attend; (2) Every such applicant shall also submit a certificate from a judge of a court of record of the county, parish or other political sub-division of the State in which he resides that he is a *bona fide* resident of such county . . . and a person of good moral character and bears a good reputation in the community in which he resides; (3) There is reserved to every institution of the University System of Georgia the right to require any applicant

for admission to take appropriate intelligence and aptitude tests in order that the institution may have information bearing on the applicant's ability to pursue successfully courses of study for which the applicant wishes to enroll and the right to reject any applicant who fails to satisfactorily meet such tests; (4) This resolution shall become effective immediately and catalogs of all institutions of the University System shall carry these requirements. Catalogs already printed shall carry inserts or addenda showing these requirements. The foregoing requirements shall apply to all applicants who have applied for admission to any institution of the University System of Georgia, but have not been actually enrolled and admitted, and to all applicants who hereafter make application for admission to any such institution.[42]

The regents were no doubt aware that it would be difficult, if not impossible, for any black applicant to produce such letters of reference from prominent white members of the state's legal establishment, few of whom up to this point had publicly expressed any willingness to open the university's doors to an African American.

If these new tests were indeed a legitimate effort to raise educational standards, it would have been just as easy to exempt Ward from them as to apply them to him. The subterfuge that the regents had devised was obvious, but only one member of the university's law school faculty was courageous enough to take issue with it. James J. Lenoir, professor of law at the university from 1940 to 1942 and from 1947 to 1953, emerged as an outspoken critic of the university's handling of the Ward affair. Although Lenoir never clamored for Ward's admission (and admitted in personal correspondence that he "did not support Ward"), he could not bring himself to acquiesce silently in what he considered a breach of ethics and academic integrity. For the next year and a half he waged a one-man crusade against the law school's exclusionary tactics.[43]

Lenoir was one of the law school's most valued faculty members, and he had earned the distinction of being a highly competent legal scholar. Perhaps it was his great respect for the law that caused him to agonize over the university's treatment of Ward's application from the outset, and he was finding it increasingly difficult to remain a member of the faculty, especially in light of the new regulations approved by the law school faculty and subsequently adopted by the regents (he had been absent from the faculty meeting when his colleagues voted to approve the new admissions requirements). As revealed in his personal correspondence, the source of much of Lenoir's dissatisfaction was the law school dean, J. Alton Hosch, whom Lenoir considered one of the principal architects of the new law school requirements. In a letter to a colleague at Columbia University Law School, Lenoir wrote that Hosch had been "working with the Board of Regents to throw the responsibility on his law faculty for the subterfuge adopted to keep the negro Ward out of the law school [while] at the same time, in the faculty meeting, professing ignorance of any motive except to raise educational standards" and that Governor Talmadge's attorney, B. D. Murphy, had told him (Lenoir) that "Alton had been working with them on a method to deal with negro applicants." Lenoir continued:

> The difficulties here in Georgia are by no means confined to this University. Vicious race-baiting politicians are in the saddle and are exercising powerful controls over the entire educational system. . . . It is my belief that the ruling politicians would not hesitate to use any means to discredit or destroy their opposition. I am likewise beginning to think that I have been singled out as a stubborn member of the opposition. I only hope that if I indeed become a target, I will have enough forewarning to get my wife and children out of the state. I think the situation is that serious. In conclusion it is perhaps unnecessary to state that I have found that Alton takes his orders from the politicians, and I do not belong to the "favored" class.[44]

The law school faculty held four meetings in all to debate the proposed new regulations. Several odd features, however, characterized these meetings. For the first time, the part-time faculty members (of whom there were five) were invited and did attend the faculty meetings. The committee that the dean appointed to study the matter was composed entirely of faculty members who consistently voted with him. With the exception of Lenoir, no faculty member was willing to acknowledge publicly that these new regulations were in any way connected to Ward's application, although this fact was understood and widely discussed in off-the-record conversations. Whenever Lenoir raised relevant questions in the meetings pertaining to the new requirements (such as, "Was it one of the purposes of the Board of Regents to have the faculty devise a system of tests which would be used as a means of keeping Negroes out of the law school?"), Dean Hosch either pleaded ignorance or simply refused to answer. Exasperated, and feeling increasingly alienated from the rest of the faculty, Lenoir made the decision to resign his post, despite having a wife and five children to support and, at least at the time, no other means of immediate employment.[45]

In one last act of defiance, Professor Lenoir expressed his views on the Horace Ward affair in an article co-written with his wife, Lora Deere Lenoir, that was published in the *Mercer Law Review*.[46] In the article, a conversation takes place between two white men—a recent law school graduate who favors abolishing segregation and an older man who wishes to preserve it (the two men are never actually identified, and may be assumed to be fictional characters). In the course of the debate, the young man presents an argument that is both logical and compelling, proving the fundamental hypocrisy of the segregationist position. The article generated many responses from the readers, most of which were positive. One reader wrote: "It is a very cogent presentation. Better than anything I have read, it reduces to the absurd all the schemes to circumvent the Supreme Court ruling. . . . It ought to be read thoughtfully by all members of the Louisiana and the Mississippi legislatures." Another reader, a congressman from Mississippi, had a different reaction: "I will have to compliment you upon the way the article was written but I must in all frankness admit that I do not agree with your reasoning nor the answers contained therein. . . . There are several points to be considered in this segregation case. The negro is far more deficient in education, morals, economics and religion. . . . Neither race is ready for [integration] in the south and regardless of what you believe and what the Supreme Court says you can rest assured it will not become a reality for some time."[47]

On August 18, 1953, Lenoir informed UGA president Aderhold of his intention to resign from the law school, effective September 1. In his letter of resignation, Lenoir wrote, "Although I am entirely in favor of a faculty adopting educational tests in an honest endeavor to raise educational standards, I am opposed to the prostitution of educational standards by the setting up of educational tests which are in reality a subterfuge to attain some other end." In accepting the resignation, President Aderhold told Lenoir that "the members of the Board of Regents make judgements in terms of what they believe to be of the best interest of the people of the state and of the University."[48] President Aderhold was not sad to see Lenoir go. In a letter to Chancellor Caldwell, Aderhold wrote: "Mr. Lenoir has been extremely critical of the way the Ward case has been handled. We have been a little concerned that he might embarrass the University and the Board of Regents in this matter.

Dean Hosch feels that this is a fortunate way out of the situation both for Mr. Lenoir and the University."[49] Lenoir and his family soon departed Athens, and in the fall he accepted a teaching position on the law faculty at Indiana University.

Despite the legal maneuvering, administrative delays, and political posturing, there was never any doubt that university and state officials were determined to keep the University of Georgia all white. Although the United States Supreme Court had ordered the admission of blacks into a handful of southern white universities, the overwhelming majority of white southerners still opposed integration, and university officials like President Aderhold realized that their support for segregation really did reflect the will of the majority, at least when measured in vocal terms. Further, the South's long history of legally sanctioned racial segregation allowed university officials the political convenience of claiming that such issues were a matter of state policy and were, in effect, out of their hands. They were, as they stated on more than one occasion, merely complying with state law. When Chancellor Caldwell first announced that Ward's application would be rejected, he claimed it was the only decision possible under state law, citing both the state constitution, which forbade integration in Georgia's public schools, and the recent actions of the state legislature, which in the 1951–52 session sought to eliminate the possibility that integration would occur in any of the state's seventeen public colleges. In a rider attached to the appropriations bill for that year—one that was attached *after* Ward's application to uga—the legislature declared that if a black person were admitted to a white school, then all state funds to that institution would be cut off. Georgia's legal proscriptions against integration, like those in most other southern states, were designed to preclude any breaching of the color line.[50]

Convinced that the University of Georgia would never voluntarily admit Ward to its law school, Ward's attorneys filed suit in the federal district court in Atlanta on June 23, 1952, alleging that Ward's application to the university had been denied solely on the basis of "race and color," which was a clear violation of the Fourteenth Amendment to the United States Constitution. Ward's attorneys asked that the court issue a permanent injunction restraining university officials from denying Ward's admission because of his refusal to comply with the new rules and regulations that were not in force at the time of his initial application. Further, this lawsuit was to be considered a class action suit filed on behalf of all black citizens who had previously been denied admission to the University of Georgia on the basis of race and color. The complaint alleged that the defendants' policy and custom of

> providing and maintaining legal training and facilities at and in the aforesaid school of law for white citizens of the state out of public funds while failing and refusing to provide adequate legal training and facilities for plaintiff and other qualified Negro residents of the state wholly and solely on account of their race and color is unlawful discrimination and constitutes a denial of the right of plaintiff and other qualified Negroes to the equal protection of the laws in contravention of the Fourteenth Amendment to the United States Constitution.[51]

University registrar Walter N. Danner, university president O. C. Aderhold, law school dean J. Alton Hosch, university system chancellor Harmon W. Caldwell, and the university system Board of Regents were all named as defendants.[52]

The following week, Judge Frank A. Hooper gave the defendants eighty days to answer the plaintiff's charges. Governor Herman Talmadge vowed to fight to the "bitter end" to defend the state's constitution and promised to assist state attorney general Eugene Cook in defending Georgia's segregation laws if it meant contesting the lawsuit "through every court in the land."[53] Having already endured repeated delays, Ward—who had spent the previous year teaching political science at Arkansas Agricultural, Mechanical, and Normal College and was currently teaching at Alabama State College—prepared himself to face yet another round of obstacles. A. T. Walden, who up to this point had been handling Ward's case alone, was now joined by nationally known NAACP attorneys Thurgood Marshall and Robert L. Carter, both of whom were seasoned litigators accustomed to legal maneuvers and courtroom shenanigans.

Like Thurgood Marshall, Robert Carter had studied under Charles Hamilton Houston. Born in Florida but raised in New Jersey, Carter graduated from Lincoln University and Howard University Law School before receiving a master's degree in law at Columbia University. After completing his service in the air force in 1944, he joined the NAACP staff and quickly became Marshall's primary assistant. Because Marshall was away from the office so often, Carter became a key player in organizing much of the litigation, and his efforts were crucial to the successful operation of both the NAACP and the NAACP Legal

Defense and Education Fund, Inc. (known later as the LDF, or simply the Inc Fund), which was established as a separate organization in 1939 to carry on the legal work.[54] The national NAACP worked closely with the local branch headed by William Boyd, who was busy crisscrossing the state drumming up both moral and financial support for the lawsuit.

Born in Morehead City, North Carolina, the seventh of eight children, William Madison Boyd graduated from Talladega College in Alabama and later earned a doctorate in political science at the University of Michigan. A prolific writer and researcher, he published widely in scholarly journals, and in 1942 as a Rosenwald Fellow, he studied social and economic conditions in several European nations. He served as professor and head of the social science department at Fort Valley State College before joining the political science department at Atlanta University in 1948. Boyd had been active in community affairs for several years and had become president of the state NAACP in 1946, a position he held until 1955. Shortly after arriving in Atlanta, however, his civic activism assumed an entirely new dimension, due in large part to his chance encounter with Horace Ward.[55]

Once Ward made the decision to apply to the University of Georgia, Boyd committed himself to the task of raising the money necessary to help pay for Ward's legal fees (and his school expenses in the event that the case was won), which was formalized with the establishment of the Ward Fund. Traveling across the state and speaking to dozens of organizations, Boyd himself raised more than $4,200 by January 1953. Other NAACP branches raised an additional $1,600. While he had always taken his community work seriously—for several years he had served as a news analyst for WERD, a black radio station in Atlanta—he devoted more and more of his time to securing additional funds for Ward's case. Gracious and charming, Boyd was considered a "people person" and had always preferred personal contacts, but physical exhaustion eventually forced him to initiate a letter-writing campaign in hopes of finding new contributors.[56]

According to those who worked with him, Boyd "carried the state NAACP on his back" during the late 1940s and early 1950s. Because of his high visibility as a community activist, and because of his close working relationship with Thurgood Marshall, Whitney Young (who would later become the president of the National Urban League), and Walter White (then the executive secretary of the national NAACP), Boyd was well known in Atlanta and throughout the entire state. Despite his involvement with Ward's case, he continued to find time to honor his many other obligations as the state president of the NAACP. Much of his time was spent on the road, visiting scores of black churches encouraging the members to register to vote, something that entailed no small amount of risk given the racist climate in the state at the time. Betty Mapp, Boyd's widow, remembers her husband's dedication to his work, something that often caused her a great deal of personal anguish. "I was so afraid for him. I always breathed a sigh of relief when I heard his car coming into the driveway. I never knew if he would get back home safely or not. I always thought he was going to go down like Medgar Evers [Field secretary for the Mississippi NAACP; Evers was shot to death in his driveway in June 1963]." Ignoring his wife's pleas to slow down, as well as her concerns about his safety, Boyd continued to press on with his work as if he sensed that he was running out of time.[57]

Boyd worked at a pace that would have killed lesser men. For most of his life he had pushed himself to the limits of human endurance, maintaining a work schedule that averaged sixteen hours a day. Mapp recalls that "William was truly dedicated to his work. He was a good husband and father who loved his family dearly, but the demands of his work meant that he spent a great deal of time away from us, on the road. I often felt he was pushing himself too hard. Later, when his illness overtook him, he would often tell those who came to see him that no matter what, they should try to spend more time with their children. I think his greatest regret was that he did not spend enough time with his own."[58]

In the summer of 1954, Boyd began experiencing fatigue, something he was not unaccustomed to, but now the bouts were more frequent and were usually accompanied by severe headaches. He was later diagnosed with leukemia, which continued to drain him of his strength and would eventually claim his life. Only then did he begin to spend more time at home, gradually relinquishing most of his duties. Although he was not physically able to continue his fund-raising activities, his interest in Ward's case did not diminish, and he remained Ward's trusted confidant. Boyd was jubilant over the *Brown* decision in 1954, but he did not live to see the outcome of Ward's case, the one that he had devoted the last few years of his life to. He died on March 10, 1956, at the age of thirty-nine. Years later, Morehouse College president Benjamin E. Mays remembered Boyd as a trailblazer and a visionary: "We held much in common. He dreamed of an America where men would be judged on the basis of their common humanity, their ability, their potential, and on what they aspired to be. I am still dreaming of that kind of America."[59] William Madison Boyd had been both mentor and friend to Horace Ward, and his death affected Ward deeply, but it also strengthened his resolve to see his case through to the end and to carry on Boyd's legacy. By late 1952, however, Ward and his attorneys were beginning to sense that they were in for a long, drawn-out legal contest.

The state took almost the entire eighty days granted by Judge Hooper to respond to the plaintiff's complaint. The state's attorneys asked that Ward's petition be denied on the grounds that he had not exhausted all administrative remedies and that his attorneys were not entitled to bring this suit as a class action on the behalf of others. After investigating the state's allegations, Judge Hooper discovered that indeed the Board of Regents had not formally acted on Ward's last appeal and ordered immediate action. Thurgood Marshall protested, pointing out that Ward had spent nearly two years seeking admission through the proper channels, only to be frustrated at every turn by repeated excuses and delays. The regents met on January 14, 1953, and officially denied Ward's application, citing his refusal to take the necessary examinations and his failure to provide character references from university alumni. Attorney General Cook also moved to have the suit dismissed on the technicality that Ward had sued the "Regents of the University System of Georgia" instead of the "Board of Regents of the University System of Georgia." The judge rejected the motion for dismissal and granted Ward's attorneys twenty days to amend the suit.[60]

Over the next several months the state's attorneys continued to use one ploy after another to delay the trial indefinitely, usually by filing motions for dismissal for various reasons. Ward's attorneys, meanwhile, were asking the judge not to allow further defense motions for dismissal and to proceed with trying the case on its merits. After meeting with the attorneys from both sides in June, Judge Hooper scheduled a pretrial hearing for September 2 and tentatively set the beginning of the trial for October 5, 1953. But on September 9, less than a month before the trial was scheduled to begin, Ward received an official letter from the United States War Department: it was his draft notice to report for induction into the United States Army. Ward had earlier received a 4-F classification because of a hernia, but had since undergone corrective surgery, which resulted in his being reclassified as 1A. As Ward prepared to take his place among the ranks of the nation's enlisted men, his case against the University of Georgia was consequently removed from the court docket.[61]

In a recent interview Horace Ward explained the timing of his surgery and why he had elected to correct a hernia that he had once characterized as "not a priority." He remembers that at the time the hernia was not causing him any physical discomfort, though he realized he would have to have it corrected eventually, and then was as good a time as any. According to draft regulations, one had to notify the draft board if there was a change in one's medical condition that might result in reclassification. Ward notified the draft board of his surgery, and he was promptly reclassified. He also acknowledged that he was not aware that having the operation would necessarily result in reclassification, though he understood that it might. Though Ward is reluctant to admit it, Dean Hosch's implication that Ward was trying to evade the draft may have prompted him—even if only indirectly—to have the surgery, which may well have been Hosch's intent. In a letter to Page Keeton, dean of the law school at the University of Texas at Austin, Hosch later wrote: "As you may know, there was an application by a Negro some time ago, but I understand that he had a hernia operation *in order to get into the Army.*"[62]

Those who had fought to keep Ward out of the university could not have hoped for a more fortuitous turn of events. But some of his supporters were of the opinion that Ward's induction into the army was a bit more than mere happenstance, leading some to speculate about the possibility of political interference, although there is nothing in the written record to suggest anything more than that Ward was the unfortunate victim of bad timing. Still, speculation about political impropriety lingers. But whether the untimely arrival of the draft notice was calculated or coincidental, university officials and the state's attorneys breathed a collective sigh of relief at the two-year stay they had been granted. Correspondence between university officials reveals that they were satisfied with the outcome. "Yesterday I learned of Ward's induction in the Army and this will leave us free of his problem for a time anyway," law school dean J. Alton Hosch wrote Chancellor Caldwell, who replied that he was "very glad that Ward is out of the picture for the time being."[63]

White Georgians believed that much of the responsibility of maintaining segregation at the University of Georgia rested with Chancellor Caldwell, who was after all the highest-ranking official in the university system. From the very beginning, Ward's application to the law school had received national attention, prompting many interested observers to write to the chancellor to express their sentiments on the matter one way or the other. Most of the respondents praised Caldwell for standing firm in the face of such a grave crisis confronting the university. One woman from Indiana wrote: "Keep up your honorable fight to keep the White race pure from negro contamination, and do not allow the *federal Missouri mule* [a reference to President Harry Truman] to succeed in his determination. . . . You Southerners have already more than amply provided splendid industrial institutions for the negro, which is all-sufficient for a *negro* to handle. The odious affair is just another dirty 'Dred Scott' rotten political affair, and if you let Truman beat you on this . . . you're a gonner." Caldwell received numerous other letters imploring him to preserve the sanctity of the white race; some of them were signed, while others were written by individuals identifying themselves as members of the Ku Klux Klan or some other white supremacist group and signed "anonymous."[64]

Not all of the letters written to the chancellor opposed Ward's admission. In fact, a few of them took the chancellor (along with the university and the state) to task for denying Ward his constitutional rights. One such letter, written by an alumnus of the university, launched a blistering attack against the chancellor and his cohorts:

> Are you an American? From what I have read and heard of your college, I don't think I'd want to meet a so called "American" like you, or anyone connected with your college. . . . In the past, I heard a lot about negroes being put in the back of the classroom, and being treated as pigs. I didn't believe it, but now I can see it sure is true. . . . Furthermore, anybody with "A" and "B" averages like *Horace Ward* is more worthy of the title *"American"* than people like you and your "staff" who don't even act *human or brotherly*. . . . I hope you aren't to blame for Horace Ward's being denied an education, but if you are, I don't ever want to meet you. If your college doesn't allow negroes or any other race to achieve goals and get an education, brother, I don't ever want to be able to say I went to the University of Georgia to learn a profession. I could say I went to learn *race segregation*, though.[65]

It is unlikely that Chancellor Caldwell replied to all of the letters he received about the Ward case, and nothing in the record indicates that he replied to this one. He did, however, respond to one letter, written by a woman from Savannah, that criticized his role in the Ward affair: "For your information please allow me to say that Mr. Ward has not been deprived of the opportunity to secure a legal education. He has been offered scholarship aid that would enable him to attend some of the foremost law schools of the country at a cost no greater than that of attending the University of Georgia in Athens. His refusal of this offer leads one to ask whether his primary concern is the securing of a legal education."[66] But preventing Ward from attending the University of Georgia merely because he was black did in fact deprive him of his rights as a citizen, and the offer of out-of-state tuition aid was an act of race prejudice and moral cowardice, not beneficence.

Chancellor Caldwell, like most white Georgians of his day, held steadfast to the notion that the races should be kept apart and that (as the above comment suggests) any black person who was serious about an education should willingly accept segregation as the price for that privilege. But for an increasing number of blacks at mid–twentieth century, segregation was much more than an inconvenience—it deprived them of their rights as American citizens. Inspired by the success of earlier university desegregation cases, Ward's attorneys remained hopeful about their chances and continued to prepare for their ultimate showdown with the state's segregationists. As his adversaries schemed to come up with new ways to keep him out of the University of Georgia, Horace Ward was on his way to Korea to fight for his country.

CHAPTER TWO

"The Color Is Black"

If they [blacks] are not willing to live
in a state of segregation and attend
segregated schools, the white people
should and must make other plans and
let the negroes scout for themselves.
And then there is another thing the
negroes ought to consider, if they have
any sense at all; when the time comes
for the white and negro children to
attend the same schools, there is going
to be a lot of people killed in this state.
If that day ever comes, we will have
bloodshed, race riots, and a race war,
and the most terrible time this state
has ever known. The negroes cannot
hope to gain anything by this thing
happening. The negroes will be the
losers in the long run. If this ever
happens, there are going to be a lot of
negroes hurt, and hurt bad in Georgia.
—Roy V. Harris, member of the
university's Board of Regents

Horace Ward's departure for Korea had granted university officials a temporary reprieve, but the possibility that blacks might be attending the University of Georgia in the foreseeable future was enough to ensure that the issue
would be continuously debated even in Ward's absence. Supreme Court decisions such as *Sweatt* and *McLaurin* had caused many white southerners
to begin to worry about the future of segregation, prompting some state officials to take measures to prevent any subversive activities. So concerned were
some white lawmakers about the activities of the NAACP and other radical
organizations that occasionally the governor would ask the chancellor about
the existence of any suspicious textbooks in the state's public institutions of
higher learning. For example, in 1952 Governor Herman Talmadge wrote to
inquire whether any of Georgia's public colleges and universities were using
the textbook *The Challenge to Democracy.* Chancellor Caldwell promised the
governor that he would look into the matter and then added that "this is just
another instance of unwarranted meddling by the NAACP. If that organization
would let us alone, we could work out our racial problems in the South much
more easily and satisfactorily."[1]

Georgia's solution to its racial problems regarding higher education had
been to offer out-of-state tuition grants—which Horace Ward had refused—
to qualified black students who applied to any of the state's white colleges or
universities. The program, the sole purpose of which was to maintain segregation, provided financial assistance to black students "only in those fields of
study which are provided white citizens of Georgia . . . but are not offered at
any of the Negro state-supported schools," namely Fort Valley State College,
Albany State College, and Savannah State College.[2] Since the vast majority
of the state's black students attended Georgia's three state-supported black
colleges for their undergraduate education, only those black students who
wished to pursue education beyond the bachelor's degree would qualify for
out-of-state aid. Once the student had submitted proof that he or she had
been admitted to a school in another state, the state of Georgia would pay
the following expenses: the difference between tuition fees at the white in-
state university to which the student had applied and the out-of-state university chosen; the differential in room and board; and round-trip transportation
once a year to the school. There was a specific formula to calculate expenses,
but the funds were made available only on a reimbursement basis, which

made it especially burdensome for poor black students who were unable to make the initial payment. First implemented in the 1943–44 school year at a cost to the state of roughly $1,044, the out-of-state tuition program cost the state more than $120,000 in 1952, by which time nearly six thousand black students had received tuition assistance totaling $405,085.09 during that eight-year period. These disbursements could not alter the fact that the arrangement was patently discriminatory, and the expenditure only served to illustrate the lengths to which some were willing to go in order to preserve segregation.[3]

Even while proclaiming that the tuition grant program was the great equalizer, university officials on more than one occasion concluded that even that was too much to offer, as the following example illustrates. In 1951, the father of a black student requested scholarship aid for his son, who was majoring in physical education at the University of West Virginia. The Board of Regents rejected the request on the grounds that Fort Valley State College, a black school in the university system, offered the same degree. But the father pointed out in his appeal to the regents that Fort Valley State College had only a B rating with the Southern Association of Colleges and Secondary Schools and that it was not fully accredited. He wanted his son to study at an institution whose credits would be accepted without question. In rejecting the father's appeal, the Board of Regents concluded, "although this institution [Fort Valley State College] has only a 'B' rating . . . at the present time, steps are being taken to have this institution fully approved *as soon as possible.*" The meaning here was clear: white parents could expect that their children would matriculate at universities that were fully accredited, but black parents could not expect the same.[4]

Blacks were not the only Georgians who objected to the state's segregationist practices. While it is impossible to determine their actual numbers, there were some whites in the state who were sympathetic to black demands for equal justice, though their voices—when they dared raise them in protest—were usually drowned out by the state's racist political establishment. In the fall of 1953, shortly after Ward's enlistment in the military, a heated controversy erupted between a prominent politician who fought to keep Ward out of the University of Georgia and a few courageous college students who sought his inclusion.

Of all of Georgia's well-known race-baiting politicians and demagogues, especially among those who never made it to the state's highest office, perhaps none was more colorful than Roy V. Harris. Born in Glascock County, Georgia, in 1895, Harris received a bachelor's degree from the University of Georgia in 1917. After two years of military duty, Harris returned to UGA to earn a law degree. He practiced law in Louisville, Georgia, until 1931 when he relocated to Augusta, Georgia, where he would practice law for the rest of his career. In 1921, at the age of twenty-six, Harris won a seat in the Georgia state legislature, which he held until 1928. Following a two-year stint in the state senate, Harris was re-elected to the Georgia House of Representatives in 1933 and wielded considerable power and influence as the Speaker of the House, a position he held from 1937 to 1940 and from 1943 to 1946. One of the state's most prominent segregationists, Harris had been the primary mover and shaker behind the scenes that had resulted in election victories for four Georgia governors, including both Talmadges. It is unclear whether Roy Harris's persona was a creation of the Talmadge political machine or whether Harris contributed significantly to the creation of the machine, but his influence in state politics was indisputable. After leaving public office in 1946, Harris continued to champion his causes, foremost among them being improving Georgia's education system and upholding segregation. It was perhaps for both of those reasons that Governor Herman Talmadge appointed Harris to the University Board of Regents in 1951. In 1947, Harris had begun publishing his own weekly, the *Augusta Courier*, which his critics considered to be more his political mouthpiece than a legitimate newspaper. The paper's main feature was Harris's editorial column, titled "Strictly Personal," which was printed in red and was devoted primarily to denouncing integration. In late 1953, Harris became embroiled in a conflict with another newspaper—the University of Georgia's student publication, the *Red and Black*.[5]

In the months leading up to Horace Ward's appointed court date in October 1953, the student editors of the *Red and Black*, demonstrating a liberal sentiment at odds with the state's political establishment and university officials, began writing editorials in support of Ward. Shortly after Ward's suspicious draft notice in September, Bill Shipp, a journalism major and managing editor of the *Red and Black*, took a far more courageous stand in a feature article titled "The Color Is Black":

Horace Ward became a casualty the day he was drafted. The Atlanta Negro who had sued for admission to the free, white University of Georgia suddenly found himself facing two years in the not-so-free, non-segregated Army. Whether some string-pulling "friend" of the University gave Ward a gentle shove toward the militia or whether Fate, nobody's friend, caught up with him remains to be seen. Nevertheless, Ward can be checked off as temporarily missing in action from the Many Years War of White vs. Black. He attempted to establish a beachhead on the vanishing white frontier. He failed. Others will try. Some won't fail. Like it or not, "that old, black nigger" who sweeps your floors, shines your shoes and picks your cotton is out to stand on equal footing with you. . . . There is absolutely no logic in excluding the Negro from the white man's way of life, especially at a university. Yesterday I strolled across campus, spoke to a Chink I knew, bummed a cigarette from a Jew and ate supper with a Kraut. And I thought what a miserable system it is when a university allows students of every race, creed and color—except black—to roam its campus and mix with us Anglo-Saxon Protestants while the southern Negro, a born U.S. citizen, is placed in a separated group as if he were a leper.[6]

A month later, the *Red and Black* fired off another editorial titled "Created Equal," this time criticizing Governor Talmadge's continuing support of segregation:

Herman Talmadge has again shown the Mr. Hyde side of his political personality. He has condemned judicial efforts to give the Negro a chance to get an education equal to the white man's as "the most foolhardy sociological calamity in our national history." In a speech at [the] Southern Governors' Conference, Georgia's chief executive said erasing segregation in schools is "a step toward national suicide." We have commended Talmadge in the past for his good work in getting Georgia on the highway to progress. But we cannot commend him for wanting to deny a segment of mankind its right to an equal education. The Governor says we are spending millions to give Negroes equal education in segregated schools. Even a schoolboy economist should realize it is impossible for taxpayers to support two "separate but equal" school systems. With communism knocking at the Negro's back door, we cannot afford to let educational segregation barriers stand. It is as plain as the Red flag in Russia that continued segregation and suppression can and will cause the death of democracy by the hands of its own leaders.[7]

This editorial was too much for university regent Roy Harris, who had a chance encounter with Bill Shipp in Atlanta a few days later. Shipp and Gene Britton, assistant news editor for the *Red and Black*, were in Atlanta to cover a meeting of the Board of Regents. After the meeting was adjourned, Harris approached them, waving a copy of the editorial in front of them. As Britton remembers it, Harris was very critical of the newspaper and told him and Shipp that "rather than sissy activities like writing for a school paper, y'all ought to be out playing football or doing something really macho." Harris then promised that if the *Red and Black* ever "stuck its nose into state politics again, particularly anything having to do with the issue of integration," he would see to it that "the newspaper's funds would be cut off."[8] Some of the other regents who were present also took exception to the editorial, asking Shipp and Britton where they came from and whether they were aware that integration would inevitably lead to race mixing. Though their regular meeting was over and some of the regents had already left, those who remained held an unofficial meeting with Chancellor Caldwell, who subsequently wrote a letter to university president Aderhold stating that the Board of Regents could not allow the *Red and Black* to operate if it persisted in spouting integrationist views.[9]

Stunned by the encounter, Shipp and Britton returned to Athens and told their fellow staff members about their unfriendly exchange with Roy Harris, who, in effect, had promised to shut them down if they persisted in expressing their ideas. The very next issue of the *Red and Black* (both the *Augusta Courier* and the *Red and Black* were published weekly) had as its front-page headline "Roy Harris Threatens *Red and Black*," in which Harris's threat against the student-run newspaper was made public. The story was accompanied by a cartoon (also on the front page) that pictured a little guy sitting at a desk typing out the words "Freedom of the Press" while a large and imposing figure of Roy Harris, smoking a cigar and holding the sword of Damocles, hovered menacingly above. This story drew a response just as heated as the earlier editorial on Talmadge, and criticism was not long in coming, especially from some university officials and the administration of the School of Journalism.[10]

Not to be outdone, Harris seized the opportunity to respond in the next issue of his paper:

> There is a little group on the staff of the *Red and Black* up at the University who recently took after Governor Talmadge and his position insisting upon segregated schools in Georgia. . . . I tried to explain to them that the people of Georgia would

not be willing to support a University which advocated mixing and mingling the races in the public schools of this state. I tried to explain to them that in their juvenile damn foolery they were hurting the University and the cause of education in this state. I frankly told them that the money for the operation of the *Red and Black* would be discontinued unless they could do a better job than they were doing. So, these little squirts went back to Athens and they got out another issue in which they made a personal attack upon me. . . . The question is whether or not the Board of Regents will be dictated to by a little handful of sissy, misguided squirts who have just enough knowledge to think they know it all. . . . Every time I see one of those little sissy boys hanging around some college, the more I think every one of them ought to be made to play football. The time has come to clean out all of these institutions of all Communist influences and the crazy idea of mixing and mingling of the races which was sponsored in this country by the Communist Party.[11]

The staff of the *Red and Black* never doubted Harris's sincerity in making good on his threat, and as the war of words escalated, the student editors, not wishing to make matters worse, decided to meet with university officials. Following the meeting, the editors issued a formal statement expressing concern "if we have created an embarrassing situation for the university or for the Board of Regents through our editorial and news columns" but insisting that "we have not retracted our stand against segregation and we do not intend to." They offered some clarification of the series of events culminating in their public disagreement with Roy Harris, but stopped short of an apology.[12]

By this time, however, political opposition to the editorial policies of the *Red and Black* had reached epic proportions, resulting in a resolution being introduced in the Georgia legislature to force the editors to resign. In accordance with the sentiments expressed by the university regents, John Drewry, dean of the School of Journalism, and university president Aderhold implemented a new policy wherein all *Red and Black* editorials would have to be cleared with a newly appointed faculty adviser. If the student editors and the faculty adviser were unable to reach an agreement, the final decision would then rest with the newly commissioned Board of Control, consisting of seven students and four faculty members, whose responsibility it was to screen any stories considered "prejudicial to the welfare of the university."[13] The purpose of this new censoring agency was not only to force the editors to modify their liberal views on integration but also to prevent further responses to Roy Harris, who had kept up a constant barrage against the *Red and Black* in his own newspaper.

It came as little surprise when on December 2, 1953, Walter A. Lundy Jr., editor, and Bill Shipp, managing editor, announced their resignations from the *Red and Black*. In his letter of resignation, Walter Lundy said that he could not "conscientiously remain in the position of editor without expounding my views on the charges of Harris." Bill Shipp's letter of resignation said that the university had denied the newspaper's staff the "right to reply to charges and names hurled at it" by Harris and that the regents had failed to recognize "the paper's right to comment on matters it feels are of vital importance to the student body." A week later, Priscilla Arnold and Gene Britton, who had stepped in to replace Lundy and Shipp, respectively, also announced their resignations.[14]

As the feud between Harris and the *Red and Black* gained increasing national attention, even some of Harris's staunchest supporters wondered privately whether he had made martyrs out of the student editors, a point that his critics were happy to make publicly. Florida's *Gainesville Daily Times* observed that "Those two lads editing the *Red and Black* . . . probably had more fun getting fired than they would have had if Regent Roy Harris had chosen to ignore their editorial. . . . Any politician who takes a student newspaper's editorials so seriously that he decides to enter combat with the authors only falls into a trap set for him by his juniors. What could possibly please a student editor so much as to have his opinions become the center of a controversy far bigger than himself." The *Cornell Daily Sun* asked, "How can they [the university administration] so easily forget that this nation was founded on the premise that 'all men are created equal'? And how can they use freedom of the press, guaranteed to them by another great tradition, to quelch [sic] another person's use of that same freedom?" And the *Miami Hurricane* lamented the fact that "Another college newspaper saw its press freedom shackled early this month with the establishment of a special control board to make editorial decisions on controversial matters. . . . A controlled press serves as a tool for its own interests rather than an objective voice. It tends to reflect the views of its puppeteers rather than the will of the students."[15] The controversy made its way into the pages of the *New York Times*, *Newsweek*, and *Time*.

For a time it appeared that Ralph McGill of the *Atlanta Constitution* was the *Red and Black*'s sole ally among Georgia's journalists. During the month of December 1953, McGill and Harris traded barbs on a regular basis. In the December 5 edition of the *Atlanta Constitution* McGill came to the defense of the *Red and Black,* criticizing Harris for a "vulgar and unfair attack on decent young men" and for helping to create a climate of "thought and press control" similar to that which existed during the Hitler, Mussolini, and Stalin regimes. In the December 14 issue of his *Augusta Courier* Harris countered by accusing McGill of waffling on the issue of segregation. "Every time you mention segregation he goes into a tailspin. He hasn't had the courage to advocate abolishing segregation, but for years he has been writing and saying that segregation is on its way out." Several paragraphs later Harris wrote that McGill would be in favor of "open[ing] the doors of the schools so that the white children and the negro children can sit down together, adjust themselves to the change and begin mixing and mingling as one race and one people." This editorial was accompanied by a cartoon titled "Mixed Schools— The Devil's Brew for Georgia," which pictured McGill stirring a boiling cauldron containing one white female student, two black male students, some books, notepads, and a ruler. Harris labeled it a "common melting pot."[16]

Walter Lundy and Bill Shipp's stand against Roy Harris drew praise from all over the world, and the letters, postcards, and telegrams poured in by the hundreds, from as far away as Japan. Many of the respondents praised the student editors for their progressive stance, while others, not necessarily in agreement with that position, defended their right to express their views without political interference. A former UGA professor then living in Freeport, Maine, wrote: "By clinging to segregation we are placing the best possible cold-war weapon in the hands of the Russians. I'm not telling the South what to do. . . . But I can't help applauding, and wildly applauding, those Southerners who've got the guts to attempt to dispose of this explosive problem." A soldier stationed in Tokyo, Japan, wrote: "Congratulations! You guys have stood firmly to principle. . . . Segregation is real fuel for Commie propaganda, and its continuance will certainly endanger the very existence of our country. . . . Incidentally, I'm white and from Texas." A college student from Michigan wrote: "Naturally, we damn-yankees agree wholeheartedly with your original editorial. Negroes room with whites in our dorms and we are proud to acknowledge the fact. . . . We realize, however, that many people south of the Mason-Dixon line are still fighting the War between the States." A person from Urbana, Illinois, wrote: "This letter is, I hope, one of thousands to offer congratulations and assistance. . . . As an outsider, the only concrete suggestion I can make is a plan to obtain enough outside subscriptions to your newspaper at a profit to you so that you can continue to publish without Mr. Harris' support and without compromising your principles."[17]

Many letters of support came from the South. A woman from Auburn, Alabama, wrote: "I just wanted to express to you my thankfulness. What you did was a pioneering and brave thing. You picked up an issue which existed and exposed it for the sake of truth. My husband did the same thing three years ago, and I remember how proud I was of him, and how proud he was of his threatening letters from the Ku Klux Klan." A UGA alumnus in Atlanta wrote: "By now you probably know that hundreds of Georgia alumni agree with your stand against segregation and that thousands of them protest the denial of your right to speak out. . . . Who appointed a man like Roy Harris to the Board of Regents? Who elected Talmadge governor? Will the people of Georgia elect in 1954 another governor whose campaign is based on race hatred? Perhaps the furor raised by your editorial will make all of us think more clearly before we vote." Another Atlantan wrote: "Whether or not segregation of the races should be maintained is a question wherein we find much diversity of opinion. Even though I might disagree fully with your opinions on the subject, I would still insist upon your right to express your views in whatever medium might be available to you."[18]

Though the vast majority of the letters sent to Lundy and Shipp expressed support for their position, not all of them did. One person from Albany, Georgia, wrote: "Instead of aiding and abetting in the suicide of your own race you would better serve yourself, your family and your country if you would about face and fight these Communist Mongrelizers before they destroy the greatest and most powerful country in the world. . . . They can't do much with us old timers, but they really mean to 'brain wash' you youngsters, and it looks like they are having some degree of success at it, as many parents in the North and West are finding out to their sorrow." Another South Georgian wrote: "Turning the University of Ga. into a Negroid school! It might even spread down here. Horrors! Do you know what this may lead to? Negro Majorettes! Can you imagine Negro Majorettes stepping in the High School band with their black skinny legs? Of course you can't. It is too awful to contemplate. . . .

Of course you've figured out a way to keep YOUR sister from dancing at the school prom with a Negro. . . . Something has got to be done to get you boys back on the right track. You are way off the beam. You are suffering from a case of what is becoming known as 'Negroietis.' . . . Hoping for an early recovery for all of you."[19]

The letters came from virtually every state in the union, and most of them were written by whites, though a good number were written by blacks, with several coming from black civic and professional organizations. Lundy and Shipp received dozens of letters of support from other student editors of various college newspapers, as well as other leading journalists across the nation, including Ralph McGill, editor of the *Atlanta Constitution,* who after World War II had emerged as one of the leading southern spokesmen for racial justice and who was himself often the target of Roy Harris's diatribes.[20] Many of the letters addressed similar themes, such as communist propaganda, an issue cited frequently by both supporters and critics of the *Red and Black.* Supporters argued that the student editors' bold stance against segregation was one clear way of subverting communist influence, while their critics charged that the *Red and Black's* liberal bent was proof positive that the newspaper had already come under communist control and that the student editors were acting as accomplices.

Despite the hundreds of letters, postcards, telegrams, phone calls, and other private expressions of support, Bill Shipp ruefully laments the fact that he and Lundy received virtually no public support. With the exception of Ralph McGill, who wrote editorials supporting their position, Lundy, Shipp, and the rest of the *Red and Black's* staff had to endure the tempest alone. Not a single university official offered any support, although some of the students were openly supportive. Shipp, who went on to become one of the state's most respected journalists and political commentators, remembers that there was "a great deal of hostility" on campus, especially at the law school, over the possibility that Horace Ward might be admitted and even greater animosity aimed at the *Red and Black* for suggesting that he should be admitted:

Many faculty members were openly hostile to the idea and went out of their way to publicly vent their hostility . . . My mother's porch was littered with garbage, and graffiti was written on the side of my house in Marietta calling me all kinds of names. It distressed my mother a great deal, as she was not in good health.

37

During this time I got virtually no support from any state or university official. Drewry was the dean of the journalism school. He and President Aderhold were instrumental in forcing the whole *Red and Black* staff to quit. Hosch was part of the establishment trying to figure out some subterfuge to keep blacks out of the law school. Caldwell was an agent of the governor and an old windbag. Dean Tate, the legendary Dean Tate, was mad as hell [at me]. He and other administrators were worried about appropriations, worried about alienating the state house. They wanted to know why was I trying to wreck the university? Why was I determined to run counter to what they perceived as public opinion? Dean Tate [who figured prominently in 1961 when the university was finally desegregated] has always been pictured as a surrogate father. But he was no surrogate father of mine. He was a mean old bastard; in my view, he was a bully. It was not a happy time.[21]

As for his decision to resign from the *Red and Black,* Shipp says that it was a forced resignation and that a journalism professor suggested that he resign voluntarily if he did not want to be fired. Several weeks later, other university faculty and administrators told him that everybody else would be a lot more comfortable if he left the university. Although he was no longer affiliated with the newspaper, Shipp was still very much a lightning rod, as he puts it. He left the University of Georgia without finishing his degree and followed Horace Ward into the army in August 1954.[22]

Walter Lundy remembers those days much the same way. He acknowledges that a good many faculty members privately supported the *Red and Black's* position but were reluctant to do so publicly. He received a few letters of support from faculty members who asked not to be identified, and occasionally some professors would come up to him and tell him very quietly to "stick with it, stick to your guns," but then walked away quickly so as not to appear conspiratorial. Although it would have been reassuring to have had some public expression of support from the faculty, Lundy understands the pragmatism of their actions better now than he did at the time, though he admits still feeling slightly annoyed at their moral cowardice. "I was a little bit bitter about the lack of faculty support, I suppose, because of my youth and arrogance. But I now realize that had these faculty members come out in support of us, their jobs might have been in danger. They may not have been fired, because I don't think the university wanted to make martyrs out of anyone, but their careers would have been damaged."[23]

Those who opposed the student editors were much more eager to share their views, in public as well as in private. Lundy recalls that the professors who were members of the Board of Control let it be known in no uncertain terms that they were "very, very unhappy" with Lundy and Shipp's actions. Other faculty members opted for a more private setting, calling the staff members into their offices to express their opposition. Even President Aderhold once called Lundy into his office to tell him that he was very disappointed in his judgment. But much of the heat that Lundy and his fellow staffers felt came from John Drewry, dean of the School of Journalism. According to Lundy, Drewry was especially angry about the *Red and Black's* editorials because the student newspaper was identified with the School of Journalism, which he saw as a reflection upon himself. As Lundy recalls it, "I think Dean Drewry was more concerned about how this would affect his own personal position. I don't think he felt strongly ideologically, but he was very upset that we had caused trouble for him and that our position made him look bad. And so he was actively involved in the effort to put a gag on the *Red and Black*. . . . To Dean Drewry, freedom of the press meant freedom only to write about those things that would not in any way embarrass the university."[24]

Walter Lundy, Bill Shipp, Priscilla Arnold, and Gene Britton all remember that their decision to resign their positions was a difficult one that caused each of them some measure of personal anguish. As Gene Britton remembers it, the decision was especially difficult for Priscilla Arnold (now Priscilla Arnold Davis) because she very much wanted to be the first woman editor of the *Red and Black*, which would certainly have enhanced her professional career. But for her, principle outweighed personal ambition, so she and Gene Britton went to a prayer service at the Methodist church and reached their decision together. They agreed to put out one more issue of the *Red and Black* in support of desegregation before tendering their resignations.[25]

The resignations of Arnold and Britton ended the brief, but intense, battle between the university's student newspaper and the most powerful member of the Board of Regents. The student editors had lost their newspaper but had won self-respect, and their actions had stirred the consciences of many who had previously been apathetic. As for Roy Harris, he eventually turned his attention to the emerging civil rights movement and devoted most of his remaining years to opposing racial equality.

There was much speculation among Georgia politicians about the future of segregation in the months leading up to the *Brown* decision. For many of the state's leading segregationists, their public confidence that segregation would remain intact belied their private concerns that the Supreme Court might possibly overturn the "separate but equal" doctrine. In the event of an unfavorable ruling, Governor Talmadge proposed to the Georgia legislature in November 1953 that the state adopt a "private school plan" that would allow the state to convert the public educational system into a private one and to channel state funds into tuition grants for students attending private schools. The legislature adopted the amendment, which the voters later approved in the general election. The governor also proclaimed his willingness to use the state militia to prevent integration, should such action become necessary.[26]

The United States Supreme Court rendered the long-awaited decision on May 17, 1954. Speaking for a unanimous Court, Chief Justice Earl Warren read the decision: "We conclude that in the field of public education the doctrine of 'separate but equal' has no place. Separate educational facilities are inherently unequal."[27] Coming fifty-eight years after *Plessy v. Ferguson*, eighty-six years after the ratification of the Fourteenth Amendment, and ninety-one years after the Emancipation Proclamation, the Court's decision in *Brown v. Board of Education* removed the legal underpinnings of the South's caste system, even though another generation would pass before the nation began to feel the practical effects of the decision.

Reaction to the decision from Georgia politicians was immediate and predictable. Governor Talmadge said that the Supreme Court had "blatantly ignored all law and precedent and usurped from the Congress and the people the power to amend the Constitution" and that the decision had reduced the United States and Georgia constitutions "to a scrap of paper." Several days later, on *The World Today* on the CBS network, Talmadge declared: "It would take several divisions of troops down here to police every school building in Georgia and then they wouldn't be able to enforce it." Senator Richard B. Russell, senior U.S. senator from Georgia, referred to the *Brown* decision as "a flagrant abuse of judicial power" and said that the Court was becoming a "political arm of the Executive Branch of the Government."[28] Other prominent politicians joined Talmadge and Russell in a chorus of dissent.

Newspapers from across the state offered various editorial opinions. The *Atlanta Constitution* said that "the court decision does not mean that Negro and white children will go to school together this fall. The court provides for a 'cooling off' period. . . . Meanwhile, it is no time for hasty or ill-considered actions. It is no time to indulge demagogues on either side or those who are always ready to incite violence and hatred." The *Dalton Citizen* said that "while this newspaper believes in segregation, it also believes in equality, and as previously pointed out, we think the majority of whites and Negroes want segregation, but certainly not without equality." The *Gainesville Daily Times* provided one of the more positive assessments: "The unanimous decision of the United States Supreme Court that segregation must end in America's public schools emphasizes what most Southerners knew in their hearts anyway: the double system of public education would not hold up in the sensitive conscience of today's world." The *Morgan County News* printed perhaps the most extreme editorial on the subject: "We are proud Herman Talmadge is the Governor of the State of Georgia at this time of crisis. . . . But we believe that it would be best for the personal safety and liberty of both the white race and the negro race that every town and county in our state and every other state ought to organize a strong and well-armed Ku Klux Klan. When the Yankees invaded the South before, our grandparents found that necessary to maintain law and order and keep their personal freedom."[29]

The *Red and Black,* with a new set of editors, endorsed the Court's decision:

> Would not Henry Grady be gladdened to know that the major stumbling block to "The New South" has been removed? Would not Thomas Jefferson be proud that the principle "all men are created equal" has finally been recognized in action as well as in theory? The Constitution of the United States has taken on a new and fuller meaning of freedom with this latest interpretation. . . . We realize the abolishment of segregation will not come soon. It will be delayed by appeals, test cases and other legal steps. These will be overruled, in time. Segregation's death seems inevitable—may it come quietly and quickly.[30]

Between 1954 and 1956 the Georgia legislature passed an avalanche of legislation designed to prevent compliance with *Brown*. Lawmakers passed an amendment (later approved by the voters) that required the governor to cut off state funds from any public school that operated on an integrated basis, a tactic used by several southern states. Legislators later won approval of a state constitutional amendment authorizing the governor to close any school threatened with integration. In 1956 lawmakers passed five bills designed to implement the "private school amendment," including one that permitted private school teachers to join the state teachers' retirement system, one that made individual tuition grants available to students wishing to enroll in private schools, and one that authorized school boards to lease school property to private schools. Acting in concert with the state legislature, the Georgia State Board of Education passed a rule that would revoke the license of any teacher who was a member of the NAACP or any related organization. The board also threatened to revoke the certification of any teacher who condoned "mixed classes" and prohibited teachers, principals, and pupils from participating in biracial meetings. The state legislature also passed laws aimed at preserving segregation in public parks and waiting rooms in interstate travel. [31]

So that there would be no doubt about their disdain for the *Brown* decision, lawmakers passed several resolutions that in actuality were more ridiculous than dangerous. The Georgia House passed a resolution demanding a return to segregation in the armed forces, and the full legislature adopted resolutions calling for "interposition," the impeachment of U.S. Supreme Court justices, and the nullification of the Thirteenth and Fourteenth Amendments. [32] In March 1956, 96 of 128 members of Congress from the eleven former Confederate states signed a Declaration of Constitutional Principles, better known as the Southern Manifesto, that formally denounced the *Brown* decision as having destroyed "amicable relations" between blacks and whites. Just one month earlier, in its own individual show of defiance, Georgia's legislature voted 41–3 in the Senate, and 107–32 in the House, to adopt a new state flag, one that would now have the state seal on the left and the battle flag of the Confederacy occupying the right two-thirds. The legislature passed numerous other laws aimed at harassing the NAACP. [33]

The Court's desegregation ruling coincided with Georgia's 1954 gubernatorial campaign. Himself ineligible for reelection, Talmadge watched his various lieutenants jockey for position. Talmadge's prestige and popularity would virtually ensure victory for whichever of his lieutenants emerged as the frontrunner. After much maneuvering and several broken commitments, Marvin

Griffin emerged as the strongest of the Talmadge candidates, eventually receiving the support of the governor himself. Although Griffin won only 36 percent of the popular vote, he carried 115 of 159 counties and received 302 of the state's 410 county-unit votes.[34]

Griffin assumed the governorship in 1955, and true to his mentor and predecessor, followed closely in Talmadge's footsteps. He became the new champion of states' rights, the county-unit system, and racial segregation. Shortly before taking office, he had vowed, "Come hell or high water, races will not be mixed in Georgia schools."[35] As Georgians would soon learn, Griffin intended to enforce his "no mixing" pledge on the playing field as well as in the classroom, and his determination to hold the line on segregation would result in a showdown with students at the Georgia Institute of Technology.

At the beginning of the twentieth century, both the University of Georgia and the Georgia Institute of Technology—the state's two athletic powerhouses—had committed themselves to a policy of rigid racial exclusion, refusing to play against any team whose ranks included a black member, even if the game were played outside the South. Both universities had successfully defended this policy during the 1920s and 1930s, but the growing presence of black athletes on nonsouthern teams after World War II forced the two schools to weigh their commitment to total segregation against their desire to win a national championship. During the 1950s, both schools began to display a willingness, albeit reluctantly, to participate in integrated contests as long as they were played outside the South. But Georgia's staunch segregationists interpreted even this regional accommodation as a capitulation to northern liberals, and Governor Griffin would have none of it.[36]

After a highly successful season in 1955, the Georgia Tech Yellow Jackets received a coveted invitation to the Sugar Bowl in New Orleans. Georgia Tech's opponent, the University of Pittsburgh, had one black player, a fullback named Bobby Grier, something Georgia Tech became aware of upon receiving its invitation. After consulting with the players and key members of the Georgia Tech Athletic Association, President Blake R. Van Leer and Coach Bobby Dodd accepted the bowl bid. As a precaution, Dodd had also contacted Governor Griffin, who responded, "Bobby, I can't come out publicly and support this. But you go ahead and do it." Georgia Tech officials considered the matter closed, but they were in for an unpleasant surprise.[37]

On November 30, the executive committee of the States Rights Council of Georgia, an influential pro-segregation organization, sent a telegram to Coach Dodd protesting Tech's acceptance of the bowl invitation and urging him to help prevent "any breakdown of our laws, customs, and traditions of racial segregation." Robert O. Arnold, chairman of the Board of Regents, defended the trip by pointing out that "Georgia and Tech both have played against Negro players in the past." A Georgia Tech spokesman tried to minimize Bobby Grier's importance to the Pitt team, inaccurately claiming that he was just a third-string fullback. Tech president Van Leer, confined to bed with the flu, told reporters that he had never broken a contract in his life and that "I do not intend to start now." University of Pittsburgh officials responded forcefully by saying that Grier was an important part of their team and that he would "sleep, eat, practice, and play" with the team in New Orleans. At this point Governor Griffin jumped into the fray and deliberately provoked a major controversy.[38]

On Friday, December 2, 1955, Governor Griffin sent shockwaves throughout the Georgia Tech community by reversing his earlier position and announcing his opposition to the game. Griffin sent a telegram to regents chairman Arnold, demanding that he call an emergency meeting of the board to consider prohibiting Tech from playing in the bowl. In apocalyptic language, Griffin declared: "We cannot make the slightest concession to the enemy in this dark and lamentable hour of struggle. There is no more difference in compromising the integrity of race on the playing field than in doing so in the classroom. One break in the dike and the relentless seas will rush in and destroy us."[39]

Griffin's action ignited a firestorm of protest throughout the state, especially among students, faculty, and administrators at Georgia Tech and Georgia who bitterly resented his intervention in what they regarded as an internal university matter. Georgia Tech students were the first to display their displeasure with Griffin's about-face. Early Friday evening, a group of Tech students burned the governor in effigy. As their ranks swelled, the demonstrators eventually headed toward the state capitol, arriving there around midnight. Upon learning that the governor had gone home, the students and their supporters, who now numbered nearly two thousand, protested loudly to reporters, hanged another effigy of Griffin, and damaged trash cans and several building doors on the capitol grounds before some of them decided to march to the governor's mansion. By the time this smaller group arrived at the residence, a phalanx of policemen and state highway patrol-men were already assembled. After a lengthy standoff, the students gradually dispersed. Students at several other Georgia colleges also staged demonstra-tions criticizing Griffin. In Athens, a crowd of over five hundred students marched through the streets displaying a banner that read, "This time we're for Tech."[40]

The controversy over the bowl game had suddenly become a major polit-ical embarrassment for the governor. The president of Georgia Tech's stu-dent government issued a public apology to the University of Pittsburgh for the governor's actions, making it clear that his fellow students were "not against segregation but against political forces which are trying to prevent us from going to the Sugar Bowl." Tech's campus newspaper, the *Technique*, charged that Griffin's actions had made the university and the state "look like fools before the entire nation." The *Atlanta Constitution* condemned the governor for creating a "teapot tempest," and several other state newspa-pers expressed similar concerns. College officials reported that Tech's pres-ident had already received more than fifty telegrams concerning the inci-dent, with all but one of them supporting Tech's participation in the bowl game.[41]

The governor's office quickly tried to counter this flood of criticism with staff members claiming that they too had received numerous telegrams, al-most all of which supported the governor. One angry state representative suggested that the legislature cut off funds to Georgia Tech if it insisted on playing the game. Roy Harris publicly backed the governor, warning that such actions were necessary because blacks were trying to undermine segregation by attacking it in the areas of entertainment and sports. This segregationist counterattack notwithstanding, public opinion seemed to be running against the governor.[42]

The Board of Regents met on Monday, December 5, to consider the gover-nor's request. David Rice of Atlanta was the only regent who argued that Tech should be allowed to play in the game, and he openly criticized the governor for making a mountain out of a molehill. Roy Harris strongly disagreed, argu-ing against any breach of Georgia's racial laws and customs, regardless of the reason. After a three-hour discussion, the regents voted to approve the trip and, in a rather surprising move, adopted a general policy governing future games that was less restrictive than expected. Under the new guidelines, state colleges were required to honor Georgia's segregation laws, customs, and traditions when playing at home, but on the road they would "respect the laws, customs, and traditions of the host state." The regents also commended the governor for his "courageous stand in upholding his oath as governor and for his inspiring leadership in protecting inviolate the sacred institution of our people" and for placing "conscience and principle above all other considerations."[43]

Historian Charles H. Martin makes the point that "Although the actual integration of both universities' football teams [Georgia and Georgia Tech] still lay over a decade away, the shift to a policy of integrated competition outside the state demonstrated that by the mid-1950s the state's college athletic establishment placed a greater emphasis on the pursuit of athletic glory than on the maintenance of total racial exclusion." However, the failure of extreme segregationists to halt the process of racial inclusiveness in college sports did not signal a softening of their position on segregation. Indeed, the regents' statement praising Griffin's actions underscored their commitment to segregation, lest there be any misinterpretation of their modest concession to the "laws and customs of other states." Feeling somewhat vindicated by the board's statement, Governor Griffin reaffirmed his commitment to segregation, a position he would embrace for the rest of his political life. As for the game itself, Georgia Tech won 7–0, capturing its fifth consecutive bowl victory. Bobby Grier, the black fullback at the center of the controversy, was the game's leading rusher and received a loud ovation from the crowd when he left the field in the fourth quarter with an injury.[44]

Marvin Griffin was first and foremost a segregationist, but equally important, he was politically astute, and in the era of massive resistance and civil rights he knew just what buttons to push. During his unsuccessful run for governor in 1962 he took aim at civil rights protestors, the Reverend Martin Luther King Jr. in particular. Always quick to turn a phrase, he told a howling crowd, "you can't give these law violators an inch, or they'll take a mile. There ain't but one thing to do and that is to cut you a blackjack sapling and brain them, and nip 'em in the bud to begin with. . . . If he [King] is still here in January and violating the law, I'll put him so far back in jail you'll have to pipe air to him."[45] Preserving segregation became the centerpiece of Marvin Griffin's administration, and like so many other southern politicians of that time, he proceeded to act as if state law and the popular sentiment of segregationists effectively nullified any federal court ruling.[46]

Herman Talmadge had proclaimed that there would be no school integration as long as he was governor. Marvin Griffin made the same promise, and he intended to fulfill it, even if it meant defying the federal courts. Georgia's lawmakers, from the governor on down, continued to act in bold defiance of *Brown;* indeed, many white southern politicians would build their careers on the segregation platform. But civil rights activists kept their eyes on the prize, sensing that change was in the wind. Segregationist forces, however, were not yet ready to sound retreat. There was far too much at stake.

CHAPTER THREE

"A Qualified Negro"

There is certainly no dispute that
no Negroes have ever attended
the University of Georgia. We will
stipulate that, but we will not stipulate
that there was any custom . . . on
the part of the authorities to exclude
them.
—B. D. "Buck" Murphy, attorney
for the defendant

The [legal] system is based on people
getting on the stand and telling the
truth. But people who talk about their
respect for tradition and integrity
and the Constitution get involved in
one lie after another. They're willing
to break down the system to keep a
Negro out. . . . This is one of the most
serious by-products of segregation.
The people get a disregard for the
law. They see supposedly important
people get up day after day on the
stand and lie. The reason the whole
thing seems funny to watch is that you
spend all that time proving something
everybody already knows.
—Constance Baker Motley, attorney
for the plaintiff

Horace Ward's two-year stint in the military was coming to an end, and he was scheduled to be discharged in August 1955. In July, state attorney general Eugene Cook released a statement to the press disclosing that he had been informed that Ward intended to reactivate immediately his suit in federal court. "It's ripe for a showdown," Cook said. "If he wins, all he will do is close down the law school." Cook was referring to sections of the Appropriations Acts, which prohibited the spending of state funds on any school unit with integrated classrooms. Cook revealed that he and other prominent Georgia attorneys, including former governor Herman Talmadge, Charles Bloch of Macon, B. D. "Buck" Murphy of Atlanta, Carter Pittman of Cartersville, and Durwood Pye of Atlanta, would attend a strategy meeting to decide how best to proceed with the Ward case. Murphy and Pye served as counsel and executive secretary, respectively, of the Georgia Commission on Education, a strategy group made up of top legislative officials and prominent private citizens and created by the legislature to continue segregation in the state's schools. Cook also disclosed that he was planning a series of meetings with representatives from other southern states who were opposing desegregation efforts and announced his intention to assign two of his assistants to segregation on a full-time basis. "I think the NAACP means just what it says about knocking out segregation, and it's being aided and abetted by a notorious Supreme Court. . . . On the other hand, I think the people of Georgia, except for a few irresponsible people and outsiders, are just as determined that it shall not happen." Governor Griffin promised Cook that state funds would be made available to any Georgia school system that resisted integration.[1]

The mere thought that the University of Georgia's law school might be forced to close if Ward were admitted was enough to create a fair amount of anxiety on the campus, among students and university officials alike. Dean Hosch sent a handwritten note to Chancellor Caldwell on July 12 expressing his concerns. "A delegation of students conferred with me this morning and expressed great concern about the segregation problem facing the Law School. It appears that the recent statements of the Attorney General greatly agitated them." Board of Regents chairman Robert Arnold was equally concerned, especially after learning from Cook that because Ward's case would be heard in the equity division of the federal court, there was at least an outside chance that Ward could be admitted. Cook quickly reassured Arnold that Ward still had "a number of hurdles to overcome before a final order is issued." One of those hurdles was a new university rule—created specifically for Ward—which required an applicant to renew his application from time to time. Cook told Arnold that he hoped that the rule "will be scrupulously followed and that the court will respect it."[2]

Part of the attorney general's strategy to thwart Ward's application process included attempts to derail the NAACP. Following the *Brown* decision, Attorney General Cook led the campaign to cripple Georgia's NAACP, placing the organization on the defensive and forcing it to fight for its very survival. Georgia refined and tightened the offenses of barratry (persistently instigating lawsuits), champerty (providing service or financial assistance in a case in exchange for a share of the proceeds), and maintenance (unlawful meddling in a suit by providing either party with the means to carry it on) in a deliberate attempt to weaken the NAACP. Additionally, the state revenue service harassed the Atlanta chapter in an investigation of purported income tax evasion. Cook aimed much of his attack at black teachers who supported the NAACP and advised local superintendents to check the records and to fire teachers who were NAACP members. He also spread propaganda linking the NAACP with communism. Overall, Cook's actions had a debilitating effect on the NAACP's ability to operate in Georgia.[3]

Cook's efforts were greatly assisted by Charles Julian Bloch, one of the state's leading legal scholars. Bloch was to the state's legal establishment what Roy Harris was to the state's political establishment, and he used his skills during the 1950s and 1960s in defense of segregation. Born in Baton Rouge, Louisiana, Bloch moved with his family to Macon, Georgia, when he was eight years old. After completing his legal studies at both the University of Georgia and Mercer University (though he never actually earned a law degree), Bloch began his law practice in Macon and was frequently retained by the state in its fight against integration. He was president of the Georgia Bar Association in 1944 and 1945, chairman of the state Judicial Council from its creation in 1946 until 1957, and a member of the Board of Regents from 1950 until 1957. He also served as chairman of the Rules committee on the state supreme court. In 1958 he published a book titled *States' Rights: The Law of the Land,* in which he argued that the federal government was unlawfully encroaching upon states' rights, especially in the areas of education and segregation. For several years he was personal adviser to U.S. Senator Richard B. Russell.[4]

Bloch's influence and prominence in the state made him especially valuable to the segregationist cause, and Attorney General Cook consulted with him regularly. Bloch's opposition to civil rights gained him a national reputation, and he was often called upon by congressional committees to give expert testimony in cases involving constitutional matters. Referring to himself as a strict constructionist, he went to Congress to testify against civil rights bills in 1957 and in 1960. When asked how he, a Jew, could be so opposed to civil rights legislation for blacks, Bloch quipped: "I believe in local self-government, customs, and traditions. I don't think the Jewish people have got anything in common with Negroes." Although Bloch's efforts to preserve segregation were ultimately unsuccessful, he kept up his opposition to civil rights until he retired from his law practice in 1970.[5]

Within a few weeks after being discharged from the army, Ward wrote to university registrar Walter Danner on September 8, 1955, requesting that his application be renewed. Almost immediately, Attorney General Cook announced that the law school would close should Ward be admitted. Ward's attorney wanted a quick reply from the regents, as Ward wanted to begin classes in the fall. The regents met on September 16 but informed the press after the meeting that the Ward case had not been discussed, as his September 8 letter had arrived too late to be placed on the regular agenda. Ward's attorneys requested a pretrial hearing, which Judge Frank Hooper scheduled for January 9, 1956. The state asked for a postponement because the attorney general had to attend the opening session of the General Assembly on that date. Judge Hooper granted the delay, and the hearing was rescheduled for February 20.[6]

For the next eleven months, the state's attorneys introduced one motion after another either to have the case dismissed or to have the proceedings delayed. At the February 20 hearing, the state argued that Ward should have to submit a new application since his original application had been interrupted by his military service. At a hearing on July 30, the state asked for a further postponement, this time arguing that six individuals who were members of the Board of Regents when Ward first filed suit in 1952 were no longer members and thus could not be held liable to litigation. The state also claimed that two other regents had previous commitments they could not be excused from and that the son of one of the state's attorneys had to undergo surgery. At a hearing on September 10, Judge Hooper acceded to the state's demand that Ward file a new application, saying that it was the only way he could determine whether the regents had acted in good faith. But Ward's attorneys objected, alleging that race was the sole reason for Ward having been denied in the first place, and that he should not be subjected to new rules and regulations passed after the fact.[7]

After one last attempt by the state on November 2 to get the case thrown out on yet another technicality, Judge Hooper set the trial date for December 17, 1956. After six and a half years of legal maneuvers and delay tactics (including a suspiciously timed military draft notice), Horace Ward would finally have his day in court.

The case of *Horace T. Ward v. Regents of the University System of Georgia* began on December 17, 1956. Ward's legal team, now consisting of A. T. Walden, Donald Hollowell, and Constance Baker Motley from the NAACP's Legal Defense Fund, set out to prove in court what had been evident to them from day one—that Horace Ward's application to the law school had been denied for no other reason than the color of his skin and that the state's political establishment, members of the University Board of Regents, and high-ranking university officials had conspired to keep Ward out of the University of Georgia. Assistant attorney general Freeman Leverett prepared the case for the state, and B. D. "Buck" Murphy, Governor Talmadge's personal attorney, handled the oral arguments as special assistant attorney general. The other attorneys for the state were Georgia's attorney general Eugene Cook, Charles H. Bruce, and G. Arthur Howell. The state's position was that Ward was simply unqualified to enter the University of Georgia and that race played no role in the university's decision not to admit him.[8]

NAACP lawyers Thurgood Marshall and Robert Carter had initially filed the lawsuit on Ward's behalf, but Constance Baker Motley represented Ward at the trial. Motley's involvement with the NAACP dated back to 1945 when, as a twenty-four-year-old law student at Columbia University, she had worked as a volunteer doing legal research. That fall, Marshall offered her a position as legal research assistant, and in 1949 she became assistant special counsel. During her twenty years with the NAACP Legal Defense Fund, she was perhaps the nation's premier black female attorney. An imposing figure, both in terms of physical stature and intellect, she became nationally known as one of the NAACP's most able attorneys and would figure prominently in numerous desegregation cases over the next two decades.[9]

Donald Hollowell joined Ward's legal team in 1956 as chief counsel. Born in Wichita, Kansas, in 1917, Hollowell earned a law degree from Loyola University in Chicago. After completing military service during World War II, Hollowell decided to settle in Georgia, in part because of his interest in using the law to break down racial barriers, and in part because of Louise Thornton, a young woman (and his future wife) he had met while stationed at Fort Benning, Georgia. There were few black lawyers in Georgia at the time (indeed, there were only a handful throughout the entire South), and many of them did not practice civil rights law. Growing up in the Midwest had not shielded Hollowell from the daily indignities of Jim Crow, and his years of service in a segregated army had only strengthened his resolve to transform American society. In the early 1950s, Hollowell became active with the NAACP and in the post-*Brown* era emerged as the leading civil rights attorney in Georgia. Civil rights activist Lonnie King referred to Hollowell as the "hired legal gun of the Movement in Georgia." While he never received the recognition that seemed reserved for the NAACP's national stars, by the 1960s his name had become synonymous with the black civil rights struggle in Georgia.[10] Tall, handsome, and articulate, Hollowell was so impressive to the local NAACP that they insisted that he become chief counsel in the case, replacing A. T. Walden, whom Constance Baker Motley later described as "typical upper-class Southern—soft-spoken, nonaggressive, and exceedingly polite to both blacks and whites."[11] Despite Walden's iconlike status among many older black Georgians, Atlanta's NAACP felt that Walden was too old (he was seventy-one at the time) and perhaps too beholden to Georgia's white political elite to dismantle segregation. Some of Atlanta's young black militants, such as Julian Bond and Lonnie King, would criticize Walden in the early 1960s for his eagerness to bargain with Atlanta's white business establishment.[12]

At trial, University of Georgia officials took the witness stand and maintained a dubious position: although they clearly wanted to preserve segregation in the university system's colleges and universities, they did not discriminate against Horace Ward in their efforts to do so. Ward's attorneys raised the issue of the Appropriations Bill of 1951, which had authorized the state legislature to cut off funds to any white school that admitted a black student. Robert Arnold, chairman of the Board of Regents, and university president O. C. Aderhold both acknowledged the state laws in support of segregation but insisted that those laws did not influence the university's decision to reject Ward's application.[13] When Ward's attorneys charged that the regents' policy of offering out-of-state aid to black applicants was tantamount to exclusion, university officials claimed that the out-of-state aid program was a gesture of goodwill and that it most certainly did not imply that blacks were ineligible for admission to the state's white universities. L. R. Seibert, executive secretary of the Board of Regents, testified that the program existed "because the colored people want it; they are delighted with it. You just ought to see some of the letters that they write me commending us and telling us what a great opportunity they have." When asked why such a program did not exist for white students, Seibert replied that white students had never requested it.[14] University system chancellor Harmon Caldwell went so far as to say that "in fact, the white students have charged we have been discriminating against them because we have been paying out over $275,000 a year for the Negro students."[15]

If Ward's attorneys were to establish that Ward was the victim of racial discrimination, they would have to prove racial motive as well as procedural irregularities. Proving the latter would not be that difficult. Under cross-examination, university registrar Walter Danner admitted that university officials handled applications from blacks differently from those from whites. The registrar's office processed applications from whites but routinely forwarded applications from blacks to the regents. In Danner's words, applications "*of that nature* were sent to Mr. Seibert, that was the practice."[16] President Aderhold initially feigned ignorance about the application process, claiming that he did "not handle the admissions of the University," but minutes later contradicted himself by saying that "as far as I know, it [Ward's application] was handled differently."[17]

Next was the issue of Ward's qualifications. At the time, the major requirement for admission to UGA's law school was two years of college; yet university officials deemed Ward unqualified, despite his being an honor student and having earned a bachelor's degree from Morehouse College and a master's degree from Atlanta University. The university's position was that while Ward had obviously been a good student, his academic record was tarnished by the fact that neither of the schools he had attended was a *member* of the Southern Association of Colleges and Secondary Schools (SACS), the regional accrediting association. Although both Morehouse and Atlanta University had received A ratings from that same association and were fully accredited using the same standards that were applied to white schools (a fact that Walter Danner himself acknowledged), black colleges and universities were not allowed to become members of SACS. Danner's own testimony had confirmed the existence of blatant racial discrimination within the university system. This exclusionary policy made it impossible for any black student in the state to be eligible for admission into any of the state's white universities. Still, attorneys for the university maintained the position (as did their witnesses, who testified under oath) that the University of Georgia did not have a policy in place that systematically excluded blacks.[18]

Aside from academic-related issues, the defendants argued that Ward was unfit to enroll at the University of Georgia because of defects in his character. The special committee that university president O. C. Aderhold had appointed in 1951 to review Ward's application concluded that Ward's interview was unimpressive and that he did not reflect the intellectual depth necessary for the study of law. As a convenient way of not having to acknowledge Ward's scholastic achievement, committee member and law school dean J. Alton Hosch testified that since Ward had already been rejected, the committee "gave most of our attention to Ward as a man," and that based on their observations, Ward's responses to their questions were "evasive," "inconsistent," and "contradictory." When asked to cite some specific examples of Ward's inconsistencies, Hosch noted that Ward seemed to waffle on the issue of who had written some of his letters. "I asked him, Ward, did you write these letters? And he said, yes. And I said are you sure? And finally he admitted he did not write some of them, as I remember." Hosch also raised the issue of Ward's hernia. "He [Ward] said that he had a rather acute hernia; well, I asked him why he didn't have an operation. He said he didn't have the money. Then I asked him did he have the money to go to school and complete three years, because after all, we have limited opportunities for our students to do part-time work, and that is one thing we are very careful about . . . I thought that was inconsistent." These "inconsistencies," along with what the committee perceived to be a genuine lack of desire on Ward's part to pursue a legal career, led Hosch to conclude that Ward "didn't show that he had the qualifications that we thought necessary for an application for admission to Law School."[19]

That Ward was invited to an interview by this special committee was ample evidence that university officials never seriously considered Ward's application, and the creation of this committee was yet another attempt at subterfuge. The most compelling example of this duplicity, Ward's attorneys argued, was the unprecedented lengths university officials went to in order to keep one black student out. No other student's application had forced university officials to go so far as to modify admission requirements and to modify them in such a way as to exclude that one student, a fact that the university steadfastly denied. At trial, Charles Bloch claimed that these new requirements—psychological and aptitude tests, as well as letters of recommendation from law school alumni and a superior court judge—were designed not to keep Ward out, but to improve the caliber of Georgia's lawyers. "I did it for the purpose of getting better students at the University of Georgia, and hoping that it would affect all other law schools in the state, and for what I thought was the betterment of the administration of justice in Georgia."[20] Bloch's testimony revealed that, as chairman of the state's Judiciary Council, he had had ongoing correspondence with university system chancellor Harmon Caldwell and the Board of Regents and that it was at the behest of the Judiciary Council that the Board of Regents became involved in the matter of law school admissions. Perhaps not coincidentally, Governor Talmadge appointed Bloch to the Board of Regents in January 1952; the next month, on February 13, the regents adopted the resolution.[21]

Dean Hosch testified that establishing entrance examinations for prospective law students had been under consideration for some time and that officials from the American Bar Association had recommended such examinations. Board of Regents member Frank Foley testified that he had supported such efforts since 1942 when he was president of the Georgia Bar Association. In his opinion, there were too many "country lawyers" who had simply memorized the code.[22] None of these witnesses, however, offered a credible explanation as to why the time suddenly appeared ripe to implement these changes or why university officials were so insistent that these new rules apply to Ward, despite his having applied before the resolution was passed.

Two major stories developed on the second day of the trial. The first resulted from the testimony of Chancellor Caldwell. On the matter of out-of-state aid, Caldwell testified that its purpose was to "encourage them [blacks] to go to other institutions, but we do not offer aid saying we are refusing to admit them." When A. T. Walden asked Caldwell about the state law that prohibited race mixing in the schools, Caldwell seemed to contradict earlier testimony of previous witnesses by claiming that such was not the case. Although he had once been under the impression that the law in question would have prohibited blacks from entering the state's universities, Caldwell testified that after having conferred with Arthur Howell, attorney general for the Board of Regents, he believed that the law applied only to the state's common schools and not to the university system: "so there is no provision in the Georgia Constitution which prohibits . . . the admission of Negroes to any institution of the University System of Georgia." After that revelation, the following exchange took place between Chancellor Caldwell and Attorney Walden:

> *Walden:* Now, in light of the statutory provisions to which you have just referred, would you admit a qualified Negro to the University of Georgia?

> *Caldwell:* I have thought about that a lot, Colonel Walden, and the Regents are here, and they can fire me as soon as the meeting is over, but I'll tell you what I think about it, the way I feel about it, what I would have done then, what I will do now. If a case comes before me on appeal, and it appears on all the facts . . . that the Negro is eligible for admission to an Institution, I will rule that he is eligible, and I'll take that decision to the Board of Regents.[23]

Chancellor Caldwell's sudden willingness to admit a black person to the University of Georgia came as something of a surprise to many courtroom observers, especially in light of his earlier testimony in which he admitted that "we do wish, in our institutions, and so far as possible, to preserve the segregation of the races."[24] Sounding like a boldly progressive pronouncement, Caldwell's comments in effect underscored the university's contention that it had never erected any barriers to black applicants, so long as they were qualified. Neither Horace Ward nor his attorneys were convinced of Caldwell's sincerity. As Ward puts it: "Over the years, much has been made of Caldwell's statement that he would admit a black who was qualified. Frankly, I considered the statement to be another ploy, because I thought of myself as being very well qualified. My experiences had taught me that they [university officials] could always find a way of 'disqualifying' any applicant." Caldwell's statement quickly became a source of amusement in black legal circles; "Would you be willing to admit a qualified Negro?" became one of Constance Baker Motley's favorite questions in future desegregation cases.[25]

While Caldwell's comments were clearly part of the overall strategy—all of the other university witnesses had said essentially the same thing—some were now eager to challenge the chancellor to live up to his new creed. The day after Caldwell's testimony, an editorial appeared in the *Atlanta Constitution* that expressed the sentiments of many in the African American community: "Dr. Caldwell is doubtless mindful of the fact that for a good many years qualified Negro students have been admitted to graduate schools of state universities in Texas and in Arkansas, and in more recent years to the state colleges of North Carolina, Tennessee, and Virginia. His forthright statement would seem to call for a re-evaluation and examination of the existing statutes on the part of the state."[26]

The next major development of the trial came when Horace Ward took the stand. Rather than concern himself with Ward's academic qualifications, Buck Murphy focused on Ward's association with the NAACP in an attempt to prove that Ward was not really interested in studying law, but was merely part of an integrationist conspiracy hatched by Thurgood Marshall and his associates:

Murphy: Do you know Thurgood Marshall?

Ward: Yes sir, I know him.

Murphy: Do you know Robert L. Carter?

Ward: Yes, I know him.

Murphy: Did you employ them in this case?

Ward: Well sir, my counsel, Mr. Walden, brought them in.

Murphy: Brought them in? They live in New York, both of them? And they are general counsel for the National Association for the Advancement of Colored People?

Ward: That is my understanding, sir.

Murphy: Have you paid anybody to represent you in this case?

Ward: Dr. Boyd arranged initially for counsel for me, and he in turn arranged for financing matters.

Murphy: Who is financing this lawsuit? Are you doing it or is the NAACP doing it?

Ward's attorneys objected to this line of questioning, arguing that the financing of Ward's suit was irrelevant and immaterial. Murphy, however, persuaded Judge Hooper to allow these questions, arguing that "the whole atmosphere of the case is indicative of the fact that the applicant is not a bona fide applicant for admission to the University of Georgia. He simply is a tool of someone else." Murphy continued his anti-NAACP barrage, accusing Ward of being on the association's payroll in the summer of 1951 when he was employed by Wilson Realty Company in Atlanta. "Isn't it true that the firm didn't pay you anything and that the NAACP paid your salary? Isn't it true that the firm merely handed you the money?" Ward denied the accusation, insisting that company officials paid his salary.[27]

During his relentless grilling of Ward concerning his ties to the NAACP, Murphy questioned him about his current residence, which led Ward to reveal that he was living in Chicago and, to the astonishment of nearly everyone present, that he had been enrolled in law school at Northwestern University since September.[28] This sudden disclosure now changed the complexion of the case. Murphy then recalled the university registrar to the stand, who testified that since Ward had already matriculated at Northwestern, he could only enter the university now as a transfer student and, hence, would have to begin the application process all over again. As Murphy saw it, Ward had "voluntarily put himself in a position where he cannot be admitted on the basis of his 1950 application." Constance Baker Motley argued that because Ward had just enrolled at Northwestern, he would not be an "advanced" student, and as such, would have no credits to transfer. Regardless of Ward's current status, Hollowell and Motley argued that Ward's application for admission to the university had been maintained continuously since 1950, and that these new developments did not change the merits of the case. But Ward's attorneys also knew that Ward's disclosure had essentially rendered their case moot, and on January 3, 1957, they amended their original complaint and asked the court to issue an injunction barring the university from denying admission to anyone on the basis of race and to declare that Horace Ward's application had been rejected for those reasons.[29] Judge Hooper set January 21 as the hearing date.

It is unclear whether Murphy had any prior knowledge of Ward's matriculation at Northwestern or whether his questioning had inadvertently produced such a fortuitous turn of events. But clearly, the manner in which Ward revealed his enrollment at Northwestern gave the appearance that he and his attorneys had purposely deceived the court; at the very least, they had been less than forthright. Both Hollowell and Motley later admitted that they had not used the proper discretion, but they held their position that Ward's enrollment at Northwestern should have been immaterial to their case, although their decision not to divulge this information to the court suggested that they suspected otherwise. Ward himself had begun to doubt that he would ever be admitted to Georgia, and during his stint in the military he had begun exploring other options. "Whenever I was on military leave, I met with my legal advisors, and I made it clear to them that I didn't think that I could invest more than one more year in the UGA case. Age was catching up with me, and I was ready to move on. After they assured me that they could get the case to trial within a year, I agreed to stay with it."[30]

But as he approached his twenty-ninth birthday, and with added family responsibilities, Ward decided in the summer of 1956 that he would enroll in Northwestern in the fall. His attorneys hoped that, in the event that the UGA case was settled in his favor, he would be able to transfer. As for the way in which the court learned of his matriculation at Northwestern, Ward says, "that revelation had both a beneficial and a detrimental effect. In our view, and in the view of others, it suggested that here is a man who must be qualified to go to law school because he's in a first-class law school. But state officials would argue that by enrolling at Northwestern, I had abandoned my application. And later, in their legal briefs, the attorneys for the state would argue that we had not been open and above-board with the judge, and he should have been told about this, and quite frankly, that probably did enter into the judge's mind."[31]

While Georgians awaited the court's decision, they had time to reflect on the events of the past six and a half years, beginning with Ward's initial application in June 1950. Given the university's diversionary tactics, some had no doubt begun to wonder if Ward's case would ever be heard. In light of recent Supreme Court rulings in other states, Georgia's segregationists had reason to be concerned that the racial barriers in the University of Georgia's system might soon be eradicated, and that loomed as a real possibility once Ward's case was placed on the court's docket. Taking no chances, some of Ward's opponents were willing to use the carrot as well as the stick to prevent him from attending the University of Georgia. Benjamin E. Mays, then president of Morehouse College and renowned educator and civil rights activist, had mentored Ward; in fact, some suspected that it was Mays who had prompted Ward to file the suit against the university in the first place, a charge that Mays denied. It was no secret, though, that given Mays's stature in the African American community, both in Atlanta and beyond, he wielded considerable influence over all Morehouse Men, including Ward. Mays remembered that "a well-known, distinguished white man came to my office to request me to advise Ward to withdraw his suit and accept out-of-state aid. My caller assured me that Atlanta University could get money to build a law school for Negroes."[32] For some at least, no price was too great to pay in order to preserve segregation.

Expectations about Judge Hooper's ruling were decidedly mixed in the days leading up to his decision. Ward had initially felt good about his chances, but his optimism waned as the trial progressed, and he suspected that the way in which his matriculation at Northwestern had been revealed had not played well with the judge. Still, he and his attorneys hoped for a definitive ruling from Judge Hooper, one that acknowledged the existence of racially exclusionary practices at the University of Georgia. Hoping to prevent a violent response from segregationists in the event that Judge Hooper ordered the university to admit Ward, the university's *Red and Black* urged readers not to repeat the violence that had occurred elsewhere: "Is it really so important to keep one man out that all the rest must be denied an education? . . . There is still an echo of a disgusting spectacle that took place at the University of Alabama not long ago. It must not happen here."[33]

On February 12, 1957, Judge Hooper dismissed Ward's lawsuit against the University of Georgia on the grounds that Ward had refused to re-apply to the law school under the new guidelines and that Ward's enrollment at Northwestern had in effect rendered moot his application to the University of Georgia. In reading his decision, Judge Hooper concluded:

It is now well established that the authorities in control of . . . any state supported law school in this country may not refuse admission to any person solely on account of race and color. . . . While [Ward's] application was filed in September, 1950 the case did not come on for trial until December 17, 1956. During this interval of time, some six and one-half years, the plaintiff had consistently failed and refused to file any new application which would give to the Board of Regents sufficient information on which to base a decision as to his qualifications . . . and as a consequence there is no action by the Board of Regents for this Court to review. . . . there is *no evidence* in the record to indicate that defendants will refuse to admit plaintiff if he should in the future file an application as a transfer student. . . . Neither does the Court see any necessity for retaining jurisdiction over this case for an indefinite time in the future. . . . Should the plaintiff file an application in the future and should it be denied, the plaintiff may again apply to the courts, but the Court should not now declare any discrimination even though it might have existed at or about September, 1950.[34]

While university officials and their attorneys breathed a collective sigh of relief, Judge Hooper's decision came as little surprise to those who had followed the trial. On its face, Judge Hooper's rationale appeared legally sound, but it was evident from the beginning—at least to Ward's supporters—that the judge's sympathies lay with the state. Not only did he allow the defense to engage in a line of questioning that often seemed irrelevant (much of which was intended to impugn Ward's character), but he also failed to acknowledge that the various administrative policy changes set up by university officials were designed for the sole purpose of excluding Ward from admission. Benjamin E. Mays later wrote that he was "shocked, stunned, and terribly disappointed when I heard top university officials swear in court that race had absolutely nothing to do with Ward's denial of admission . . . I supposed these top officials had to lie, since [admitting] that Ward was kept out because of his race would have forced the university to admit him."[35] Despite the testimony offered by the state's witnesses, it was clear that the resolutions that were passed with the stated purpose of improving the quality of the University of Georgia's law school were timed to derail Ward's application. Donald Hollowell summed it up: "I don't think the judge was ever inclined to support our position. It was almost as if he knew deep down that Ward should be admitted, but instead looked for any reason to avoid making that decision.

But that was the kind of social and legal climate in which we operated in the 1950s."[36]

There were many who felt at the time—and are even more convinced today—that the deck was stacked against Ward from the very beginning. Bill Shipp, the former student editor of the university's *Red and Black* whose commentaries in support of Ward eventually led to his forced resignation from the newspaper, minces no words in denouncing the hypocrisy of the politicians and university officials who conspired to keep Ward out of the law school:

> The tests were not designed to qualify Ward for admission; they were set up to disqualify him. The judge himself couldn't have passed those tests. If Ward had gotten a perfect score, they would have claimed he had signed his name incorrectly. The university was never serious about these new requirements, because as soon as Ward went into the military, they went back to admitting white students the same way they had always done. If "Daddy" had gone to law school, then it didn't make any difference if "Junior" couldn't pass high school. Buck Murphy was Talmadge's lawyer, and it was Murphy's charge to keep any blacks from getting into the school system, or into UGA. Talmadge's position was "Don't let anything happen while I'm governor." He later admitted—or virtually admitted—that he had arranged the draft [of Ward into the army].[37]

In the post-*Brown* era, racism and segregation had become principal themes in southern politics; Georgia was no exception. Prejudices and fears that lay smoldering beneath a facade of gentility erupted with cataclysmic force in the aftermath of the United States Supreme Court's decision ending legalized segregation in the nation's public schools. If civil rights proponents viewed *Brown* as a long-overdue affirmation of the nation's commitment to racial and social justice, opponents interpreted the decision as a declaration of war. Some historians have argued that the most immediate effect of *Brown* was not to bring about an end to segregated classrooms but to galvanize the opposition into making its last stand in defense of segregation. An entire generation of southern white politicians built careers largely upon their opposition to any change in the existing racial order. Clearly, there was a profound southern white backlash against *Brown,* and the unification of this racial intransigence, known as "massive resistance," temporarily destroyed racial moderation in the South and helped create a climate in which racial fanaticism flourished. As Michael J. Klarman has observed, "In this extremist political environment, men who were unswervingly committed to preservation of the racial status quo were catapulted into public office. These massive resistance politicians were both personally and politically predisposed to use whatever measures were necessary to maintain Jim Crow, including the brutal suppression of civil rights demonstrations."[38] Georgia's political establishment, from the governor on down, reflected the racial intransigence of the region at large.

In Atlanta and other large cities in the state, black Georgians sought to influence public policy by increasing their numbers at the voting booths as well as forging political alliances with white moderates, especially white business leaders who feared the economic repercussions of trying to promote industry and growth in a region beset by racial strife. The Atlanta Negro Voters League, formed by A. T. Walden and John Wesley Dobbs in 1949 primarily in response to the reactionary Talmadge regime, organized African Americans into a viable political force. Black voter registration, which stood at 145,000 in 1952, had climbed to 163,000 by 1956. In 1953, the league was influential in electing Atlanta University president Rufus E. Clement as the first black member of the Atlanta School Board. Atlanta's black community also pressured the city to desegregate the police force in 1949, city buses in 1953, and golf courses in 1958. Pointing to Atlanta's black colleges and their influence, the increasing political power of the city's black population, and the liberalism of the city's newspapers (and no doubt mindful that Horace Ward's lawsuit against the University of Georgia had originated there), Roy Harris described Atlanta as the Achilles heel in the fight to preserve segregation in Georgia.[39]

After Judge Hooper dismissed Ward's suit, Ward and his attorneys pondered whether they should file an appeal. The decision was Ward's, and as he remembers, it really was not that difficult. He felt that he had invested as much time in the case as he could and that it was time for him to move on with his life. His lawyers were disappointed, but they understood his reasons. Ward said that he had gotten tired of people "assailing my character and questioning my integrity," and he and his family were eager to return to Chicago, which he thought of at the time as a place of refuge. He described that period in his life as "a real low point for me."[40]

Back in Chicago, Ward resumed his studies at Northwestern. As for his classroom experiences at Northwestern, Ward remembers them as being positive, though there was little in the way of racial diversity. He was one of only four black students in the entire law school, and there was no black faculty. He studied diligently, not only out of a desire to succeed in his chosen profession but also because he felt the added burden of having to prove himself. University of Georgia officials had said that he was not qualified to enter their law school, that he did not possess the character to be a lawyer. With the constant support of his wife, Ruth, he was determined to prove them wrong on all counts.[41]

Meanwhile, Ward's detractors, undoubtedly encouraged and emboldened by the trial's outcome, redoubled their efforts to stave off school desegregation. In Arkansas, Governor Orval Faubus was facing a showdown with President Eisenhower over the desegregation of Central High School in Little Rock, and Georgia governor Marvin Griffin and Roy Harris came to the state to lend their support to the segregationists. Faubus invited them to stay with him at the governor's mansion. Speaking to large crowds, Griffin and Harris railed against integration and proudly proclaimed that Georgia had successfully avoided integration and would keep up the fight. Days later, a mob of angry whites gathered outside Central High School to prevent nine black students from entering. Federal troops, dispatched reluctantly by President Eisenhower, would eventually guarantee the safety of the black students. When the school year ended in June, Governor Faubus closed all public schools in Little Rock for the 1958–59 school year. One by one, public schools in other southern states followed suit. By 1958, massive resistance to school desegregation helped define the southern landscape, and Georgia's political establishment, at least publicly, remained confident and defiant.

Roy Harris boasted that "as a result [of our efforts] sentiment became so unified in Georgia that there was no real effort made over five years to integrate the schools in Georgia. So far as I am concerned, I propose never to surrender. I may be hung. I may be shot. But regardless of what happens there will be no surrender on my part. . . . If one little nigra is entitled to go to Henry Grady High School in Atlanta, then all nigras are entitled to go to some high school with whites."[42] Even as massive resistance lay dying across the South by 1959, southern politicians continued to identify segregation as the one issue that most distinctively set the South apart from the rest of the nation. Having witnessed the futility of openly defying the federal government, segregationists now saw the necessity of changing their tactics—but there would be no retreat.

Horace Ward's efforts to enter the University of Georgia represented a major challenge to the state's political establishment, but at least for the time being, the segregationists had prevailed. As was evident from Ward's trial, those who ardently defended segregation were willing to go to any lengths to preserve it, even if meant subverting the legal system in the process. But here a critical distinction needs to be made: some, like Governor Talmadge and Regent Roy Harris, controlled the state's political machinery and had staked their careers on the preservation of segregation; others, like registrar Walter Danner and Board of Regents secretary L. R. Seibert, were merely tools of that establishment; and others, like President Aderhold and Chancellor Caldwell, who had a greater moral responsibility to the larger university community, chose the path of least resistance.

Those who hoped to end segregation at UGA would have to fight another day, and that day was not long in coming. In July 1959, two black Atlanta high school students, Hamilton Holmes and Charlayne Hunter, declared their intention to seek admission into the University of Georgia. Horace Ward's sojourn in Chicago was coming to an end and, with law degree in hand, he would soon be heading home.

A crowd of newsmen and students surround Charlayne Hunter, 18, and Hamilton Holmes, 19, as the two students arrive to register at the University of Georgia. Just ahead of Holmes and Hunter, carrying a folder and wearing a hat, is Horace Ward. AP/Wide World Photos.

Alfred Holmes, left, escorts his son Hamilton, right, and Charlayne Hunter (center) to the registrar's office. Vernon Jordan is in front. AP/Wide World Photos.

Hamilton Holmes displays the *Atlanta Journal*'s headlines on January 6, 1961, after he and Hunter were ordered admitted immediately to the University of Georgia. AP/Wide World Photos.

University of Georgia students wave a
Confederate flag as they demonstrate
through the streets of Athens against
the integration of the school and the
ordered closing by Governor Vandiver.
AP/Wide World Photos.

Holmes and Hunter on graduation
day, June 1, 1963.
AP/Wide World Photos.

Horace T. Ward being sworn in as U.S.
District Court Judge by Chief Judge
Charles A. Moye on December 27,
1979. Photo by H. C. Williams.

Horace Ward and Donald L. Hollowell
at the federal courthouse at the
swearing-in ceremony, December 27,
1979. Photo by H. C. Williams.

Horace Ward, Charlayne Hunter, and
Hamilton Holmes in the late 1980s.
Courtesy of Horace Ward.

Hamilton Holmes and Charlayne Hunter-Gault together on the University of Georgia campus for the last time during the 1992 Holmes-Hunter Lecture. Courtesy of the Georgia Center for Continuing Education.

Charlayne Hunter-Gault and Marilyn
Holmes unveil the marker that now
graces the front of the newly renamed
Holmes-Hunter Academic Building.
Courtesy of the Georgia Center for
Continuing Education.

CHAPTER FOUR

"Journey to the Horizons"

We will not bow our heads in sub-
mission to naked force. We have no
thought of surrender. We will not
knuckle under. We will not capitulate.
I make this solemn pledge. . . . When
I am your governor, neither my three
children, nor any child of yours, will
ever attend a racially mixed school in
the state of Georgia. No, not one.
—S. Ernest Vandiver, governor
of Georgia, 1959–1963

I had considered [the University of]
Georgia, but not really seriously. It
seemed such a remote possibility. . . .
When Hamp [Hamilton Holmes]
brought up Georgia . . . I said sure,
I'd like to go. It seemed like a good
idea. . . . I guess it always was in my
mind that I had the right, but Hamp
and I never had any discussions about
Unalienable, God-given Rights. . . . in
the back of my mind I kept thinking
this would never really happen.
—Charlayne Hunter-Gault

Rosa Parks's refusal to surrender her seat to a white passenger on a city bus in Montgomery, Alabama, on December 1, 1955, set in motion a series of events that would eventually transform a nation. The success of the Montgomery Bus Boycott, and Martin Luther King Jr.'s leadership role in it, signaled an awakening of African Americans' determination to be treated as first-class citizens, and it inspired an entire generation to confront the ugliness of American apartheid. Those who opposed change would meet this challenge with equal conviction, and nowhere was their determination greater than in their desire to preserve segregated schools. The crisis in Little Rock represented the high point of massive resistance, and all across the South white politicians closed schools rather than operate them on an integrated basis. Georgia was no exception.[1]

In 1958, Samuel Ernest Vandiver was elected governor of Georgia. In comparison to some of the state's previous governors, Vandiver seemed almost moderate on the race question. But when William T. Bodenhamer, one of his opponents in the Democratic primary, accused Vandiver of being weak on segregation, and then later claimed that the NAACP had endorsed Vandiver after whites and blacks stood together in line to be served barbecue at a Vandiver rally, Vandiver was stung by the charge. As was the case with previous elections, the candidate judged to be the best qualified to lead the state was usually the one who seemed to be the most committed to maintaining segregation, and Vandiver could ill afford to be "out-segged" by any opponent. While avoiding the virulent race-baiting that had characterized previous political contests, Vandiver nonetheless managed to convey his sentiments in clear and unmistakable language. He promised voters that if he were elected governor he would use the "state patrol and national guard troops if needed to maintain segregation," and in an oft-repeated statement he promised that "no school or college classroom [would] be mixed" during his administration. His segregationist slogan, "No, not one," proved successful, enabling him to capture better than 80 percent of the popular vote.[2]

Like most Georgia politicians of his day, Vandiver was stridently opposed to the *Brown* decision, which he maintained was unconstitutional. As lieutenant governor in 1957, Vandiver called the *Brown* decision a "judicial monstrosity fabricated upon sociology and psychology rather than legal precedent." In the same year, he told an audience, "[There is] not enough money in the Federal treasury to force us to mix the races in the classrooms of our schools in Georgia." When President Eisenhower sent troops to Little Rock, Arkansas, to enforce the desegregation of Central High School, Vandiver denounced him as a "modern-day Caesar" and even called for the president's impeachment.[3] But a series of decisions handed down by the federal courts in 1959 made it apparent that massive resistance in blatant defiance of federal law would not succeed.[4] Still, the rhetoric played well politically, especially since segregation remained grounded in the laws of the state. Just prior to his inauguration, Vandiver proclaimed on a television program, "If there is any integration, the schools must be closed under Georgia laws and the constitution of the state." He suggested that he would propose "an arsenal of legislation" allowing the governor to close individual schools rather than entire school systems, as well as any school which blacks transferred to or from. Ten months later Vandiver characterized desegregation as "the most overriding internal problem ever to confront the people of Georgia in our lifetime" and went on to attack the "advocates of surrender."[5]

By 1959, the civil rights movement was quickly capturing the nation's attention, and the crisis in Little Rock and the intensity of massive resistance signaled that the struggle to desegregate the schools would likely be a protracted one. Black leaders in Atlanta had been meeting among themselves, trying to figure out how best to proceed in their own local movement. They had organized themselves into a group called the Atlanta Committee for Cooperative Action, known as ACCA. Among its members were college professors and deans, insurance and real estate executives, and other professionals. Though most of them either were self-employed or worked in black institutions, they still were not immune from reprisals from the white community, and their activism—as was true of the movement as a whole—always carried with it an element of risk.[6]

It was this element of risk that led many within ACCA to focus their desegregation efforts on the Georgia State College of Business Administration rather than the University of Georgia. Georgia State was in Atlanta and was primarily an urban campus, which eliminated the problems of travel and housing. The University of Georgia, located seventy-five miles away in Athens, had a traditional college campus that was all-white and potentially dangerous, and its distance from Atlanta posed strategic problems for Atlanta's black leaders, who were understandably concerned about their children's safety. Jesse Hill, an actuary at the Atlanta Life Insurance Company and an influential member of Atlanta's NAACP, remembered that "in those days, people hesitated to send a seventeen-year-old kid into that hostility [referring to the crisis in Little Rock]."[7] Georgia State also seemed like an ideal place to strike because a federal judge had recently dealt the state its first setback in a desegregation suit involving the Georgia State College of Business Administration. On January 9, 1959, Judge Boyd Sloan declared that Georgia State's rule requiring that applications to the college be endorsed by two alumni was illegal. In a ruling that stunned the state's segregationist legal establishment, Judge Sloan wrote:

> The Court finds, under the evidence here, that the plaintiffs have scholastic credits sufficient to qualify them to make application for admission to the college. While the evidence indicates that the plaintiffs, Barbara Hunt and Myra Elliott Dinsmore Holland, may not be of good moral character and for that reason may not be qualified for admission to the college, the evidence shows the other plaintiff, Iris Mae Welch, to be of good character and not lacking in qualifications for admission. . . . The effect of the alumni certificate requirement upon Negroes has been, is, and will be, to prevent Negroes from meeting this admission requirement. . . . The alumni certificate requirement is invalid as applied to Negroes because there are no Negro alumni of any white institution of the University System of Georgia, and consequently this requirement operates to make it difficult, if not impossible, for Negroes to comply with the requirement, whereas white applicants do not face similar difficulties.[8]

Attorneys E. E. Moore Jr., Donald L. Hollowell, and A. T. Walden hailed Judge Sloan's decision as one "supported not only by the law and evidence, but also by the higher dictates of justice and equity." As expected, both of Georgia's United States senators viewed the decision differently. Senator Richard B. Russell expressed outrage that "any judge of any race" would order "the admissions of such persons to any college over the rejection of the governing board." Senator Herman Talmadge was equally shocked and urged white Georgians to use "every resource at their command to maintain segregation in Georgia colleges and public schools."[9]

In response to Judge Sloan's ruling, Governor Vandiver asked the legislature to strengthen the state's existing anti-integration laws. One bill permitted the governor to close any public school under federal orders to desegregate. Other laws prohibited cities with independent school systems from levying property taxes to support desegregated schools, permitted the state to pay legal counsel to defend segregated schools, permitted the closing of any college in the university system to avoid desegregation, allowed state income tax credit for financial contributions to private schools, and established maximum age limits for admission to colleges within the university system. All of the bills had the governor's blessing, and they all passed with only minor opposition.[10]

The maximum age bill, however, did raise a few eyebrows. State lawmakers believed that this bill, which established twenty-one as the maximum age for admission as an undergraduate and twenty-five as the maximum age for admission into a graduate program, was a good way of reducing the number of African Americans eligible to serve as plaintiffs in desegregation lawsuits. Representative J. Roy McCracken justified the bill on the grounds that the NAACP had difficulty finding young blacks willing to get involved in litigation and that, for various reasons, blacks tended to start college later (he reminded his colleagues that the plaintiffs in the Georgia State case were all in their forties). But Georgia Tech's president, Edwin Harrison, feared that such a law would cripple his school's graduate program, and UGA president O. C. Aderhold was equally concerned about the impact that the law could have on his university. Some lawmakers felt that the bill discriminated against students who waited until after marriage to pursue their education, while others believed that the state should be encouraging people to continue their education rather than discouraging them. Those who defended the law, however, pointed out that the bill made exceptions for veterans, teachers pursuing additional education, and others who exceeded the age limits but who possessed "ability and fitness" to further their education. Representative George T. Bagby was more blunt; reassuring his colleagues that the law would not discriminate against a single white student, he proclaimed unabashedly that the law was "designed to keep the nigger out!" The bill passed with only twenty-eight negative votes.[11]

Undeterred by the state's new segregationist legislation, ACCA activists began to compile a list of outstanding seniors in Atlanta's black high schools. These students had to have stellar records of academic achievement and be morally above reproach so that it would be virtually impossible for university officials to disqualify them for any reason other than race. The two best candidates were soon identified: Hamilton E. Holmes, a star athlete and valedictorian at Atlanta's Henry McNeal Turner High School (which had the rep-

utation of being *the* school for black Atlanta's upper crust), and his classmate
Charlayne A. Hunter, who had finished third in her class, was the editor of
the school newspaper, and had been voted Miss Turner High. Initially re-
cruited as applicants to Georgia State (where ACCA activists were optimistic
about their chances, especially since Judge Sloan had retained jurisdiction in
the case), neither student expressed much interest in going there. Holmes,
who wanted to study medicine, and Hunter, an aspiring journalist, were disappointed after reviewing Georgia State's course offerings, and both agreed
that they would rather attend the University of Georgia. As Jesse Hill remembers it, their decision to apply to the University of Georgia, which many ACCA
activists initially greeted with a great deal of apprehension, turned out to be
the right decision because it "got straight to the heart of the matter."[12] As the
flagship university of the state, the University of Georgia seemed to many to
be the ideal place for a federal-state showdown over integration.

Born in Atlanta on July 8, 1941, Hamilton Holmes seemed perfect for the
part. He was an honors student, co-captain of the football team, and senior
class president; his father and grandfather were both college graduates; and
his willingness to serve as a plaintiff was no doubt inspired by his family, one
of the most respected in Atlanta. His grandfather, Hamilton Mayo Holmes,
was a prominent Atlanta physician and family patriarch. Along with two of
his sons, Alfred Fountain "Tup" Holmes (Hamilton's father) and the Reverend Oliver Wendell Holmes, he successfully filed suit to desegregate the
Atlanta public golf courses in 1955.[13] Hamilton Mayo Holmes had worked
his way through Shaw Medical School in Raleigh, North Carolina, and had
been practicing medicine in Atlanta since 1910. "I trained my children from
infancy to fear nothing, and I told my grandson the same thing," Holmes told
journalist Calvin Trillin in 1963. "I told him to be meek. Be meek, but don't
look too humble. Because if you look too humble they might think you're
afraid, and there's nothing to be afraid about, because the Lord will send his
angel to watch over you and you have nothing to fear." To his grandfather's
delight, Hamilton had always wanted to be a physician.[14]

By contrast, Charlayne Hunter's origins were more humble. Born in Due
West, South Carolina, on February 27, 1942, she and her family moved to
Covington, Georgia, when she was very young. Her father, Charles S. H.
Hunter Jr., was an alumnus of Morehouse College and an army chaplain.
Her mother, Althea, whom she refers to as her "ideal woman—smart and

strong, creative and feminine," did not attend college but worked at various jobs, though her main job was caring for her family. The family moved to Atlanta in 1951 and Charlayne enrolled at Turner High School in the fall of 1954. She had hardly gotten settled in at Turner when she, her mother, and her two younger brothers moved to Alaska to be with her father, who was stationed there at the time. But in the spring of 1955 the family (with her father staying in Alaska) returned to Atlanta and Charlayne happily returned to Turner High.[15]

By the time they had entered their senior year, both Holmes and Hunter had distinguished themselves as being among the brightest and the best of Turner High's students. He was handsome and had an athletic build. She was slender and attractive and had hazel eyes. Though they were never romantically linked—they were more rivals than anything—they seemed ideally suited for the task before them. As Trillin put it, "Both had always been considered perfectly cast for the role. Good-looking and well dressed, they seemed to be light-complexioned Negro versions of ideal college students, models for an autumn Coca-Cola ad in a Negro magazine."[16]

Once Holmes and Hunter had decided on the University of Georgia, they requested application forms and course catalogs by mail (Hunter-Gault denies published reports that a black janitor sneaked the forms out of the office for them). M. Carl Holman, ACCA member and English professor at Clark College (now Clark University) in Atlanta, made sure that the applications were filled out properly, and Donald Hollowell made sure that no legal details were overlooked and that all correspondence was sent by registered mail. Several days later three ministers (two white and one black), a black physician, and a black YMCA official accompanied the two to the office of the Fulton County Superior Court clerk to obtain the affidavits of good character that were a part of the admissions process. Clerk J. W. Simmons signed the affidavits, setting the process in motion.[17]

On July 11, 1959, Holmes and Hunter made the front page of the *Atlanta Constitution*: "2 Negroes Try Doors at Athens." University of Georgia officials already had their strategy mapped out, and the registrar's response to Holmes's and Hunter's applications was to be the tack they would use for the next year and a half: "Registrar Walter N. Danner said the university is full up and already is turning down would-be freshmen. He said that because dormitories are full the only freshmen he can admit are those who are bona

fide Athens residents." Since the University of Georgia required all freshmen to live in dormitories, the lack of dormitory space meant that Holmes
and Hunter could not be admitted. Danner claimed that five hundred other
applications had been rejected for the same reason. Making sure that all bases
were covered, other university officials indicated that Holmes's and Hunter's
applications would not be considered because the previously announced August 10 deadline for admissions had been pushed back to July 15, several
days before Holmes and Hunter mailed their applications to Danner. With
their plans to enter the University of Georgia temporarily on hold, Hamilton
Holmes enrolled at Morehouse for the fall semester and Charlayne Hunter
enrolled at Wayne University (later Wayne State University) in Detroit. Both
students, however, informed Danner that they wished to be considered for
admission in the winter quarter 1960.[18]

Meanwhile, the civil rights movement continued to gain strength, encouraging the efforts of blacks and more than a few whites who had grown weary
of Jim Crow. The state's determination to keep blacks out of colleges and
universities meant that an increasing number of white applicants were being
hurt by this wave of anti-black legislation. The built-in loopholes that were
designed to allow whites to slip in saved some of them, but not all. Particularly burdensome were the age-limit statutes, which prompted some whites
to clamor for repeal of that legislation. Some members of the Board of Regents were concerned that the age-limit statute could have an adverse effect
on the entire university system, especially at Georgia State, which had lost at
least one thousand students in the last year. Hardest hit were the nontradi-
tional students, many of whom for various reasons could take classes only at
night. In 1957 the average age of students in the college was twenty-seven,
but three years later it had fallen to twenty for day students and twenty-
five for night students. Furthermore, Georgia State College officials pointed
out that, despite the built-in safety net that was supposed to protect white
students, very few whites had been admitted under the new guidelines, an
indication of how cumbersome it could be to maneuver the law in such a
way as to make it applicable only to blacks. State Representative Chappelle
Matthews of Clarke County tried to have the law repealed but encountered
stiff opposition from other legislators and Governor Vandiver, who insisted
that the state had a right to "determine at what age it wants to stop educating

persons." When the 1959 legislative session ended, the law was still on the books. [19]

Now that Holmes and Hunter had been forced to enroll elsewhere for the fall of 1959, they could only enter the University of Georgia as transfer students. University officials seized this opportunity to modify the rules again, making it more difficult in the future for transfer students to be admitted. As stated in the new policy, Holmes and Hunter now fell into a category of students who wished to transfer but did not "need the change in order to continue their academic program." Surely such a policy seemed justifiable, especially in light of the crowded conditions that existed at the University of Georgia. On November 24, 1959, Registrar Danner informed Hamilton Holmes by letter that he would not be admitted in the 1960 winter quarter because of "limited facilities" and because of his new classification as a transfer student whose matriculation at the University of Georgia was now deemed nonessential. A similar letter was sent to Charlayne Hunter a few weeks later. [20]

The two renewed their applications to the University of Georgia each quarter during the 1959–60 calendar year, and Danner replied each time that there was simply no space available. Holmes and Hunter's attorneys were aware that a substantial number of transfer students (who fell into a variety of categories) were being admitted to Georgia every quarter. But, as university officials pointed out, there were other reasons why the two could not be admitted. Because both Morehouse College and Wayne State University operated on the semester system and the University of Georgia was on the quarter system, officials argued that it was unlikely that their transcripts would arrive in time to permit admission in the middle of the academic year. When Holmes's transcript did arrive in time for him to be considered for the 1960 summer quarter, university officials discovered that the Morehouse transcript had inadvertently failed to specify that Holmes was a student in good standing, which UGA officials used as another reason not to admit Holmes. As the 1960–61 school year approached, the university's claim of inadequate housing space would no longer be relevant in Holmes's case, since male students were permitted to live off campus after their freshman year. When Holmes completed his freshman year at Morehouse, he was informed that limitations on "other facilities" now prevented his admission to UGA. Hunter's application for the summer quarter was denied because UGA officials claimed she had failed to file a formal request to have her application renewed, despite her letter to the registrar the previous December in which she had made her intentions clear.[21]

Herbert Holmes, one of Hamilton's younger brothers, who was a high school junior at the time, says that when it became apparent that Hamilton and Charlayne would not give up, some whites were willing to stoop to any level to keep UGA all-white. He recalls an incident at Morehouse College that convinced him of their determination. As Hamilton told Herbert later, some white people had approached a black student at Morehouse and had convinced him to go along with a plan to arrange for Hamilton to be caught in a compromising position with a white female. "Hamp told me that the black student got scared, and rather than go through with the plan he reported it to Dr. Mays [Morehouse president]. Mays then tipped Hamp off, and that was the end of it. But I remember that Hamp was shaken by the affair, and that probably helps to explain why he never got really close to any white students at UGA. He was just being careful."[22]

As fall approached, attorneys Donald Hollowell and Constance Baker Motley concluded that since the University of Georgia seemed determined to keep up the shenanigans a lawsuit was inevitable. Hollowell and Motley understood that if they were to have any chance of prevailing in court they would still have to go through all the motions or run the risk of having their suit dismissed because they had not "exhausted all administrative remedies," an increasingly popular and convenient legal excuse for those judges not inclined to rule against segregation. After being rejected for admission in the fall quarter, Holmes and Hunter appealed to Chancellor Caldwell; when he refused to act, they appealed to the Board of Regents. While the regents stalled, Hollowell and Motley, on September 2, 1960, petitioned the United States District Court for the Middle District of Georgia for a preliminary injunction that would prohibit the university from denying admission to the plaintiffs solely on the basis of race.[23]

Meanwhile, Horace Ward, who had completed law school at Northwestern in January 1959, was getting ready to come home. Ward had always known that Chicago was a brief stopover for him, and he was delighted when Donald Hollowell invited him to join his Atlanta law firm. He was even more thrilled when Hollowell asked him to assist in this new desegregation suit against the University of Georgia. Ward returned to Georgia in August 1960 and promptly became associate counsel in the lawsuit.[24]

Judge William A. Bootle began the hearing on September 13, 1960. Georgia attorney general Eugene Cook argued that the plaintiffs had filled out the application forms incorrectly and that by appealing to the Board of Regents they had in effect removed the registrar, against whom the suit had been filed, from the case. Since the regents had not yet met to consider the appeal, all administrative remedies had not been exhausted. Attorneys for the plaintiffs argued that the two black students had been denied admission repeatedly for no reason other than their race and asked the judge to issue an injunction forbidding such racially discriminatory action. Judge Bootle agreed that the plaintiffs had not exhausted administrative remedies, and refused to order their admission into the university; he did, however, leave the door open and ordered the Board of Regents to rule within thirty days on whether the applicants could proceed with personal interviews by university admissions officers, the next step in the admissions process.[25] The regents took nearly the entire thirty days before rejecting the applications of both students. In a meaningless gesture, the regents ruled that the applicants could reactivate the admissions procedure "without prejudice," obviously another delaying tactic. Such ploys continued to be effective, as by now fall classes had already begun and Holmes and Hunter had returned to their respective universities as sophomores. Judge Bootle scheduled a pretrial hearing for November 18, 1960, and ordered the university to allow the two students to proceed with the admissions interviews in the interim.[26]

In early November, Holmes and Hunter finally had their much-anticipated interviews with university officials, which Charlayne Hunter-Gault later described as a "going-through-the-motions waste of time," which was especially true in her case since she had to fly from Detroit to Atlanta and then drive over to Athens. She remembers her meeting with the three-man panel as being "pretty routine" but recalls that the interviewers were "rough on Hamp." Reminiscent of a similar panel's inquisition of Horace Ward nine years earlier, the interview committee completely ignored Holmes's academic qualifications and chose to focus exclusively on his personal life, asking him, for example, if he had ever visited a house of prostitution. Never known as an eloquent speaker, Holmes was unnerved by the intense grilling, which caused him to become even more flustered and inarticulate and, as Hunter-Gault remembers, almost proved disastrous. "It was so patently ridiculous to be asking Turner High School's 'Mr. Clean' such questions that it came close to undoing Hamp, who reverted to the kind of stuttering that used to grip him in high school when he was under pressure or angry. Only, in this case, his speech problem fed the perception of the opposition that he had something to hide." And, as was true in Ward's interview, the three-man panel concluded that Holmes's answers to their questions had been evasive and that there was "some doubt as to his truthfulness."[27]

At the pretrial hearing on November 18, Hollowell and Motley asked the judge to allow them to inspect the records of the registrar in hopes of finding a smoking gun that would prove definitively what was obvious—that university officials had treated the plaintiffs' applications differently from those of white applicants. As Ward recalls, he and Jordan had begun searching the files (discreetly and infrequently) prior to Judge Bootle's ruling, but after a while university officials refused to cooperate with their requests for information, necessitating the court order. As Ward puts it, "We knew university officials were not being truthful in the reasons they gave for refusing Charlayne and Hamilton, but we also knew that we'd have to convince a judge of that if we stood any chance of winning the case."[28] The state's attorney, Buck Murphy, argued that opening the files for public examination would seriously disrupt the registrar's office, because nearly seven thousand of the forty thousand files kept in that office would have to be made available. Judge Bootle rejected Murphy's argument and ruled that the plaintiffs' counsel could begin their inspections immediately. He also set the trial date for the second week in December.[29]

Horace Ward, who took great satisfaction in his new role as associate counsel in this case, was dispatched to Athens to help Motley pore through the registrar's files. They were assisted in this special assignment by Vernon Jordan, a recent graduate of Howard University Law School who had come to work for Hollowell in the summer of 1960. Not yet having passed the bar exam, Jordan spent the summer of 1960 as a law clerk for Hollowell. His immediate assignment was to examine University of Georgia application files in hopes of discovering evidence that would prove that the university handled applications from blacks differently than they did those from whites.[30]

The racial climate in the South at the time that was so openly hostile to desegregation was no friendlier to those dedicated attorneys, black and white, who sought to overturn the status quo. If Donald Hollowell (often referred to in the white press as the "Negro lawyer for the plaintiffs") and Constance Baker Motley (often referred to as "that Motley woman") could not command respect from their white peers, then certainly two brash upstarts like Ward and Jordan were bound to encounter difficulties, especially if they did not show the proper deference demanded by white southerners. Vernon Jordan remembers an exchange between him and Georgia's attorney general, Eugene Cook, that took place in Judge Bootle's chambers in the summer of 1960, shortly after Jordan had taken the bar exam. As Jordan remembers it, Attorney General Cook told him, "You know, you can't pass the bar this time." Before Jordan could reply, Cook continued: "You don't show any respect. Before you could get out of law school good, you were serving the governor with papers, me with papers. Trying to be a lawyer before you were a lawyer." As Jordan struggled to maintain his composure, Cook continued: "You know, Horace Ward made the highest score ever on the bar exam." Unable to resist any longer, Jordan asked: "How did you know that? That's supposed to be kept by the numbers, so that it can be confidential." With a sly grin, Cook replied, "We keep up with y'all."[31]

The 150-mile round-trip from Atlanta to Athens kept Motley, Ward, and Jordan busy for the next two weeks. But finally their search turned up several pieces of incriminating evidence. During the time the University of Georgia was reportedly facing a housing crisis, the dean of the agriculture department had gone to upstate New York to recruit students for the university's food-technology program. Ward and Jordan also discovered that the admissions interviews of some students were held *after* they were already attending the university. But it was Vernon Jordan who found the smoking gun: a white female student whose situation was almost identical to Hunter's had been allowed to transfer to the University of Georgia. A letter had been written to Chancellor Caldwell asking him to use his influence to get the student admitted; attached to the letter was a handwritten note from Chancellor Caldwell to President Aderhold, which read: "I have written Howard [Howard Callaway, a member of the Board of Regents] that it is my understanding that all of the dormitories for women are filled for the coming year. I have also indicated that you relied on this fact to bar the admission of a Negro girl from Atlanta."[32] The lawyers also discovered that many white students were hardly interviewed at all and that few of them had academic records as good as

Hamilton Holmes. Armed with this new evidence, attorneys for the plaintiffs felt that their case was as solid as they could make it.

The trial of *Holmes v. Danner* began on December 13, 1960. Among the first witnesses were those who had conducted the interviews with Holmes and Hunter: university registrar Walter Danner, assistant registrar Paul R. Kea, and admissions counselor Morris Phelps. Phelps testified that though he found Charlayne Hunter to be "very cooperative," Holmes had been "evasive." The counselor also raised questions about Holmes's candor in responding to certain questions. When asked if he had ever been arrested, Holmes said that he had not, whereupon the team of interviewers presented evidence that Holmes had been given a traffic citation for speeding (which Holmes did not consider an arrest). Assistant Registrar Paul R. Kea testified that Holmes "seemed to have a chip on his shoulder" during the entire interview process. "He was not as cooperative as we would have liked him to have been," Kea declared. "Holmes directed answers more to the floor than to us, and answered, in many cases, in monotone, mumbling, and slouched in his chair. It seemed he had the attitude that now, you folks have something to sell me and I am here." In describing the interview with Hunter, Kea said that she was "well-mannered, and answered questions forthrightly."[33]

In all likelihood, university officials were predisposed to react more favorably to a black female than to a black male, who from a historical and sociological perspective was generally perceived as more threatening.[34] Still, there were other reasons why Holmes and Hunter came across so differently in their responses to interviewers' questions. For one thing, Charlayne Hunter was smooth and articulate, chose her words very carefully, and was, at least publicly, always in control of her emotions. Holmes, on the other hand, was more excitable, and his slight speech impairment perhaps fueled the perception that he was being uncooperative. Furthermore, whereas Hunter's self-confidence was perceived as charm and wit, Holmes's was often interpreted as arrogance and contempt. And because his family was one of the most influential in Atlanta and boasted a proud history of civil rights activism, Holmes was perhaps less inclined than Hunter to be gracious or deferential.

Lawyers for the plaintiffs tried to prove in this case what they had been unsuccessful in proving in Ward's case—that the University of Georgia did not admit blacks. When Chancellor Caldwell took the stand, he was asked to read the note he had written to President Aderhold acknowledging the university's subterfuge in using housing shortages to justify its denial of admission to Charlayne Hunter. Still, Caldwell refused to admit that his note reflected the existence of legally sanctioned segregation at the university. When Donald Hollowell questioned President Aderhold about his denial of Horace Ward's appeal for admission years earlier, Aderhold said he felt that Ward, like Holmes, had been "evasive and inconsistent" and that he did not possess the necessary qualifications to enter law school. When asked to compare the standards of Northwestern University, where Ward earned his degree, with those of the University of Georgia, Aderhold claimed to be unfamiliar with the standards at Northwestern.[35]

Responding to questions from the state's attorney Buck Murphy, Aderhold sought to clarify his position for the record:

Murphy: Now I'll ask you if, as an official of the University of Georgia for the period you have stated and as President of the University of Georgia since 1950, do you know of any policy of the University of Georgia to exclude students on account of their race or color?

Aderhold: No sir, I do not.

Murphy: Do you know of any policy to discriminate against Negro applicants?

Aderhold: I do not.

Murphy: Have you ever had any instructions from the Chancellor of the University System or the Chairman of the Board of Regents or anybody else to exclude Negroes as applicants to the University of Georgia?

Aderhold: I have not.

Murphy: Have their applications, so far as you know, been considered on the same basis as the applications of white people?

Aderhold: On exactly the same basis, as far as I know.[36]

On the afternoon of the third day of the trial, Horace Ward called Hamilton Holmes to the witness stand. The two had much in common, because in so many ways Holmes's experiences paralleled Ward's, and both men knew from day one that they were kindred spirits. Without dismissing Hunter's personal anguish (which later took on even greater dimensions) Ward understood better than most the kind of inner turmoil Holmes was enduring. "There were times when he said he really didn't want to be a part of this process," Ward said of Holmes years later. "I knew what he was feeling, and I could understand why there were times when he didn't want to go on. The way they interviewed him, asking him about red-light districts and such, and bringing up other indiscreet personal matters, was rough on him. But we had to explain to him that these kinds of things were to be expected, because the bottom line was always that they were not seeking to qualify you, but to *disqualify* you, and at that time it really didn't matter to them how they did it."[37]

Under direct examination from Ward, Holmes testified that the interview committee had subjected him to an intense grilling on personal matters. All of the questions focused on his morals, and no one asked him anything about academics. He was asked if he had ever attended any "mixed" social affairs and if he had an opinion on the various integration crises in Atlanta and New Orleans. Holmes testified that he had never attended any racially mixed parties, though he did admit to taking part in interracial cultural groups, which he described as lectures and debates at universities, including Emory and Georgia Tech. He did not offer any comment on integration crises in other parts of the country. The interviewers also asked him if he was familiar with Athens's red-light district or if he had attended any beatnik parties. Holmes testified that he had never taken part in so-called tea house parties in Atlanta, nor had he ever visited any house of prostitution. Ward's direct examination was designed to prove that Holmes had been questioned in a manner totally different from that which any white student encountered. The final day of testimony was highlighted by Constance Baker Motley asking Registrar Danner the one question she referred to as "the old clincher": "Would you favor the admission of a qualified Negro to the university?" In a tone eerily reminiscent of Chancellor Caldwell's declaration four years earlier, Danner's reply in the affirmative hardly surprised anyone.[38]

The long-awaited decision came down on Friday afternoon, January 6, 1961, roughly one month after the trial ended. Judge Bootle ruled that "although there is no written policy or rule excluding Negroes, including plaintiffs, from admission to the University on account of their race and color, there is a tacit policy to that effect" and that the plaintiffs "would already have been admitted had it not been for their race and color." In his ruling Judge

Bootle noted that "No Negroes have ever been enrolled at the University of Georgia, and, prior to September 29, 1950, no Negro had ever applied for admission. At the time of the trial only four Negroes [Horace Ward, Hamilton Holmes, Charlayne Hunter, and Ida Rose McCree, who had applied on June 4, 1960], including plaintiffs, had made application for admission to the University, all on or since September 29, 1950, none of whom has yet been admitted." Acknowledging that housing space at the University of Georgia was certainly limited, the judge minced no words in stating his belief that the real reason behind the limited facilities at the university was best expressed in that handwritten note from Chancellor Caldwell to President Aderhold. Judge Bootle discovered similar intent in a letter to university officials from Breedlove Arrington, a transfer student denied admission to the university, who wrote:

> Upon receiving your letter, stating that I could not be accepted to the University, I made a trip to Athens and talked to one of the counlesors [*sic*] about what prevented me from being accepted and what I could do to be accepted. He said that there were several reasons why I could not be accepted. One of them was because of my poor record at Tech and the other was that they did not have a quota for students from senior colleges due to segregational problems. . . . If there is any reason why I can not be accepted, due to segregational problems, I would appreciate any advice you might give me which would enable me to penetrate this barrier.

As for the interviews, Judge Bootle noted that "Although, in most cases, an interview record was completed on an applicant, in at least one case, a letter from an alumnus stating that the applicant was 'an excellent student' and 'one of the outstanding young ladies in her class' and that she 'would be a definite asset to the University' was accepted in lieu of the regular interview. . . . Some students were accepted for the Winter Quarter, 1960 or subsequently whose files contain no record of interview."[39]

Judge Bootle's decision did contain one surprise: the plaintiffs were to be admitted not by the following fall, as some had predicted, or for the spring quarter, beginning in March, but immediately. The lawsuit had also sought five thousand dollars in damages, but the judge refused to grant that award. Still, plaintiffs' attorneys were jubilant, finally having gotten the verdict they had been seeking for so long. But Judge Bootle's order clearing the way for the two students to enroll immediately meant that neither they nor their attorneys had much time to celebrate, since registration for winter quarter would end in just three days.

Herbert Holmes remembers that Judge Bootle's ruling, as welcome as it was, created a lot of tension in the Holmes household. "We got several harassing phone calls every night. There was this one guy who kept at it for weeks; he called so often that we could recognize his voice. So I started talking back to him, trying to mess with him. After I started talking about his mama he stopped calling." Herbert says that while his family was not the type to scare easily, they were all extra careful during that time. Just to be on the safe side, several of Atlanta's black police officers provided unofficial surveillance of their home, just as they had done in 1955 following the furor created by the desegregation of the golf courses.[40]

Gary Holmes, Hamilton's younger brother, had enlisted in the air force in September 1960 and was stationed in Texas in January 1961. He knew that his brother and Charlayne Hunter were about to enroll in the University of Georgia, but he did not know how close they were to being admitted until the evening of January 9. "I walked into the lounge area where the other guys were sitting watching the evening news, and one of them turned to me and said, 'Do you have a brother named Hamilton?' and I said yes. He then told me that he'd just seen him on television, and I could feel all these other white guys staring at me. Later in the evening it came across the news again and I caught it that time. I can't describe in words how proud I felt at that moment. Though nobody at the base ever said anything to me directly, I could sense that some of the guys resented me for what my brother was doing."[41]

News of Judge Bootle's ruling spread quickly around the nation and across the state. With all eyes now on the University of Georgia, some student leaders pleaded for calm, and at least initially it appeared as if the ruling would be met with little fanfare, especially since only four days earlier two black students had enrolled at the University of Tennessee without serious incident. But on the evening of January 6, just hours after Judge Bootle's desegregation order, the uneasy quiet that had settled over the campus earlier in the day gave way to angry demonstrations. That night a crowd of some 150 to 200 students gathered by the historic archway entrance to the campus and hanged a blackface effigy of Hamilton Holmes. The students "serenaded the effigy with choruses of *Dixie*," and sang "There'll never be a nigger in the ———[fraternity] house," whose various names they inserted. They also chanted, "Two, four, six, eight, we don't want to integrate." Hundreds of students began to burn gasoline-soaked crosses and throw firecrackers as they screamed in anger, replete with all manner of racist epithets. William Tate, the Dean of Men, single-handedly tried to restore order, but no sooner would he disassemble one flaming cross than another would ignite. Later that night, students sought to burn a fifteen-foot-high cross in front of President Aderhold's home, but campus officials prevented them from doing so. Hope and optimism for an easy integration process quickly vanished as Athens, Georgia (dubbed by many as "the classic city"), showed its ugly side.[42]

By the time that Hamilton Holmes and Donald Hollowell arrived in Athens on Saturday morning, January 7, to begin the registration process, the campus had quieted down, but Hollowell remembers that it still felt very much like enemy territory. Accompanying them were the Reverend Samuel Williams, pastor of the Friendship Baptist Church in Atlanta and president of the Atlanta NAACP; Holmes's father; and Julian Bond, a reporter for the *Atlanta Inquirer*, a new black newspaper that had grown out of the civil rights movement. Without hesitation, the Atlanta entourage strode past reporters and curious onlookers to the registrar's office. Just before the noon closing time, Hollowell placed a copy of Judge Bootle's order on Walter Danner's desk. Danner, who had not seen Hollowell since the trial, said nothing, but quietly handed Holmes a packet of registration materials and reminded him that he would have to return on Monday to select his classes for the winter term. As they left the registrar's office, Hollowell informed the reporters who had gathered to witness this historic moment that Charlayne Hunter, who was still in Detroit, would be present to register on Monday.[43]

Meanwhile, groups of university students were meeting around the campus to discuss how they would respond to the integration that now seemed imminent. Dean of Students Joseph A. Williams met with a group of student leaders and urged them to accept the judge's order. This ad hoc student group, including presidents of the leading campus organizations and the editor of the *Red and Black*, pledged their cooperation in what they hoped would be a peaceful process.[44] Pete McCommons, vice president of the Student Council, helped draft a petition that opposed closing the university in the event that Holmes and Hunter were admitted. "Most of the students were not enthusiastic about integrating," McCommons said in a recent interview. "They were mostly segregationists, products of their environment, who accepted 'our way of life' without questioning it. But there were still a good many that did not want to see UGA closed if it came to that. I cannot remember the exact number, but we must have collected over two thousand signatures on that petition, which we later presented to the Speaker of the [Georgia] House of Representatives."[45]

Not all University of Georgia students, however, shared those sentiments. The day after Bootle's ruling a group calling themselves Students for Passive Resistance circulated the following proclamation:

> We, the student body of the University of Georgia, fully deplore and resent the court-ordered intrusion of two negroes into this century-old white institution. . . . While we disavow the use of violence in any form, we hereby pledge ourselves to the use of the ultimate weapon so widely and effectively used by these people— the weapon of "passive resistance." We will NOT welcome these intruders. We will NOT associate with them. We will NOT associate with white students who welcome them. We love our school. We WILL save it.[46]

At about the same time, the Demosthenian Literary Society was meeting to discuss the issue. Over the years the Demosthenians had discussed the possible integration of the university, and the minutes from their meetings revealed that the membership was overwhelmingly segregationist. In 1957 the group had passed a resolution in favor of closing the law school if Horace Ward were admitted, and a year later they applauded the writings of a student journalist who had berated a federal judge in another integration case for trying "to present his foreign ideas and to implement the infamous 1954 integration decision of the left-wing liberal Supreme Court." In their January 7 meeting the Demosthenians restated their opposition to desegregation in any form. When their president, Tom Linder, was contacted by the *Red and Black,* he said: "I know that the people of Georgia and the students want this University segregated. I have deep faith in the legislature and in their ability to maintain for us both segregation and open doors. I hope that every student will express his disappointment in the federal decision and will support the legislature in this time of crisis."[47]

Earl T. Leonard Jr., recently retired senior vice president of corporate affairs for Coca-Cola in Atlanta, was a third-year law student at UGA at the time and a member of the Demosthenians. In a recent interview he acknowledged that the Demosthenians were every bit as segregationist as the record suggests. White supremacy and states' rights was the order of the day, and the Demosthenian Literary Society played a major role in preserving both on UGA's campus. "The mood in virtually all of the white South was hostile. Most white southerners believed that the courts, through judicial edicts and judicial activism, were taking away something that belonged to us, and that what they were doing was unconstitutional. Fast-forward that to the University of Georgia. We felt it was perfectly legitimate to defend that which was ours. That was the view shared by most white southerners, and most white students. It was probably as ugly a time of 'us vs. them' as anything we would witness again until the Vietnam War."[48]

Even before Hollowell and Holmes arrived in Athens on Saturday morning, Governor Vandiver was meeting with his legal advisers (namely Attorney General Eugene Cook, special counsel Buck Murphy, associate counsel Freeman Leverett, chief-of-staff Griffin Bell, and legal aide Henry Neal) and had decided to appeal Judge Bootle's decision. Vandiver was hoping that Bootle would temporarily stay his order so that the General Assembly would have time to act. (At issue here was Section 8 (d) of the 1956 Appropriations Act, which called for the mandatory cutoff of state funds to any institution that admitted black students.) And, of course, the governor himself was hoping for an opportunity to make one last defiant gesture in support of segregation, since, after all, it was he who had promised "not one, no not one." After the meeting, Attorney General Cook drove to Macon to deliver a motion for a stay of the desegregation order, which according to the motion was necessary in order to prevent "the possibility of great hurt and damage to more than 7,000 students." Judge Bootle set a hearing for 9:30 A.M. Monday morning in his Macon courtroom and sent word to attorneys Hollowell and Motley requesting their presence.[49]

On Monday morning, January 9, as Donald Hollowell and Constance Baker Motley headed toward Macon for their scheduled appearance in Judge Bootle's chambers, Charlayne Hunter, who had arrived back in Atlanta on Sunday, and Hamilton Holmes prepared to head to Athens to complete their registration. As Hunter remembers, "It was decided that we would go to the campus early Monday morning, in part because there were no hotels for blacks in Athens, and even if we could find a black home courageous enough to take us in, we had no security. We weren't afraid, but we weren't crazy." They were accompanied by Charlayne's mother, Hamilton's father, Vernon

Jordan, and Horace Ward. Also scheduled for that Monday was the opening session of the state legislature, where it was most certain that the current integration crisis in Athens would dominate the day's proceedings.[50]

When the Atlanta entourage arrived in Athens (the University of Georgia had no security force and no provisions had been made for security, despite the potential for violence), six-foot five-inch Vernon Jordan led them to the registrar's office past a crowd of waiting reporters and students, some of whom were shouting, "Nigger go home." Upon leaving the registrar's office, the group proceeded toward the Henry W. Grady School of Journalism, where Charlayne would select her courses. She remembers being greeted by George Abney, a member of the journalism faculty who, despite his apparent nervousness, was friendly and cooperative. They had no sooner begun discussing her schedule when they heard students cheering outside. Seconds later George Abney received a telephone call that explained this sudden outpouring of jubilation. In a surprising move, Judge Bootle had issued a stay of his own order (to give the state a chance to appeal, or as Bootle put it, to "test the correctness" of his decision). The group was dumbfounded, and Vernon Jordan, his face now grim, looked behind him through the door where students were waving and cheering. He heard one of them proclaim, "That big nigger lawyer ain't smiling no more."[51]

Stunned by this setback, Hollowell and Motley were clearly concerned that any more delays would seriously jeopardize their clients' chances of enrolling for winter classes. Motley immediately placed a call to Judge Elbert P. Tuttle, chief judge of the U.S. Fifth District Court in Atlanta, and asked him to vacate Judge Bootle's stay. Judge Tuttle told Motley that she and Hollowell would have to file a notice of appeal, and he agreed to meet with them in his Atlanta office at 2:30 P.M. Hollowell and Motley arrived in Judge Tuttle's chambers at 2:32, and to their delight, quickly discovered that Judge Tuttle had run out of patience with the state's never-ending legal maneuvers. Judge Bootle's stay, he declared, had been "improvidently granted," and he promptly overturned it. His order noted "that the quickest disposition that can be made of this case . . . is the best solution not only for the Negroes, but for all concerned."[52]

Born in California in 1897, Elbert Parr Tuttle grew up in Hawaii and attended multiracial schools there. When he began to practice law in Atlanta in 1923, he brought his liberal views on race with him. When President Eisenhower appointed him to the Fifth Circuit Court of Appeals in 1954, Tuttle helped transform the federal judiciary in the Deep South into an agent for change, and he interpreted the *Brown* decision as a broad mandate for racial justice. The Fifth Judicial Circuit, which encompassed six states of the old Confederacy—Alabama, Florida, Georgia, Louisiana, Mississippi, and Texas—became the largest court in the nation, in both caseload and number of judges, and became the lightning rod for cases dealing with racial discrimination. As chief judge in the 1960s, Tuttle was to the Fifth Circuit what Earl Warren was to the United States Supreme Court. He understood that state officials were using delay tactics to forestall desegregation, and he, along with a handful of others, such as John Minor Wisdom of Louisiana, John Robert Brown of Texas, and Richard Taylor Rives of Alabama, ordered segregationist federal district judges to comply with federal law. "I never had any doubt that what I was doing would be affirmed by the Supreme Court," Tuttle once said. "The truth is, the black person in the litigation that I sat in on was entitled to the result he got, under what the Constitution required." In a tribute to Tuttle some years later, Supreme Court Chief Justice Earl Warren wrote: "Since the day he assumed office, the Fifth Circuit has been in the very eye of the storm."[53]

Judge Bootle's decision to stay his own order surprised some and confused others; but, as Bootle himself explains it, it was all part of a larger plan. Like Tuttle, William Augustus Bootle was also appointed to the federal bench by Eisenhower in 1954, and he also shared Tuttle's belief that the courts were society's great levelers. Born in South Carolina in 1903, he admits that from an early age he accepted segregation as the law of the land. But after the *Brown* decision, he believed it was his sworn duty to uphold the law. "The university didn't have a case," he said in a recent interview. "There was no legitimate reason for the university to keep them out." As for his issuing the stay of his own order, he believes that was the quickest way to have the matter settled once and for all. "After I issued the stay, I got the backup I wanted from the Fifth Circuit, and then from the U.S. Supreme Court. So you see, I got what I wanted, and I got it more quickly than I thought possible." At age 98, he's still not comfortable discussing the case and insists that his actions should not be considered heroic but that he was merely following the law. "As I once explained to my law clerks, the beauty of being a judge is the freedom. He's under no obligation to any side, and if he is, he should recuse himself.

In every case before him he's at liberty to look for justice, and that's a source of great pleasure."[54]

Relieved by Judge Tuttle's ruling, Hollowell telephoned Jordan at the home of Ray Ware (a black Athens businessman at whose apartment the Atlanta group sometimes convened), gave him the good news, and told him to escort Holmes and Hunter back to campus to continue with registration. Shortly thereafter Holmes and Hunter did return to campus, completing their registration without serious incident and securing forever their place in history. Both students returned to Atlanta that night with plans of beginning classes Tuesday morning. Meanwhile, Attorney General Cook announced immediately his intentions to fly to Washington, D.C., and appeal to United States Supreme Court Justice Hugo Black (the justice who heard appeals from the Fifth Circuit) to set aside Judge Tuttle's order.[55]

Monday had seemed like an eternity, but it was not over yet. Amid rumors that Governor Vandiver was planning to order the university closed the next day, roughly one thousand students took to the streets in protest. Some were angry about the anticipated closing of the university, while others were just plain mad, searching for any excuse to vent their frustrations. The sounds of exploding firecrackers filled the night air, and a group of freshmen burned crosses near the tennis courts and the track field. Other students waved Confederate flags and chanted racist slogans. Some drove their cars through the campus and the town, blocking traffic along Route 78. By most accounts, the local police showed up but did little. The only attempts to restore order came from Dean Tate, who waded through the crowd in an attempt to identify the leaders. The rowdiness continued until well past midnight, and two students were arrested.[56]

At midnight on January 9, calling it "the saddest duty of my life," Governor Vandiver released a statement ordering the University of Georgia closed in accordance with the funds cutoff law (Vandiver's statement indicated that he had already signed the order, when in fact he stated on the morning of January 10 that he was waiting for the black plaintiffs to enroll before actually signing the order). In any event, the university did not close on Tuesday because President Aderhold never received any official word from the governor's office. On that same day, the U.S. Supreme Court denied the state's motion to overturn Judge Tuttle's desegregation order. Although the petition had been made to Justice Black, he chose to present it to the entire court, which was then in session. Two days later, Judge Bootle overturned Vandiver's order to close the university. In their victory celebration, the plaintiffs and their lawyers chanted, "From Bootle to Tuttle to Black and back."[57] All of the state's last-ditch efforts to prevent desegregation had failed.

Both Holmes and Hunter returned to campus on Tuesday, January 10, and got settled into their respective residences. Since he was no longer a freshman and did not have to reside on campus, Holmes stayed with the Killians, a black family who owned a local restaurant. The Killians were one of Athens's most prominent black families and over the years had earned a reputation of independence and fearlessness, especially where whites were concerned. The Reverend Archibald Killian, now a minister, co-owned the restaurant with his younger brother Alfred, and he remembers well the events leading up to Holmes's arrival on their doorstep. "We had never met Hamp until the day he showed up at our house. Another black family in town had agreed to house him, but later changed their minds after the powers that be told them that it would not be in their best interest to do so. Then somebody, I can't remember who, called my mother [Mrs. Ruth Moon Killian] and asked if we could keep him. We all decided that we would; we knew that our space would be cramped, but we said yes. We were advised, for security reasons, to have Hamp sleep on the front side of the house; so Mama gave up her bedroom to Hamp and she took the bedroom in the back."[58]

No doubt, university officials would have preferred that Hunter live off campus as well, but since university rules required that all females under the age of twenty-three reside on campus, university officials concluded that they were obligated by law or court order to find dormitory space for Hunter. She was assigned to Center Myers Hall, the central dormitory of three adjoining buildings. Not wanting to place her in a room with a white female student, officials agreed that Hunter should have her own private suite (formerly the offices of the Women's Student Government Association), where she would have as little contact with white students as possible. Her room also had a kitchenette, which was where officials hoped she would take her meals rather than use the university's dining facilities. On her first night, a few of the girls stopped in to welcome her to Myers dorm. After shyly introducing themselves and commenting on the spaciousness of her new quarters, they left. Alone in her room now for the first time, and emotionally drained from the events of the past several days, Hunter was much too tired to pay much attention to a group of rowdies who had gathered outside her window. She finally drifted off to sleep, having been serenaded by constant chants of "Two, four, six, eight, we don't want to integrate . . . Eight, six, four, two, we don't want no jigaboo."[59]

All was quiet when Hunter emerged from her dormitory on Wednesday morning, January 11, the official first day of class. Dean Tate, who had driven to the Killians' home to pick up Holmes, found him already walking toward campus by himself. (President Aderhold had assigned Dean Tate to be Holmes's personal escort, and Dean Williams was assigned to protect Hunter.) By 9:00 that morning, the two students were seated in their first classes. As Hunter would write years later, "Although nearly two hundred years of segregation had just officially died, in my classroom in Meigs Hall, at least it was a quiet death. No words were spoken to mark the moment. . . . In a way, though, this was a relief to me, because at that point I just wanted to get on with being a student as quickly as possible." Aside from various episodes of racist taunts from scattered clusters of students, for most of that first day Holmes and Hunter were besieged by reporters, most of whom were white and, as Hunter writes, "seemed always to be trying to convince me that they weren't 'like the rest of them.'" But of all the reporters they encountered, Calvin Trillin was by far their favorite. Then a reporter for *Time* magazine, Trillin (who preferred to be called Bud) had covered the trial, and for a time was almost a constant companion for the two students. Hunter recalls, "I really liked him, and so did Hamp . . . he had a way of interviewing that was unobtrusive, that made you feel he really cared. I think it was because he listened more than he talked. . . . Trillin stood out in my book. And he was all over the place; every time I looked up, even in the middle of a rambunctious crowd, he never seemed far from my side." (Shortly before Holmes and Hunter graduated in 1963, Trillin returned to Georgia to do a follow-up on their experiences. Because of the trust the two students had placed in him, Trillin was able to conduct interviews with the students' families, friends, fellow students, professors, attorneys, and university administrators, which he published as a book later that year.)[60]

As Holmes and Hunter finished their classes on that first day, they both began to feel as if they might survive this ordeal after all. In that day's edition of the *Atlanta Constitution,* columnist Ralph McGill expressed optimism that Georgia's students would "save the honor of the South and warm the hearts of good people everywhere" by welcoming their first black classmates. A similar sentiment was expressed in the university's student newspaper, the *Red and Black,* where one columnist urged his classmates to treat the two black students with "the proper respect they deserve," and thereby "show the rest of the United States that we in Georgia are the true leaders of the new South." Charlayne Hunter later described herself as being "upbeat about the reception I had received throughout the day both in class and at the dorm." Even Hamilton Holmes, who was always less sanguine than Hunter about their prospects for peaceful coexistence on campus, told one reporter, "I have faith that they won't turn to violence." Later that evening on the NBC network news, Chet Huntley praised Governor Vandiver, the university, and the students for their behavior, which, he said, "has made this whole country feel good." But all of these expressions of hope and optimism proved premature.[61]

The first indication that there might be trouble had come earlier in the day when several UGA officials and local white city leaders paid a visit to the Killian home. As Archibald Killian remembers it:

> That morning, [Police] Chief Hardy, the sheriff, Tommy Huff, the city attorney, and some other big shots, came to the house. They told us that they had gotten word that the Klan was coming that night, and that they had said that they were going to burn a cross in our yard. . . . At that point I told them that since they had brought the message they could take the message back. I said, "Y'all call them, and tell them that I said that if they come over here tonight, ain't nobody going to have to ask who came; all you'll have to do is turn their bodies over in the yard tomorrow morning and pull the sheets off, because we intend to kill every one." And I meant that thing. I was just like Patrick Henry; give me liberty or give me death. And all the white folk around here knew it.[62]

Killian says that once word got out in the community that there might be trouble at his house that night, a number of black men, armed with shotguns, began to gather at his house around nightfall. "We waited for them, and we were ready for them, but they never showed up."[63]

Shortly after 10:00 P.M. (right after Georgia had lost a basketball game to arch rival Georgia Tech in overtime), a crowd of students, described as a "howling, cursing mob" and numbering at various times between 500 and 2,000, laid siege on Center Myers dormitory and unfurled a bed sheet bearing the racist slogan "Nigger Go Home." Several members of the group then ran toward the dormitory, flinging bricks and bottles through scores of dormitory windows (aiming for Charlayne's, whose room was located on the ground floor), while others set fires in the woods near the dormitory, threw rocks and giant cherry-bomb firecrackers at reporters, and scuffled with police. Another group led cheers: "Two, four, six, eight, we don't want to integrate . . . One, two, three, four, we don't want no nigger whore." Dean of Students Joseph Williams was present but made no attempt to break up the riot. As more people filed out of the gymnasium following Georgia's disappointing loss, the crowd swelled and was soon out of control. The first Athens policemen to arrive on the scene spent more time directing traffic than dispersing the mob. After about thirty minutes Dean Williams reluctantly agreed to call in the state police, who did not arrive until an hour after the riot was over and, according to most estimates, nearly two and a half hours after they were called. The angry mob was finally dispersed with fire hoses and tear gas, but not before several policemen, at least one girl inside the dorm, and Dean of Men William Tate (who had waded through the crowd seizing identification cards) were injured in the melee. Hunter remained in the dormitory during the disturbance and escaped without injury, but Center Myers Hall sustained extensive damage, including sixty broken windowpanes. Adding insult to injury, Dean Williams, acting on direct orders from Governor Vandiver, suspended Holmes and Hunter "for their own safety."[64] In his letter to Holmes (with a similar copy sent to Hunter), Dean Williams wrote:

> I am withdrawing you from the University of Georgia in the interest of your personal safety and for the safety and welfare of more than 7,000 other students at the University of Georgia. . . . Last night the events which took place on the University campus were due to the enrollment of you and Charlayne Hunter at the University of Georgia. These events placed in jeopardy the lives of you and Charlayne as well as University students, University officials and city police. In addition to the factors of safety and welfare, the educational program of the University has been and would continue to be seriously affected should you remain at the University at this time.[65]

The day after the riot Roy Harris issued a series of denunciations. In a statement on WGST radio he said, "If the Board of Regents had had nerve enough to . . . fire President Aderhold and Dean William Tate, the violence wouldn't have happened. . . . Aderhold, Tate and the house mothers have tried to conduct a successful experiment of race mixing . . . I protested that action; the students protested it; but the house mothers and the dean [Tate] brow-beat the students. They tried to force them to accept the Negroes on a social basis and they refused." On the same radio station, Governor Vandiver's executive secretary Peter Zack Geer praised the student rioters for being "possessed with the character and courage not to submit to dictatorship and tyranny."[66]

In the aftermath of the riot many segregationists blamed Dean Tate, who apparently did everything he could to keep the riot from getting any worse than it did. Many were also angry with Tate because despite his views toward integration—and most who knew him considered him a segregationist—when the order came to admit Holmes and Hunter, Tate complied with the law. Because he had seized student identification cards at the riots, many whites held him personally responsible for the expulsions of white student rioters, and he received a great deal of angry mail. One postcard, addressed to "William Tate, N.A.A.C.P. Agent," read: "Judas received 30 pieces of Silver for the Betrayal of ONLY ONE MAN. How much did the N.A.A.C.P. Pay you for the Betrayal of YOUR OWN RACE? JUDAS HAD A CERTAIN SENSE OF HONOR, HAVE YOU?" Others criticized Dean Tate for what they termed a "nigger-loving atmosphere" and the "seemingly enthusiastic acceptance of the two Negroes." Some complained about "the plush suite set up for the Girl" and "the deference and unusual treatment shown the boy." Nearly all of the angry respondents lamented the fact that the communists had won, that "our white children are being subjected to police methods," and that Tate and others were "brainwashing our children into social acceptance." One writer asked, "What has become of the rights of white people?" Several respondents promised to withhold all future monetary contributions as long as Tate remained dean.[67]

Not all of the letters Dean Tate received were negative. Many praised him for the courageous stance he had taken on behalf of the university. One person wrote, "To me it is not a question of whether or not we approve of integration or segregation, but whether or not we will abide by the laws of the land, and . . . I feel you should be congratulated on the stand you have taken." Another wrote, "A great many of us have a keen admiration for the way you have steadfastly supported law, order and decency. I assume that the court orders were personally distressing to you, but the way in which you have put personal feelings aside in order to attain broader and more far-reaching goals has increased my already considerable respect for your integrity and vision." More than 1,200 Athens citizens signed a petition expressing confidence in President Aderhold, Dean Tate, Mayor Ralph Snow, Police Chief E. E. Hardy, and others for their actions and their handling of the crisis.[68]

Following the suspension of Holmes and Hunter, the university also suspended four riot leaders and placed eighteen on disciplinary probation (ten of whom were suspended, three who refused to attend school with blacks, and five others who "wanted to drop out until the crisis was over"). Clearly embarrassed by the student connection to the planning of the riot, university officials were eager to blame outsiders for starting the riot, including members of the Ku Klux Klan, several of whom were spotted in the crowd. Although eight Klan members (along with two university students) were eventually arrested in connection with the riot, the FBI documents on the Klan's involvement suggest that the local Ku Klux Klan merely joined in on what university students had already organized and that they were apparently *invited* to participate by university students. There was also at least one confirmed report that a Klansman had visited a university fraternity house prior to the riot, though it is not clear whether the Klansman actually initiated the visit or was merely responding to an invitation.[69]

Referring to the Klansmen as "sullen, ugly, and properly ominous," Calvin Trillin believes that their mere presence on the campus could have made the situation much worse had tear gas not been used to break up the riot. He does point out, however, that although they had guns in the car, they did not bring them onto the campus and in fact took no real part in the riot. But because of their "guns and bad reputations," they were "more logical suspects than respectable law students." It is worth pointing out that none of the segregationist student leaders placed any blame on the Klan, even though a few of the student leaders later admitted to having had contact with Klan leaders. Regardless of who was responsible for organizing the riot, the university's image had been severely tarnished, and the fact that Holmes and Hunter had been suspended certainly gave the appearance that violence could achieve what the state's last-minute legal maneuvers could not.[70]

The riot was front-page and prime-time news, and the national media denounced the rioters as bullies and racists.[71] In an attempt to downplay the spectacle, some university spokesmen tried to explain the riot as a spontaneous outburst created by a handful of students, ignited by an upsetting basketball loss to Georgia Tech.[72] But a significant body of evidence exists to disprove that assertion. According to Calvin Trillin:

> By Wednesday just about everybody on the campus knew there was a riot sched-uled in front of Charlayne's dormitory after the basketball game that night. It had been organized by a number of law-school students. All day Wednesday, the or-ganizers scurried around making plans and bragging about the promises of help and immunity they had received from legislators. Some students got dates for the basketball game and the riot afterward. Reporters, faculty members, and even some students warned Joseph Williams, the dean of students, about the riot and suggested that he ban gatherings in front of the dormitory, or at least cancel the basketball game. But Williams said that neither step was necessary.[73]

There is overwhelming evidence to dispel the myth that the riot was the result of postgame frustration. When questioned later by the FBI, several students admitted that they had known about the riot well in advance. Char-layne Hunter later discovered that the girls in her dormitory had been told by the riot organizers to turn off the lights in their rooms when it got dark; that way, with the rest of the dormitory in total darkness, Hunter's brightly lit windows made for an easy target.[74] The subsequent FBI investigation also revealed that some students had distributed firecrackers the day before the riot and that the Athens police chief was so certain of the riot that he urged the dean of students to cancel the basketball game, which the dean refused to do on the grounds that too many tickets had already been sold. Still, there is a connection between the basketball game and the riot that followed, if for no other reason than the game itself (and the huge crowd that it drew) presented riot organizers with a golden opportunity to recruit more anti-integrationists to their ranks.[75]

There is little doubt that some of the university's law students, possibly dur-ing a meeting with the Demosthenians, actually organized the riot. During the meeting, Cecil Davis, a law student and a member of the Demostheni-ans, promised that Holmes and Hunter "would receive the same greeting Autherine Lucy got at the University of Alabama." In a fiery address to his fellow Demosthenians, Davis made reference to the American Revolution in pointing out that the nation had been founded on violence, inspired by patriots who rebelled against what they perceived as unjust laws. Another law student bragged to reporters that "action will be taken within the week" to get rid of the black students and that "the money is already in town."[76] On January 15, just days after the riot, the *Atlanta Journal and Constitution* offered its own interpretation of the events:

> It is generally believed by university students and a number of faculty members that 15 or 20 hard-core segregationist students planned, directed and encouraged from afar the unlawful resistance to the Negroes. Moreover, persistent reports indicate that this group—some law students and some top campus students—got encouragement from big names in state politics. . . . Judging from the wild disregard for law and order, the open flouting of city police and university officials, the demonstrators must have had reason to believe they could raise the roof with impunity to punishment. Who are these instigators . . . ? Their names are on the lips of many a student and professor, but they will go unnamed here.[77]

According to several eyewitnesses, some of the militant students in the riot crowd egged others on by boasting that they had gotten assurances that the state patrol would not show up and that if any of the student rioters were expelled their political allies in Atlanta "would take care of the situation." The most damning piece of evidence pointing to such a conspiracy was revealed when riot leader John Thomas Cochran, under intense FBI questioning, admitted that he had been in daily contact with several top state officials (whom he refused to name; the names of other likely suspects have been deleted from the FBI files) during the week leading up to the riot. By his own admission, the riots had been planned, and their purpose was clear. Cochran told the *Macon Telegraph*, "The suspension of the two niggers here was caused by the demonstration. . . . If we caused them to leave one time, we can do it again." Interestingly, neither Cochran nor anyone else was ever charged with conspiracy to incite a riot.[78]

The closest public acknowledgment of collusion between Georgia officials and UGA student riot leaders came when Roy Harris told the press that "it was people holding high official positions in the Capitol" who encouraged the riot. Harris declined to name names at the time but threatened to do so if any of the student rioters were expelled for their part in the riot. A more zealous FBI investigation might have resulted in criminal prosecution for conspiracy, but federal officials did not pursue it. To this day, no state official has ever admitted to conspiring with UGA students to resist desegregation.[79]

Although the smoking gun may never be found, Charlayne Hunter-Gault is among those who remain convinced that the January 11 riot was a carefully planned act, deliberately designed to force her and Holmes from campus permanently; in fact, her convictions on this point are perhaps stronger today than they were at the time. In a recent interview, Hunter-Gault bristled at the notion that top state and university officials were embarrassed by the riot:

> I don't believe they were embarrassed. There were some who said they were, but Peter Zack Geer was inciting it [Geer, who at the time was Vandiver's executive secretary, would be elected lieutenant governor in 1962]; other top officials of the state were inciting it. There may have been a few people who were embarrassed, but they certainly weren't the leadership, because the leadership did not condemn it. As I understand it, they were on the phone encouraging the students not to take this lying down. In fact, many of the state's leaders were hoping that this would be the end of our efforts to integrate the university, and they were clearly hoping to use the Autherine Lucy case as a precedent. When Autherine was suspended from the University of Alabama she was outspoken and critical of the university [actually, it was her attorneys], which gave Alabama officials a hook on which to hang her suspension. But Hollowell and Motley had done their homework, and they told us not to say anything. And we didn't. But had we said the wrong thing, then our case might have ended the same way hers did. So I don't know where people get this notion from that state officials were embarrassed. I do not accept that for one minute.[80]

The Autherine Lucy incident at the University of Alabama was foremost in the minds of many during UGA's crisis, and there are some striking similarities between the riots at Alabama and Georgia. When Autherine Lucy arrived on campus to register in January 1956, she was met by an angry mob that within a few days was nearly out of control. On the evening of February 6, the Board of Trustees voted to suspend Lucy on the grounds that her presence represented a threat to public safety. Lucy's attorneys, one of whom was Constance Baker Motley, later charged that university officials had conspired with the mob to prevent her from attending school and asked that university officials be held in contempt. Claiming that the charges against the university were unfounded, the Board of Trustees permanently expelled Lucy on March 5. District Court Judge H. Hobart Grooms sided with the Board of Trustees, ruling that Lucy's expulsion was for disciplinary reasons, not racial ones.[81]

Hence, the message that many took from this episode was that violence could be effective where legal resistance had failed, even if only to prolong the inevitable: the University of Alabama would remain all white for the next seven years.[82]

Local residents, some of whom professed shock and dismay over the events of January 11, were reluctant to acknowledge that there existed in Athens a social and political climate (present also among the university's student body) in which racial intolerance and bigotry flourished. As veteran political observer Bill Shipp has noted, "the Klan prospered and thrived on violence in the city of Athens, Georgia, in the 1960s, while the townspeople looked on in apathy and sometimes encouraged the hooded thugs in their vicious doings." Underneath the facade of gentility—in this college town of oak-lined residential streets and stately antebellum homes that gave the appearance of culture and refinement—existed a class of poorly paid white workers who labored in the city's textile mills and whose socioeconomic status was only marginally better than that of Athens's black population. Shipp writes: "Ignorant and oppressed whites in Athens and elsewhere in the South sensed in the early 1960s that their last claims to superiority were about to be challenged. Simply being white would no longer be enough to give them status and a feeling of superiority over all black men and women." Many of them sought refuge in the Ku Klux Klan, which billed itself as the savior of the white race.[83]

For much of the 1950s and 1960s, Athens, Georgia, was a hotbed of Klan activity. The best-known incident during that period was the murder of Lieutenant Colonel Lemuel Penn on July 11, 1964. Penn, forty-nine years old, had just completed two weeks of army reserve training at Fort Benning, near Columbus, Georgia, and was driving to Washington, D.C., with two black companions. Part of their journey took them through Athens, where they stopped long enough to change drivers; unfortunately, these three black men in a car with Washington, D.C., license plates drew the attention of several Klansmen, who began following the car. Outside of Colbert, Georgia, one of the Klansmen fired into the car now being driven by Lemuel Penn, and the shotgun blast tore away the left side of his face. Despite a mountain of evidence against the carload of Klansmen (including the eyewitness testimony of the Klansman who drove the car), an all-white jury acquitted six Klansmen of all charges.[84]

On the night following the verdict, at a rally of the National Knights of the Ku Klux Klan at Stone Mountain, Georgia, Imperial Wizard James Venable declared: "You'll never be able to convict a white man that killed a nigger that encroaches on the white race in the South." Given the fact that either Klansmen (or Klan sympathizers) usually dominated the all-white juries, there was certainly some measure of truth to Venable's bold declaration, at least as far as state courts were concerned. This grim reality of an often brutally racist and unrepentant South prompted the federal government to become more aggressive in prosecuting such acts under new civil rights laws. Two of the men charged with Penn's murder were later convicted of federal civil rights charges, though neither would spend more than a few years in jail. Because they had virtually no fear of prosecution, the Ku Klux Klan in Athens, Georgia, as well as numerous other white supremacist organizations throughout the South, continued to terrorize and intimidate with impunity until the end of the 1960s.[85]

Although there was never any doubt that the state's lawmakers and university officials were committed to preserving the all-white character of the University of Georgia to the bitter end, what was less well known at the time (but has been brought to light in recent years) was the depth of white student resentment toward integration.[86] Just a few days after the rioting, thirty-five students in a Math 254 class were asked to write essays explaining their views on integration. Professor Thomas Brahana, who had been an outspoken critic of the riot and an advocate of Holmes's and Hunter's reinstatement, asked his students to write the essays rather than take their scheduled calculus test. Here is a brief sampling of their responses, which were almost uniformly segregationist:

Many students, parents, and Georgians feel hurt because our federal government . . . has shown us that it (fed. govern.) can force people to do things which we dislike. . . . I feel as many students do at the University of Georgia that we as citizens should have a right to go to segregated schools. It seems to me the federal government has gotten too powerful. . . . Perhaps in another hundred years integration would have come about voluntarily in the South but why must something we resent be crammed down our throats?

The main reason I say I do not want integration is that I believe the Negroid race is inferior to the Caucasian race. . . . The Negro has an average of one eighth more

101

bone thickness on his skull. This leads one to believe that the Negro has not come as far through evolution as the "White" man. It is virtually impossible to remove someone or a race from a most primitive culture and replace him in one that has advanced over fifteen hundred years above his and expect him within two hundred fifty years to adjust himself to the new culture as well as the descendants of the founders of the old culture have. . . . The Negro . . . is shiftless and undependable. Why does the average Negro have almost double the rhythm of a "white" man if he has become equal to the white man in his culture. This leads me to believe it is still the "jungle instinct."

I personally do not desire to associate with persons of low moral character. . . . Southern Negroes have a lower moral standard in general than I care to associate with. This is shown by 1 their brand new Cadillac standing in the yard of their one room tennant home (neither paid for yet), 2 the statistical percentage of taxes paid by Negroes as compared to Whites 3 The frequent number of court cases involving Negroe stabbings, wife beating, driving drunk and disorderly, etc. 4 Lack of trust among themselves 5 General sanitation.[87]

One student wrote, "Personally I would like to choke both of them [Holmes and Hunter] to death," while another warned that integration "will build up so much friction in the south that there will be an outright war over race. We know that the NAACP will go all the way on getting the negro in *all* of the white schools. Then *Hell* will break loose, and the University of Georgia riot will simply be a little party compared to what will happen."[88]

In his insightful analysis of these student essays some years later, historian Robert Cohen makes the points that when the students mentioned those in the riot who were victimized by force, "most were referring to themselves rather than to Holmes and Hunter," and that "stereotypes of black inferiority pervaded the most strongly segregationist essays." While such racist rhetoric was hardly surprising given the social climate of the times, Cohen writes that "the fact that college students, among the state's best educated youths, expressed with such seriousness absurd ideas about black skull size, jungle rhythm, and shiftlessness should give us pause to consider the sources of these ideas and the nature of Georgian and southern education—or more precisely miseducation—about race. . . . Georgians did not have to be taught about segregation in school; they learned about segregation and were indoctrinated in white supremacy by merely living on the white side of the color line."[89]

One additional aspect of the January 11 riot needs to be reconsidered. Part of the lore surrounding the UGA riot is the widespread belief that it was not really a serious riot and that most of the students in the crowd never intended to harm anyone. While it is not always easy to determine intent, it is clear that the riotous mob was larger and more violent than local residents and university officials wanted to admit. (In a recent interview, former governor Vandiver cringed when the word "riot" was used to describe the events of that evening; he referred to it as a "disturbance.")[90] In light of the embarrassment and the avalanche of negative publicity that the University of Georgia endured as a consequence of being scrutinized by the national press, it is certainly understandable that Athenians would want to minimize the seriousness of the affair.[91] But recently uncovered evidence suggests that earlier accounts (both oral and written) greatly understated the dangerous dimensions of the riot and that the Athens police had a vastly different interpretation of the events.

Some Athens policemen remember that on at least two separate occasions, the crowd prevented them from arresting those individuals who appeared to be leading the riot. The policemen also noted that rocks and bottles were being thrown not just at the windows, but at them as well. One of the injured officers recalled that "it appeared [that] the students were trying to enter the dormitory," and the only thing that prevented them from doing so was the tear gas. The entire Athens police force (thirty-nine men) was eventually mobilized against the mob of nearly two thousand, and both tear gas and fire hoses were eventually needed to quell the disturbance.[92] Pete McCommons, who remembers being "in the middle of it" along with Marcia Powell, who was then the society editor of the *Red and Black,* and Calvin Trillin, agrees that the crowd had become dangerous. "When the students charged the dormitory, Marcia got hit by a rock, and that just ripped it for Trillin," said McCommons. "Later, we were back at Trillin's room at the Holiday Inn, where he had written his story. When he called it in to his editor in New York, the editor was asking him questions about the riot. And I could hear Calvin saying, 'President Aderhold, he's a shit. Dean Williams, he's a shit. Registrar Danner, he's a shit; no wait a minute, hold that, he's just a clerk.' I will always remember that exchange, and he [Trillin] was furious. It is interesting in retrospect to see how a reporter can get personally involved in a story."[93]

Ray Moore, who was then news and program director at WSB television station in Atlanta, was on campus the night of the riot, and his recollection confirms that the crowd was dangerous, that the riot had been planned well in advance, and that Governor Vandiver's office knew about it. According to Moore, he had decided to cover the events at the University of Georgia after one of his newsmen, Dick Goss, was hit in the face with a rock and knocked to his knees on the night of January 6, when UGA students staged their first protest in response to Judge Bootle's ruling. "I couldn't very well send someone else to cover an assignment if I was unwilling to go myself," Moore said recently. So on the evening of January 11, Moore and his chief cameraman, Joe Fain, arrived on UGA's campus to cover the riot, which they knew was going to happen. "I walked through the gym during the basketball game with Georgia Tech and got hooted out of the place. The students were shouting at me, 'You better not show up at Charlayne's dormitory, because we're going to be there, and we're going to get you in particular.'" When the game was over, Moore and Joe Fain proceeded to campus. By the time they got near Center Myers dorm, rocks were flying all over the place. As Moore remembers it:

> In light of the earlier threats they had made against me, I was afraid to turn the camera lights on, fearing that I would become a target. I could hear the rocks pounding against the sides of the fire trucks. I caught a rock in the chest; luckily, I was wearing an overcoat, so the rock didn't wound me. Suddenly, I looked up, and a whole group of them was converging on me, and they were chanting, "Get that camera, get that camera." John Furman, a reporter for the *Red and Black*, and Larry Aldridge, who later became an instructor in the journalism school, interposed themselves between me and the mob, and said, "Look, this guy is not a network guy, he's a local guy, don't do anything to him." At about that time, the Athens police threw the tear gas, and that tear gas explosion was enough to cause some of them to scatter and gave the rest of us an opportunity for a judicious escape. We all ran into the lobby of Center Myers, and we were given refuge there. [94]

Moore says he was furious that the Georgia State Patrol never showed up, especially because they were only a few minutes away and had to have known what was happening on the campus. "That afternoon, we had all kinds of information and tips that there was going to be a riot after the basketball game. Everybody, everybody, including university officials, knew there was going to be a riot. We called the governor's office and asked them to be alert, and we were confounded by their [the state patrol's] lack of response, especially when they were so nearby. But I'm glad I got out of there with my neck."[95]

There was never any doubt in Charlayne Hunter's mind that the riot was serious, and she dismisses any claims to the contrary as convenient amnesia and historical revisionism. "Of course it was a riot," Hunter-Gault said in a May 2000 interview. "If they didn't think it was a riot, why did they use tear gas? When I finally did go outside, the smell of tear gas was everywhere. The so-called 'disturbance' at UGA has been deliberately minimized because nobody got killed. I'm familiar with some of the accounts that claim that most of the damage was done to buildings; while that may be true, some of those bricks came through my window, and I was on the other side of that window. But that's that old style of historical revisionism. You can't find anybody in South Africa today who supported apartheid; they'll always tell you, 'It was those others, it wasn't me.' Believe me, it was a nasty riot, and any assertions to the contrary are absolute bullshit."[96]

While the UGA riot never reached the level of violence that occurred on the campus of Ole Miss in 1962 when James Meredith tried to enroll, the situation in Athens was undoubtedly a volatile one, made especially so because the Athens police had to try to restore order without any assistance from the Georgia State Patrol.[97] Despite the fact that Athens's mayor, Ralph Snow, and the police chief personally requested assistance from the state patrol, none came until after the riot had ended. The state patrol refused to intervene until it received verbal authorization from Governor Vandiver— authorization that came far too late to be of any use to Athens police. By the time that the state patrol arrived the riot was over; at that point, their only official duty was to remove Hamilton Holmes and Charlayne Hunter from campus.

The actual time when the state patrol was requested is a matter of debate. According to Colonel William P. "Bill" Trotter, the director of the Georgia Department of Public Safety who was on duty at the state patrol headquarters in Atlanta, the Athens Police Department requested tear gas around 10:00 P.M. that evening. Trotter approved the request but said that he was surprised that troopers were not requested "because events were getting out of hand around Myers Hall." FBI files indicate that a Georgia Bureau of Investigation lieutenant and a Georgia state trooper did arrive at the riot scene and left a sack full of tear gas missiles but then left immediately, although it was obvious at that point that the Athens police needed assistance. According to Trotter's recollection several years later, troopers were eventually requested, but he could not recall the exact time of the request. "At no time," he insisted, "was there the least hesitation on the part of the governor to use the troops we had assembled." In a memo to the governor sent the day after the riot, Trotter estimated that Mayor Snow's request came "at about 10:50 P.M. or 11:05 P.M." According to the memo, Trotter immediately contacted the governor, who called him back within ten minutes to authorize deployment of the state patrol. But Mayor Snow and Dean Williams maintained that they had requested assistance from the Athens Patrol Post around 10:00 P.M. For his part in the episode, Vandiver maintains that he never hesitated to send the state patrol and that he acted as soon as he received notification.[98]

Governor Vandiver received widespread criticism for his poor handling of the riot, and it was clear that some were not buying his explanation. In a front-page editorial, the *Athens Banner-Herald* asked, "Why was the State Patrol not immediately available to assist local officers in preventing trouble?" The *Macon News* editorialized that Georgians were not proud of a governor who could not "offer an adequate explanation of why state troopers were not on the scene to break up the mob before the demonstration was over." The *Atlanta Constitution* criticized state officials who "failed unforgivably to provide state police when only they could keep the law from being broken." And the faculty at Morehouse College believed that the riot was "aided and abetted by what appears to [have been] the planned negligence" by those in authority. Assessing Vandiver's role in the crisis years later, *Atlanta Constitution* reporter Hal Gulliver observed that rather than exercise leadership during the riot, Vandiver "felt caught that night by his own rhetoric [and] his campaign pledges to permit no integration while he was governor."[99]

Most of the university's faculty members had maintained silence throughout the desegregation crisis, but a good many of them found their mettle in the aftermath of the riot and the suspensions of Holmes and Hunter. A majority of them, as well as many students, publicly condemned the rioters and the actions of the university administration. The day after the riot many of the faculty members met in the university's chapel, and over the next few days more than four hundred of them—roughly 80 percent of the university's faculty—signed a resolution deploring the violence and demanding that Holmes and Hunter be reinstated. Messages of support and goodwill also came from the faculties of Georgia Tech, Agnes Scott College, Emory University, and Morehouse.[100]

One of the faculty members who signed the petition was Horace Montgomery, a professor in the history department. Reminiscent of law professor James J. Lenoir's actions on Horace Ward's behalf several years earlier, Montgomery was in the forefront of the petition drive and consequently placed his personal reputation on the line. He remembers being terribly embarrassed by the riot and was disgusted by the administration's decision to suspend Holmes and Hunter. The day after the riot, Montgomery and five other faculty members gathered in his office to draft a resolution condemning the university's actions. The resolution was presented to the faculty later that evening at the University Chapel, where faculty members had their first opportunity to sign it. As Montgomery recalls, copies of the resolution were later placed in the main library so that those faculty members not at the meeting could sign, but some of the copies disappeared. After Roy Harris's threats, several of the faculty members admitted to Montgomery that they regretted having added their names to the document, though no one ever claimed responsibility for removing the lists.[101]

A day after the resolution was adopted, Montgomery and Frank Gibson, a faculty member in political science, were later called to President Aderhold's office and asked to explain their actions. "You see that stack of letters on my desk," Aderhold said to Montgomery. "They are from some of the people who are very upset about what y'all are doing. Some of them are saying that the university's faculty members are unreliable and should be disciplined." As Montgomery put it, "I expected to get the pink slip any minute, but I never did. I explained to Aderhold that what we were doing was a matter of principle, and we all felt that it was morally right. I think he [Aderhold] was a decent man who was caught in a tough situation. He was also smart enough to understand that if the officials did not follow the court order [to desegregate] that the university would be in a mess."[102] The university never took any disciplinary action against the faculty members who had signed the petition.

President Aderhold may have been sympathetic to the signers of the petition, but the Georgia legislature clearly was not. A few days after the riot, Georgia lawmakers passed two resolutions: one urging reinstatement of the students who had been suspended for their parts in the demonstrations, and another commending UGA professors who had not signed the petition calling for Holmes's and Hunter's reinstatement. The first resolution was authored by Senator D. B. Blalock of Newnan who said he wanted "to associate myself with those students who have been expelled." The resolution passed the Senate 39–9, while the House gave voice approval. The second resolution, authored by Senator Dan Hart of Quitman, commended those faculty members who had not signed the petition for "much courage, loyalty and interest in doing a good job," and for refraining from "being pressured or browbeat into the matter of intergration [*sic*]." It passed the Senate by a vote of 29–19.[103]

On Friday, January 13, two days after university officials suspended Holmes and Hunter from the University of Georgia, Judge Bootle ordered that the two students be reinstated immediately. "The constitutional rights of plaintiffs are not to be sacrificed or yielded to violence and disorder. Nor can the lawful orders of this court be frustrated by violence and disorder. The court does not find and does not conclude that law and order in this state have broken down or that the law enforcement agencies of this state are inadequate to maintain law and order at the university. The court is therefore of the opinion that the order of suspension or withdrawal of plaintiffs should be lifted and vacated by 8 A.M. January 16, 1961." Bootle also enjoined state and university officials from suspending the two students for any reason related to mob action or violence.[104] Governor Vandiver pledged that as the two black students returned to campus, peace and order would be maintained. But there was still strong sentiment against his decision to keep UGA open. In a meeting with about fifty or so of his leading political advisers and allies at the executive mansion, all but two of them—Frank Twitty, Vandiver's floor leader in the House, and Carl Sanders, his floor leader in the Senate—urged him to close the university.[105]

In a speech to the General Assembly, Governor Vandiver asked the legislature to repeal the law that required funds to be cut off to any public school that desegregated and to replace it with an amendment that would prevent white children from being forced to attend desegregated schools. The governor requested a tuition-grant program for white parents wishing to use state funds in order to send their children to private schools and a local referendum provision that would allow any community to vote to close its schools rather than accept integration. These proposals, which had been recommended by the Sibley Commission—a special legislative committee created in 1959 to gather opinion on segregation across the state—passed overwhelmingly.[106] The governor's proposals made it clear that while the vast majority of white Georgians were still not prepared to accept integration, shutting down the University of Georgia was no longer an option.

Indeed, it was the belief (especially strong in the black community) that state officials would never seriously consider closing the University of Georgia that had made it the ideal place to challenge Jim Crow. Jesse Hill, Atlanta businessman and activist who had advised Holmes and Hunter early on, understood the symbolic importance of the University of Georgia. "I think the governor might have closed Georgia State or the Atlanta high schools if they had come first, but Georgia, with all those legislators' sons over there and the way everybody in the state feels about it, was different. He wouldn't dare close it."[107] Writing some years later, Vandiver admitted as much. "Almost every family in Georgia has some connection with the University of Georgia. A father, mother, brother, sister, uncle, or aunt, somebody in the family group had attended. The university would have been more difficult to close down than any other school—the people of our state just could not imagine the University of Georgia being closed."[108]

Hamilton Holmes and Charlayne Hunter returned to campus on Monday morning, as Judge Bootle had ordered. The events of the previous week had left both of them a bit shell-shocked, but they were determined to press on. Hunter tried to remain upbeat, saying that the friends she had made far outweighed the ugliness of the past few days. Holmes, however, was less sanguine, saying "I'll go back with an open mind," but then added, "I don't think anything could compensate for what happened Wednesday night."[109] For the most part, their return to campus provoked no major protests, though Kappa Alpha fraternity did lower its Confederate flag to half-mast, which it had also done on the first day of classes. Hoping to return to some semblance of a normal campus life, the university temporarily banned reporters, but Holmes and Hunter were protected by armed plainclothes government escorts. Hunter remembers that both she and Holmes were somewhat uncomfortable with the escorts and that she in particular felt that their presence "made us stand out at a time when we needed to try to blend in." By the end of their first week back, both students felt sufficiently at ease to walk the campus alone without their police escorts.[110]

The University of Georgia's first black students had endured the tempest and they were now hoping that they would be allowed to be normal students. But deep down they knew that the likelihood of that happening was remote, for their presence had changed forever the racial dynamics on this once all-white college campus. Writing years later, Charlayne Hunter-Gault perhaps summed it up best: "White sons and daughters fac[ed] their most apocalyptic moment since Sherman marched to the sea, Black sons and daughters their most liberating moment since the Emancipation Proclamation."[111]

CHAPTER FIVE

Tolerated, but Not Integrated

The general attitude on the campus
is an attitude of tolerance, but, as
yet, there are no signs of social
acceptance. . . . The atmosphere is
definitely not cordial.
—Hamilton Holmes

During the early 1960s young people throughout the South were trying to create and sustain the spirit of the civil rights movement. The success of the Montgomery Bus Boycott and the subsequent creation of the Southern Christian Leadership Conference (SCLC), along with Martin Luther King Jr.'s inspiring leadership, motivated thousands of people across the nation to combat the forces of Jim Crow. On February 1, 1960, four black freshmen from North Carolina Agricultural and Technical College in Greensboro, North Carolina, staged a sit-in at an F. W. Woolworth Company store. On February 18, black students from Fisk University in Nashville, Tennessee, led by Diane Nash and John Lewis, held their first sit-in. Thousands of other young people in cities across the nation soon followed suit. Inspired largely by the success of the sit-in movement, the Student Non-Violent Coordinating Committee (SNCC) was founded after a two-day meeting on April 15–16, 1960, at Shaw University in Raleigh, North Carolina. Despite overtures from SCLC to become a part of its organization, the young lions of SNCC, with encouragement from veteran activist Ella Baker, voted to remain independent of the movement's traditional leadership. In May 1961, just months after Holmes and Hunter had been admitted to the University of Georgia, the Congress of Racial Equality (CORE) sponsored a freedom ride from Washington, D.C., throughout the Deep South, testing the legality of a recent U.S. Supreme Court decision banning segregation in interstate travel. The vicious beatings that the freedom riders suffered in Alabama, and the incarcerations many of them later received in Parchman Penitentiary in Mississippi, eventually prompted the Interstate Commerce Commission, on September 22, 1961, to provide executive approval (and enforcement) to the earlier Supreme Court decision. As 1961 ended, these young and courageous pioneers who had captured the imagination of African Americans across the nation continued to press on in their tireless crusade for freedom, preparing themselves for future bloody confrontations in Alabama and Mississippi where, unfortunately, some of them would lose their lives. But there were still battles to be fought in Georgia.[1]

Now that Hamilton Holmes and Charlayne Hunter had survived the riots and the glare of the media, they were trying to settle into a normal routine, or something as close to normal as they could expect under the circumstances. While the unwanted media attention had been a distraction, in some ways it provided a measure of security, as the students and their attorneys felt that they would be relatively safe as long as the eyes of the nation were upon them. When the cameras left, however, the black students were on their own, and there were few friends in Athens that they could rely on for protection. Even on a much quieter UGA campus, the potential for violence still existed, and there were times when Holmes and Hunter were not always aware of it.

Mathematics professor Thomas Brahana recalls one incident in particular, one that left him feeling frightened and numb. He remembers getting out of his car across from Center Myers dorm on the night that Holmes and Hunter returned to campus, and he noticed eight white men, all armed with rifles, lined up in front of the dorm. He also noticed that Center Myers dorm was dark except for the light in what appeared to be Hunter's room (as it had been during the night of the riot). "A sick feeling came over me," he said in a recent interview. "These men looked like a squad, and I took them for Klansmen, probably some of the ones who later killed Lemuel Penn. And I believe that if Charlayne's silhouette had come across that window, they might have taken a shot at her. Now I don't know that for sure, but they looked serious. They could have done it." Brahana notified the police, and later that night, the FBI arrested the men on concealed weapons charges.[2] At the time, Hunter was completely unaware of the situation. (A day before Hunter's return to campus, a white man had walked into her dormitory carrying a gun and asking for her. The man was arrested and recommitted to an insane asylum.)[3]

Because she lived on campus, and because it was her tearful exit from the university that had been photographed and circulated across the nation, Hunter naturally received more attention (and generally more sympathy) than Holmes. In her first two weeks back at the university, she received about a thousand letters—three or four times the number Holmes received—from all over the United States and several foreign countries, with most of them coming from Georgia and New York. A few of the letters were abusive, but the vast majority of them expressed admiration for her "courage and dignity."[4] On campus, a few of the students appeared more friendly, and both she and Holmes would now be greeted by an occasional "Hi" or "Hello." Several students also stopped by Hunter's dorm room from time to time to sit and chat with her and to offer their support. Still, there were the diehards who refused to give in. Hunter remembers that "for roughly a week, girls on the second floor above my room would take turns pounding the floor for hours at a time." Sleep deprivation eventually caught up with her, and her coursework suffered as a result. In yet another interesting twist, some of the students who had visited her before the riot—some of whom were motivated, at least in part, by curiosity over her living quarters—began to complain that they were being discriminated against because of the lavish segregated suite the university had created for Hunter. It was not the first time that whites had claimed victim status as a result of Jim Crow laws imposed upon blacks, nor would it be the last.[5]

The absence of physical violence did not mean that overt hostilities would cease, a fact that became painfully evident to Hunter when she sought to eat in the cafeteria. Although the university was now officially desegregated, there was some ambiguity over just how much integration would be required. Suffering from chronic stomach problems, Hunter pressed her right to eat in the cafeteria, which Judge Bootle later affirmed, saying that the black students were entitled to use all university facilities, including the swimming pool (which set off another round of mild protests from white students who "didn't want to have to get in the water with the 'nigger' "). While she had no desire to take swimming, she was pleased that Judge Bootle's ruling had opened the cafeteria to her.[6]

On the first day that she ate in the cafeteria she sat alone at an empty table until being joined by Marcia Powell, by now the *Red and Black*'s editor-in-chief, whose face had become a familiar one. As Hunter writes, "Marcia Powell had been there at every critical stage of my desegregation of the university, and once again she was on the scene. . . . We talked about the story of my eating in the cafeteria for the first time . . . simply as two nineteen-year-old aspiring journalists who took themselves very seriously." On this particular occasion, it was Marcia Powell, more so than Hunter, who was the target of the white crowd's abusive epithets, for in their eyes she was a race traitor, deserving of the taunts of "nigger lover" they hurled at her. But she remained undaunted and tried not to notice her classmates' ugly behavior. She and Hunter would remain friends for many years to come, and Hunter later credited her with helping "to create and sustain some of the spirit that most college students take for granted."[7]

Joan Zitzelman was another white student who befriended Hunter. Their first encounter came in a journalism ethics class taught by Professor John Drewry, dean of the School of Journalism. Zitzelman was in the class and she knew that Hunter had registered for it. When Zitzelman entered the class and took her seat she noticed that someone had scrawled on the blackboard in large letters "Nigger Go Home." Knowing that Hunter would walk in at any minute, Zitzelman felt compelled to do something. "I stood up, walked back down the stairs to the blackboard, picked up an eraser, and erased the phrase. My mind was churning, wondering what my fifty or so classmates were thinking and doing as they watched me. I turned and walked back up the steps and took my seat. I was shaking. I wondered whether anyone would have the audacity to walk down there and write the phrase again in full view of the class; and, even more, I wondered if I would be able to walk down and erase it again." No one did write the phrase again. When Hunter walked in a few minutes later, Dean Drewry pointed out a seat where she could sit for the first class. As Zitzelman recalls, "I tried to concentrate on his words and make helpful notes, and I tried not to look over at Charlayne Hunter, sitting in a side section of the auditorium, with empty seats all around her."[8]

Marcia Powell's and Joan Zitzelman's acts of kindness proved to be the exception rather than the rule. The federal courts could order black students admitted to the University of Georgia, but they could not force white students to accept them. With but very few exceptions, UGA's white students shunned Holmes and Hunter as if they were pariahs, and this calculated determination to be unfriendly was deep-seated and pervasive. Caroline Ridlehuber was ostracized by her sorority in 1961 merely for walking Charlayne Hunter across campus.[9] Hunter remembers finding her car tires flattened on more than one occasion, and in one particular instance, someone had scratched the word "Nigger" on the driver's door.

Because of his superior scholastic ability, Holmes was the more frequent target. In one instance, a columnist in the *Red and Black* attacked him as an "alien," complaining that he was "merely a serious student" and took no part in extracurricular activities.[10] On another occasion, Holmes had to pretend to have a gun (actually a flashlight in his coat pocket) in order to keep from being assaulted by about thirty members of Kappa Alpha fraternity (Hunter later characterized the Kappa Alphas as notoriously racist). Even the more moderate white students, fearful of being ostracized by their peers, remained aloof, contributing to what they must have known was a cold and hostile environment for the university's first black students. Holmes and Hunter told journalist Calvin Trillin that they had "underestimated how long the unfriendliness would last," and in a speech in Savannah in March 1963, Holmes lamented the fact that he had "made no friends while attending the University," noting that the atmosphere for black students "is definitely not cordial."[11] UGA's white students had sent their message loud and clear: black students might be tolerated, but they would most certainly not be welcomed.

While they were almost always lumped together as "the first black students to desegregate the University of Georgia," Hamilton Holmes and Charlayne Hunter did not have identical experiences. For one thing, the fact that Holmes lived off campus gave him a greater degree of independence, whereas Hunter's living on campus created a stronger sense of interdependence, which resulted in Hunter having at least a few white friends. No one can remember Holmes spending a single weekend in Athens during his entire stay at the university, and at least initially, Hunter accompanied him on his weekly treks to Atlanta. But after a while, Hunter began to spend more weekends on campus, returning to Atlanta only if she had a speaking engagement or if she had to fly somewhere. The fact that Holmes was a serious scholar also seemed to work against him. As Hunter recalls:

Hamp felt all along that he had something to prove at Georgia, that he wanted to show whites that they were wrong in their attitudes that Blacks were inferior. . . . The fact that Hamp always scored the highest on most tests in all his classes may have convinced the white students that he was not inferior, but it also caused them to dislike him all the more, since his grades raised a normally modest curve to a level that was beyond the reach of many of them. On the other hand, a strange phenomenon occurred in my classes when I got a D or flunked with the other students. There was such a feeling of relief that I hadn't pulled a Hamilton Holmes on them that mutual commiseration ensued, and so did real communication. [12]

The extent to which there was actual communication is debatable, but one easily gets the impression from reading her memoirs that Hunter was clearly more willing than Holmes to work at gaining white acceptance, something that Holmes apparently could not have cared less about. And while she never comes out and says it, she intimates that their differing attitudes toward integration were one of the reasons they began to drift apart. She writes: "Hamp and I were beginning to change a little bit, however, possibly because . . . each of us had developed different ideas about how we wanted to approach the next year and a half at Georgia. . . . I had come to the realization that this was the only college experience I was ever going to have . . . I wanted to get the most out of everything, and I decided that the way to do that was to get personally involved." [13] All her youthful idealism notwithstanding, there were still times when the harsh realities of racism came crashing down on her with a force that left her physically weakened and psychologically demoralized. There was, for instance, the time when she wanted to bring a date with her to the university to attend a play. Upon learning that her date was a black man, university officials reassured her that the university was completely integrated as far as she and Holmes were concerned but that the desegregation order did not include "other Negroes." As Calvin Trillin remembers, this particular incident made Hunter "angrier at the university administration than she had ever been before." These kinds of daily slights and indignities eventually took their toll, and even Hunter's eternal optimism was tested. [14]

Another problem that Hunter faced was one of perception among certain segments of Atlanta's (and to a lesser extent, Athens's) African American community. Holmes made regular visits to Atlanta, which kept him in constant contact with his supporters there, and when in Athens he lived with a black family and was more closely connected to the black community. But because of Hunter's desire to get the most out of her college experience, she spent more time on UGA's campus and less time in either community's black social circles, creating the impression among some that she was snobbish. Local black activists remained unwavering in their support, but some were beginning to magnify the subtle distinctions they had made initially between the two students. Trillin identifies a pro-Hamp group and a pro-Charlayne group, and supporters of one were not necessarily supporters of the other. Holmes and Hunter had not been especially close at Turner High School, and the widening rift between their respective support groups strained their friendship even more; there were times, in fact, when the two were not speaking. But their differences were always secondary to their larger common goal, and the two of them always came together in times of crisis.[15]

To be sure, there was occasional tension between Holmes and Hunter, but Hunter-Gault believes it was sometimes blown out of proportion.

> The truth of the matter was that while Hamp and I were close, in many ways we were very different. Hamp invested his total self in the process; he was a scientist, an absolutist, and I think he was angrier than I was because his family was angrier. His father and grandfather had been civil rights pioneers. My parents were pioneers of another sort; they were capable of expressing anger against injustice, but they managed to deal with it a different way. As for me, I needed to see this as a process, one that was not going to be the definitive experience of my life, although it probably was, now that I look back on it.

As for them occasionally not being on speaking terms, Hunter-Gault remembers that "Hamp and I had our fights and spats, kind of like brother-sister fights. He could be judgmental of me and my behavior, and I'd let him know it. But whenever I had a problem, he was always there. Whenever I got sick, Hamp was always the first one in the infirmary. We had what I would call intellectual tiffs. I thought he should have tried harder on campus, but he would rather go play basketball with the brothers, and he felt reassured by that. I just tried to make my place in my space."[16]

Holmes and Hunter would remain the only African American students at the University of Georgia until the summer of 1961, when they were joined by Mary Frances Early, a music teacher from Atlanta who had transferred her graduate work from the University of Michigan, thus becoming UGA's first black graduate student. Like Holmes and Hunter, Early had attended Henry

McNeal Turner High School in Atlanta, and the three of them had actually known each other; in fact, as a member of Turner High's newspaper staff, Hunter had once interviewed Early, who at the time was doing her student teaching there. While matriculating at Michigan, Early had been following the desegregation crisis that was unfolding in her native state, and the events surrounding the riot compelled her to take a personal stand:

> When I learned that Hamilton and Charlayne had been evicted from the campus, supposedly for their own safety, I was very upset. And when I saw the photo of Charlayne clutching the statue of the Madonna, getting into that police car on her way back to Atlanta, I was furious. I decided right then and there that I was going to transfer to the University of Georgia. Since Hamp and Char were in the undergraduate school, I felt it was time for someone else to go to the graduate school. When I told my mother about my decision, she asked me if I was sure I knew what I was doing. I told her it was something that I had to do. Three days later I wrote a letter to the dean requesting an application.[17]

But getting into the University of Georgia proved almost as difficult for Early as it had been for Holmes and Hunter, and she had to jump some of the same hurdles, though without the benefit of press coverage. The application forms she requested were sent promptly, and they contained a certificate of residence, which had to be signed by two UGA alumni and the clerk or judge of the superior court, certifying that the applicant was of good moral character. Jesse Hill accompanied her to the court, where she was able to obtain the signature of the clerk, but she did not get any alumni signatures because she did not know any. And then the wait began. Her initial application packet mentioned that she would have to complete an on-campus interview, but no one ever contacted her, so she arranged her own interview. During the interview, conducted by registrar Walter Danner and which Early describes as "not pleasant," she was asked a series of degrading and inappropriate questions, questions that no university official would have dared to ask a white female student. Perhaps the most offensive question Danner asked her was whether she had ever been a prostitute. Danner also told her that she should reconsider her decision to transfer because if she did she would lose all of the credit hours she had accrued at the University of Michigan. Early replied that it really did not matter to her if she lost her credits because she was determined to enter UGA. On May 10, 1961, Mary Frances Early finally received official notification that she had been admitted to the University of Georgia. She arrived on campus on June 12, set to begin the summer session.[18]

During her first term at UGA, Early was assigned to live in Hunter's room, which Hunter had vacated for the summer. The following spring, both young women requested single rooms that were private but not isolated, but university officials denied their requests, citing a lack of space. (A week later, Early and Hunter had lunch with a white graduate student who said she was changing dorms because of vacancies in a new dorm that had opened.) Early and Hunter would end up sharing Hunter's room during the spring and summer of 1962. Early remembers that life in Center Myers dorm was no fun, and the fact that all of the other girls were freshmen certainly did not help matters. She and Hunter had little in common with the younger girls, who generally kept to themselves, monopolized the television in the lobby, and quickly became versed in the art of giving the cold shoulder. Early also remembers that some of the girls wanted to be friendly but told her that they were rushing sororities and had been warned by some of their big sisters that fraternization with blacks might hurt their chances. Isolation became a part of Early's life on UGA's campus, and she soon became accustomed to students leaving tables as soon as she sat down. And wherever she went on campus, some white person always demanded to see her student ID, even when they recognized her as a student. "Isolation and ostracism came with the territory," Early recalls, "and we dealt with it as best we could. But when things on campus got too rough, we sought refuge at Killian's," the black-owned restaurant in Athens where Holmes ate most of his meals. "Killian's was our respite, because it was a place where we could see our own folk and eat our own food."[19]

Early could not spend all of her time at Killian's, however; while on campus, she was subjected to a never-ending torrent of abuses, which were compounded that first summer by Holmes's and Hunter's summertime vacation, leaving Early as the lone black student on campus. Football players once threw lemon slices at her while she stood in the dining hall line. On another occasion, a group of white boys formed a line across the entrance to the library and prevented her from entering. When one of the boys said, "I smell a dog," another one shouted, "That's not a dog, that's a nigger." Even now, recounting that incident is especially painful for Early, and she recently described it as perhaps the single most humiliating experience she had to endure while a student at UGA. "Just calling me a nigger was not enough for them," she said.

"They had to compare me to a dog. It's still hard for me to understand how some people could be so cruel to another human being." She credits James Popovich, a speech professor who had also tried to be helpful to Holmes and Hunter; the Reverend Hardin W. "Corky" King, the chaplain at the Presbyterian Westminster House; and a few other faculty members (all of whom "caught some flak") for doing what they could to make her feel welcome.[20]

Like Hunter, Early soon learned that though the university was at least partly desegregated, it was not open to blacks who were not students. When she wanted to bring her mother and some friends to a concert of the chorus (of which she was a member), she was advised to check with Dean Williams before bringing other blacks to campus. As it turned out, she was unable to get an appointment with the dean until after the concert was over, so her family did not make the trip. When she finally did get to see him, Dean Williams told her it would not have been a good idea anyway because the university was not ready for such a step.[21]

As he began his final ten-week quarter at Georgia, Hamilton Holmes was still very much an outsider. He had never eaten in a university dining hall, studied in the library, used the gymnasium, or entered the snack bar. No white students had ever visited him, and he had never visited one of them. He had not spent a single weekend in Athens during the entire period of his enrollment. He had had little contact with campus organizations, though he was initiated into Phi Kappa Phi, a scholastic honorary society. (Another medical honor society, so as not to have to accept Holmes for membership, stopped initiating new members after Holmes applied.) Holmes felt that his instructors were decent, though he did single out history professor E. Merton Coulter as a notable exception. According to Holmes's brother Herbert, Coulter—who had served on Horace Ward's special committee back in 1951—never went out of his way to conceal his racist views in the classroom and, at least during the term that Hamilton was in his class, seemed to spend a lot of time denouncing Henry McNeal Turner (after whom Turner High School in Atlanta was named) as a "radical Negro" who was an example of the failures of Reconstruction. Turner, a bishop in the Methodist church and a member of Georgia's legislature during Reconstruction, was one of the state's foremost political leaders at that time.[22]

As for his fellow students, Holmes told Calvin Trillin in 1963 that they respected him as long as they were in the classroom, but that was as far as it went. "I guess they think that outside the classroom I'm just another nigger. It used to bother me. But all I can see now is June first [graduation day]." Holmes's personality was almost the complete opposite of Hunter's, and most whites who came into contact with him described him as being surly, aloof, unfriendly, or as having a chip on his shoulder.

> I'll admit I didn't try too hard. About this time last year I sort of gave up. I just figured I'd make it on my own. . . . Char wanted me to eat on campus, but it just didn't interest me. That just isn't in my personality. . . . It just wouldn't have been me to go down there just to be noticed. . . . I haven't gone out of my way at all to make friends. And I don't expect them to go out of their way . . . [But] I'm used to speaking to almost everybody I see. That's the way I was brought up. . . . [Here] I look up at people, wanting to speak, and people turn their heads. I guess that bothers me more than anything else.

But then he was quick to add that socializing was never his top priority. "I've concentrated on getting some good grades; I was so determined to show them that what they said about me wasn't true."[23]

The one thing that Holmes wanted to do at UGA other than study was to play football. When he broached the subject shortly after being admitted, the dean strongly advised against it, telling him frankly that there was a real possibility that someone (from either the opposing team or his own) might try to kill him. Holmes's desire to play football was widely known across the campus, but the opposition to him was intense. But Georgia's recent string of losses apparently caused a few to reconsider, if perhaps only for a moment. One Georgia alumnus is said to have commented, "The more I look at that nigger, the whiter he gets."[24]

As her matriculation at UGA wound down, Charlayne Hunter became much more at ease in her environment, and her engaging personality enabled her to befriend those who were interested (generally those who were unconcerned with the pressures associated with fraternities and sororities) while ignoring those who were not. By now, she had become accustomed to curious stares and racist remarks and had accepted the reality that no matter how hard she tried, she would never gain universal acceptance. Even when she was allowed into a particular circle, she was not always accepted into it. Such was the case with her brief and unrewarding stint at the *Red and Black*. Her journalism school faculty adviser suggested that she work at least one quarter on the student newspaper to get some additional experience, to which Charlayne agreed. In the fall quarter of her senior year she worked in the advertising section, making up dummies for ads and devising an advertising filing system. But her desire to try her hand at other tasks was ignored, and the editor seemed determined to deny her any kind of mobility. Frustrated, she eventually left the paper. Later, one of the boys on the newspaper's staff ran for student office and sent around letters to his classmates soliciting their support. The letter he sent to Hunter had the salutation "Dear Nig." These kinds of slights and slurs persisted until she graduated.[25]

Hamilton Holmes and Charlayne Hunter were not the first dark-skinned students to attend the University of Georgia; in fact, they were actually lighter in complexion than some of the foreign students who had been attending the university for years, a fact that Bill Shipp points to as an example of the contradictions and absurdities inherent in racial segregation. "I thought it was ridiculous that blacks were kept out of the university, when just about every other ethnic group I could think of was here," Shipp said recently. As editor of the *Red and Black* in 1953, Shipp had criticized the university's policy of excluding blacks while admitting foreigners. "Racial segregation is illogical in the first place, and that policy proved it," says Shipp. According to Calvin Trillin, 116 foreign students from 37 countries were enrolled at UGA in the fall of 1962. The students came from Cambodia, India, Pakistan, the Philippines, Thailand, as well as a host of other countries from all across the world; the only area of the world not represented, of course, was black Africa. The darker foreign students on campus could generally expect to be well received, but apparently that was true only as long as they accented their foreignness, usually by their speech or dress (stories of American blacks donning turbans to get into Jim Crow establishments, while perhaps largely apocryphal, certainly have some basis in fact). Those who tried to assimilate too much—sometimes by abandoning their traditional attire—ran the risk of being misidentified as American blacks, which could be especially dangerous if the students ventured off campus and into the town of Athens itself.[26]

Part of the frustration that the university's first black students encountered stemmed from the fact that while the university may have been desegregated, the city of Athens was not. When Holmes and Hunter first enrolled at the university in January 1961, segregation was the rule in practically every facet of life in Athens, Georgia, although a few changes had occurred by the time they began their senior year. Some of the town's department stores and its bus station had quietly desegregated, but there were still certain places where blacks were not welcome. Harold Black, one of the African American freshmen admitted in the fall of 1962 and the first black male to live on campus, recalled that it was with some trepidation that he ventured downtown to visit some of his white classmates. "Athens was an interesting place, because there was a fairly active, or at least reputed to be active, Ku Klux Klan presence there. There was a redneck bar by the Trailways bus station called 'The Old South.' Ironically, friends of mine who were white rented apartments above the bar, and I had to walk past the bar to get upstairs. I was aware of the potential for danger, but fortunately, I never encountered any hostility."[27] Blacks could not go to any of the white-owned restaurants, movie theaters, or pubs. In fact, the university itself remained off-limits to blacks, except for the handful who had been admitted and those who worked there either as cooks or janitors. Only the black students (there were eight by the fall of 1962) were allowed to sit among the whites in the football stadium; local black Athenians still had to sit in the segregated "crow's nest." Signs reading "White" and "Colored" still dotted the local landscape.[28]

With hardly any exceptions, the local churches remained bastions of segregation, as Harold Black discovered when he accepted an invitation from some of his white classmates to attend First Presbyterian Church in Athens. Black recently described the circumstances leading up to his decision to attend First Presbyterian:

> I was attending Westminster House, the Presbyterian center on campus [during the first months of UGA's desegregation, Westminster House had been the headquarters for the Students for Constructive Action and the scene of many discussions about race relations]. The kids that I met during my first week at Georgia were Presbyterians, and they went to Westminster House to study. Westminster House turned out to be sort of a haven for black students, a place where they could go and study, and not worry about being harassed. And so, when we started going to Westminster House, it was only natural that we would attend Sunday school there as well. It was after Sunday school that the Westminster House students would then go to First Presbyterian Church; but I wouldn't go, knowing that 11:00 A.M. on Sunday morning was then, and probably still is, the most segregated hour in America. But those kids were persistent, and every Sunday they would ask me. Finally, I said yes, that I would go. Westminster's minister, the Reverend Roland

Perdue, was very supportive, and by now I felt that I was a part of the Westminster family, so I felt comfortable accompanying them to First Presbyterian.[29]

On his very first visit to First Presbyterian, Black remembers that the service seemed quite normal and that he did not perceive any animosity or hostility. He went in with his white friends from Westminster House, and they all felt very comfortable. But he suspected that his presence might create some controversy, especially once he recognized university registrar Walter Danner as one of the ushers. "Walter Danner had made it plain that he did not welcome us on that campus; as a matter of fact, the black students felt that the only University of Georgia administrator who was not hostile toward us was Dean Tate. And it was not that Dean Tate actually welcomed our presence, but he loved the University of Georgia so much that he did not want to see anything that would in any way besmirch the University of Georgia." Despite Danner's presence, Black recalls feeling good about the service, so much so in fact that he looked forward to returning the next Sunday. He did return, but his worship experience at First Presbyterian would be a brief one.[30]

During the wave of "kneel-ins" across the South, First Presbyterian's board of elders had agreed to welcome all visitors in the church, regardless of race. But when Harold Black put this policy to the test, many of the white parishioners apparently did not believe that Christian love extended that far. "Some people don't come on the Sundays he's here," First Presbyterian's minister Reverend William Adams told Calvin Trillin in 1962. "We have had people get as far as the vestibule and realize he was here and turn away. . . . The real antagonism has been toward the students who brought him—some of them sons of our members." It was apparent early on that Black's presence did not sit well with many of the white parishioners, and when he sat beside a white girl one Sunday, the controversy escalated. Reverend Adams received an avalanche of abusive letters and phone calls, some of which inveighed against the perils of intermarriage. Two Sundays later, Black brought one of the black freshmen girls with him. Initially, Reverend Adams had supported the church's policy of seating all visitors, but these latest episodes had forced him to capitulate. While he did not forbid Harold Black from coming back to the church, he did explain to him that his presence in the congregation offended many of his white parishioners and that his continued presence in the church could lead to violence, which would damage the church's reputation. Black decided not to return.[31]

Harold Black approached desegregation at the University of Georgia in much the same way that Charlayne Hunter did. Despite his status as one of the black pioneers on campus, he still hoped to have a college experience as close to normal as possible under the circumstances. UGA officials were considering waiving the residency requirement for Black, which would have permitted him to live off campus, and he remembers that he and Hamilton Holmes had discussed the possibility of him living at the Killians', the same place where Holmes stayed. But then Black changed his mind. "I decided not to live at the Killians' because I figured if I did that, I would never be a part of the campus. My friends didn't even know that Hamilton was still at Georgia; they never saw him." Living on campus could certainly make one feel a part of the larger university community, but it had its down side, especially for black students, who were easy targets. Black recalls that the single most negative experience he endured was having rocks thrown at his window in Reed Hall following yet another basketball game in which UGA had narrowly lost to Georgia Tech. "After the basketball game, for whatever reason, a large crowd gathered at my dormitory window. There was a lot of shouting, and rocks were being thrown through my window, which really was nothing new; my windows were broken out nearly every night during my first quarter, but usually it was done surreptitiously. But on this occasion, people were bold about it, and were doing it out in the open. I never felt really threatened, but it was a little unnerving."[32]

In the early 1960s Athens was the typical southern, segregated city and remained so even after the first black students had arrived on campus. But unbeknownst to these black students at the time, their presence was having a profound impact on local black residents, many of whom later credited Holmes and Hunter with inspiring civil rights activism in Athens. Longtime Athens resident and retired postal worker Rubye Potts remembers that black Athenians rallied around UGA's few black students and that Ebenezer Baptist Church, West, one of the city's most prominent black churches, was the center of much of the activity and the site of weekly mass meetings. "Our pastor at the time was Reverend [William] Hudson, and he was a character," Potts recalls. "He actually led the sit-in movement and was so brazen in his actions that some in the church didn't think his behavior was appropriate for a minister. It was widely rumored that on Sundays he packed a pistol underneath his robe, and knowing him, he probably did. But because of him, things began to change around here."[33]

In 1961 Rubye Potts worked as a cook at Woolworth's in Athens. She says that the black and white employees had always gotten along rather well, but all that changed with the beginning of the sit-ins, which started shortly after Holmes and Hunter's arrival. "When the sit-ins began the white management told us not to have anything to do with those troublemakers, as they put it. We weren't even allowed to speak to them. The waitresses, who were white, were ordered not to serve them. And then the waitresses stopped speaking to any of the black help." Racial tensions in Woolworth's took on a new dimension after Potts's oldest daughter, Chandra, became one of the sit-in leaders. "When our children got involved in the movement, many of us older folk began to reassess the kind of life we had been living under Jim Crow. We had just gotten tired of things as they were, and many of us had reached the point where we no longer cared if we lost our jobs or not. We were ready for change."[34]

Athens businessman Homer Wilson remembers those days much the same way. One of the most successful black families in the city, the Wilsons have operated businesses in downtown Athens for more than fifty years, including a barber shop and a soul food restaurant. Wilson recalls that black Athenians were overjoyed when they first got wind of the news that the University of Georgia was about to desegregate. "At that time, the people were glad to see some things happening. We had been going into back doors, side doors, no doors, and all the rest. So, yeah, we were in the mood for change." As Wilson remembers it, there was very little in the way of civil rights activism in Athens prior to 1961, but the arrival of Holmes and Hunter galvanized the masses. "What I remember most was that black people stopped taking some things. Fear left them, and the people were now saying, 'I ain't taking that no more.' Blacks began to confront the system more. If a white person referred to a black man as 'boy' after 1961, that black man was now very likely to respond, 'I got a name.' We had a new attitude."[35] While whites in Athens may have taken notice of that new attitude, they gave no indication that they were prepared to accept any change in the existing social order.

There were hardly enough African American students at the University of Georgia in 1962 to cause administrators to agonize over the possibility of widespread interracial dating, but concerned they were nonetheless, and Charlayne Hunter's suspicions that her relationships with white males were being monitored would soon be confirmed. At least two white boys (that she knows of) were called into the dean's office and grilled about their closeness to her; one friendship was completely innocent, but her friendship with the other, Walter Stovall, had turned serious, and apparently Dean William Tate had gotten wind of it. He summoned Walter Stovall to his office and proceeded to lecture him about the dangerous ground on which he and Hunter were treading. Claiming not to be unsympathetic to black hopes and aspirations (Tate told Stovall that he had once been invited to speak at a "nig funeral"), he pointed out to Stovall that public knowledge of their relationship could trigger an incident, and that they should not rock the boat. Stovall denied that there was any truth to the rumor. But it was true. In fact, the two of them would get married in the spring of 1963, but for obvious reasons (the most important of which was that interracial marriage was still illegal in Georgia and in twenty other states) they dared not disclose it. That story did not break until both of them had graduated from the university and were living safely in New York.[36]

On June 1, 1963, Hamilton Holmes and Charlayne Hunter endured yet another media blitz as they graduated from the University of Georgia. With considerably less fanfare, Mary Frances Early had graduated on August 16, 1962, with a master's degree in music education, becoming the first African American to earn a degree from the University of Georgia. (In 1966, Shirley Mathis McBay became the first African American to receive a doctorate from the University of Georgia, earning a Ph.D. in mathematics. Thomas Brahana served as her major professor.) Holmes achieved two other milestones: he became the first African American elected to UGA's Phi Beta Kappa and the first African American admitted to Emory University's School of Medicine.

Three months after her graduation, Charlayne Hunter acknowledged publicly that she and Walter Stovall, the twenty-five-year-old army veteran with whom she had often been seen, were indeed married. News of Charlayne Hunter's marriage to this white man from Douglas, Georgia, set off another round of protests from angry whites who had expressed fear all along that the NAACP would never be satisfied with anything less than intermarriage with whites. Some of her black supporters were none too happy about it either, fearful that her interracial marriage might not play well with some of their white allies, whose liberal attitudes stopped well short of the bedroom. But racial politics was no longer her top priority, and Hunter felt that she had given more than enough for the cause, as she made clear to television reporters the day after she revealed her marriage. "This is a personal thing," she said, "and my personal life should not have anything to do with that which affects the masses of people. . . . I have my own life to live." It may well have been her own life to live, but some in Georgia were making it pretty clear that she would not live it there. The state attorney general reminded the interracial couple that such unions were in violation of state law and that they faced prosecution if they returned to Georgia. University of Georgia president O. C. Aderhold proclaimed that neither Hunter nor Stovall would be allowed to return to campus. Stovall lacked a few credits for his degree, but he had no plans to return; by now, the newlyweds were residing in New York and expecting a baby.[37]

The desegregation of the University of Georgia had now become another chapter in the nation's ongoing struggle to deal fairly and equitably with its African American citizens. To be sure, there were hurdles yet to overcome, but this important first step had been taken; and that first step, as civil rights attorney Donald Hollowell reminds us, was no easy walk. "Charlayne's and Hamilton's entry into the University of Georgia gave me fulfillment," Hollowell said recently. "It was a proud moment in our history, and certainly one of the highlights of my legal career." Hollowell cites the desegregation of the University of Georgia as one of his two greatest legal victories. (The other was his successful defense of Preston Cobb, a fifteen-year-old black boy from Monticello, Georgia, who had been sentenced to death for allegedly killing a white man on whose land he and his family lived and worked. Fearful of white reprisal, Cobb's mother did not contact the NAACP until five days before her son's scheduled execution in the electric chair. Following a series of appeals and reversals, Preston Cobb was finally released from prison in 1968 after having spent seven years on death row.)[38]

Looking back on that period in her life nearly forty years later, Charlayne Hunter-Gault said recently that her attorneys, especially Donald Hollowell and Constance Baker Motley, made all the difference. "I knew my family would be there, and I could always count on Hamp. But my faith and confidence in our legal team was a big part of my own confidence." In a May 2000 interview, she summed it up this way:

Hollowell was like a father figure; he was very close to my family, very avuncular, and very reassuring, always slow and deliberate in his speech. I never hesitated to call him at home, because he really felt like a family member. He always appeared to be in total control; he never panicked. He was attentive to little things, like making sure that I was eating right. As for Constance Motley, she was the hard-charging intellectual, with a brilliant legal mind. She wasn't someone that you just walked up to and cuddled up with, like I could do with Hollowell. But the courtroom was her element. For me to see this black woman up there just ripping Walter Danner to shreds in ways that were so smooth and searing that he didn't even know what hit him, that was something to witness. I'm sitting there thinking that I want to be like that when I grow up. Here was a black woman taking on the system and kicking its butt; she was the epitome of dignity and confidence. But what I remember most is that neither she nor Hollowell were intimidated by white people; they didn't bow to white supremacy, and I cannot emphasize enough what kind of impact that had upon me as an impressionable nineteen-year-old. Today, we often talk about the importance of role models. It is very important for young blacks to see other black people in all kinds of positions. Good role models don't have to be warm and cuddly, just competent.[39]

For his part, Horace Ward takes exceptional pleasure in his role in the case and remembers that at the time he shared vicariously in the monumental journey on which Holmes and Hunter were embarking. "Their victory was my victory," Ward said recently. "My case ended in defeat, but theirs ended in triumph, and I gained a great deal of personal satisfaction knowing that my case had helped pave the way." But what was seen as a great victory by Ward, Hollowell, Motley, and all the others who had waged a long and often bitter campaign against segregation was denounced by those who had opposed them as a flagrant violation of states' rights and a clear-cut case of unwarranted intrusion by the federal government. As the events of the 1960s unfolded, many of the South's white sons and daughters made it known, in no uncertain terms, that their defiance was far from over. As Ward walked off UGA's campus after Holmes and Hunter had completed registration in January 1961, a white man in the crowd shouted to him, "Hey you, nigger lawyer, get off this campus, and don't ever come back."[40] It would be more than thirty-five years before Horace Ward would again walk through the arch of the University of Georgia.

CHAPTER SIX

"Wouldn't Take Nothing for My Journey Now"

A poet once wrote, "I knew where
the lamplighter was by the lamps he
had lit." I say to you to continue to
light lamps by which others may be
guided. I congratulate you today for
myself. I congratulate you, Horace,
for Austin T. Walden, who with me
and others, in this [very] courtroom,
handled your case when you were
seeking to enter the University of
Georgia. I congratulate you for Dr.
William Madison Boyd, who worked
his heart out going back and forth
across this state trying to raise money
to support that case. I know that
wherever good men go, they are
smiling upon us here today. . . . So it
is my privilege and my pleasure to be
a part of this robing ceremony, as you
are robed with this beautiful gown,
and that which represents the message
of your office.
—Donald L. Hollowell, at the
Oath of Office Ceremony, on the
Appointment of Horace T. Ward as
Federal Judge, United States District
Court, Northern District of Georgia
(December 27, 1979)

The desegregation of the University of Georgia was one of the great triumphs of Horace Ward's career. By the time that Hamilton Holmes and Charlayne Hunter graduated in 1963, Ward had spent thirteen years of his life trying to crack segregation at UGA. Even while finishing his law degree at Northwestern University, the University of Georgia was never far from his mind. When the victory finally came, Ward recalls that, in addition to experiencing the general euphoria of the moment, for the first time in his life he really understood the power of the law to right the nation's wrongs and was more convinced than ever that he had chosen the right career path for himself. Like his mentor Donald Hollowell, Ward saw himself in the early 1960s as a civil rights lawyer because it was one sure way of effecting social change. But breaking down segregation at the University of Georgia was, as Ward put it, "a very important piece of a much larger puzzle." There were other battles yet to be fought, and greater victories still lay ahead.[1]

Ward had joined Donald Hollowell's law firm in 1960, serving as associate counsel in the UGA desegregation case. Over the next two years, Hollowell's practice would become the law firm of Hollowell, Ward, Moore, and Alexander. Howard Moore Jr., now an internationally famous trial lawyer, joined Hollowell in 1961; William H. Alexander, now a superior court judge, joined the firm in 1962. Most of their cases dealt with issues of constitutional law and civil rights violations, several of which were eventually argued before and decided by the United States Supreme Court, most notably the Preston Cobb case. The law firm represented Martin Luther King Jr. on a couple of occasions, as well as the plaintiffs in the bus desegregation case in Augusta and in the school desegregation case in Macon. Ward was the principal attorney in the Grady Hospital case in Atlanta and in the case involving the medical and dental societies of Fulton County and the state of Georgia.[2]

Prior to the passage of civil rights legislation by Congress in the mid-1960s, the medical and dental associations in Georgia were no less segregated than other establishments, and they often claimed to be exempt from federal civil rights statutes because they were private organizations. In 1964 Ward and Hollowell successfully challenged this form of segregation in *Bell v. Georgia Dental Association*, in which a district court held that the state dental association, although a private group, was an agency of the state to the extent that it had the right to nominate members of state agencies. The dental association's policy of excluding black dentists from membership, therefore, was a state action, and as such, violated the Fourteenth Amendment. This decision, along with a consent decree in related cases, resulted in the admission of black physicians and dentists to the staff of Grady Memorial Hospital in Atlanta and the desegregation of the Grady Hospital nursing school, as well as the admission of blacks to the medical and professional societies in Georgia.[3]

Ward's involvement in these cases taught him that although practicing law could be rewarding, making the law might even be more gratifying. In 1964, with the encouragement of his wife, Ruth, Ward decided to seek election in the thirty-ninth senatorial district in Fulton County. After winning the Democratic primary in the majority white district, he defeated his white Republican opponent in the general election, becoming the second African American to serve in Georgia's state senate since Reconstruction. (In 1962, his friend and classmate Leroy Johnson had become the first African American elected to the state senate since Reconstruction.) Ward won re-election four times, running unopposed in 1966, 1968, and 1970. In 1972 he defeated a black challenger in this district, which had become majority black in 1970.[4]

For the nine years that he served in the state senate (1965–74), Ward considered himself a liberal Democrat and an activist legislator who was committed to fairness in government. He served on several key committees and sponsored or supported several pieces of important legislation, including election-laws reform, revision of the state constitution, reapportionment of the House of Representatives, establishment of a human rights commission, and the abolition of the death penalty.[5] In 1968, in one of the highlights of his political career, Ward was selected as a delegate to the Democratic National Convention in Chicago, where he witnessed Vice President Hubert H. Humphrey win the party's nomination for president. In 1969, he was appointed deputy city attorney of Atlanta, a position he held for about eighteen months. In 1971, he was named assistant Fulton County attorney, a position he held for three years. No longer a member of his original law firm (Hollowell had left the practice in 1966 to head the Equal Employment Opportunity Commission in the southeast), Ward continued to work during this period as a sole practitioner, representing the Atlanta NAACP and the Atlanta Urban League on various issues. Even though he was now an elected lawmaker, Ward kept his ties to the city's black legal establishment. In 1972 and 1973, Ward served as president of the Gate City Bar Association. Founded in 1948 by Ward's early mentor and legal adviser A. T. Walden, the GCBA served as the official affiliation for Atlanta's black attorneys who, until 1963, had been barred from membership in the all-white Atlanta Bar Association.[6]

More than just a party stalwart, Ward was shrewd enough to forge the kinds of alliances necessary to get things done. One of Ward's closest allies in the state senate was Jimmy Carter, a native of Plains, Georgia, then in his second term. Carter befriended Ward early on and offered to assist the newcomer in any way that he could. The two legislators worked together on several important pieces of legislation and usually voted the same way. Their time together in the Georgia legislature was cut short, however, when Carter decided to run for governor. Jimmy Carter's subsequent election as Georgia's seventy-sixth governor in 1970 did not mark the end of his relationship with Horace Ward. As fate would have it, the ties between these two sons of the South would afford Carter an opportunity to cement his legacy as someone worthy of the appellation "New South governor," reflected in his willingness to embrace a new racial order by boldly proclaiming himself as the governor of all Georgians, black as well as white.

Jimmy Carter's election as governor in 1970 signaled the dawning of a new era in Georgia politics and is often referred to as the transitional period between Georgia's departure from the Old South and its emergence into the New, especially in the area of race relations. The game rules of Georgia politics had changed drastically since the days of the Talmadges and the county-unit system in which a few rural bosses controlled the state's political apparatus. The Supreme Court's "one man, one vote" ruling in *Baker v. Carr* and the Voting Rights Act of 1965 forever altered the political landscape in the South, and no future candidate for statewide office would be able to disregard the region's African American voters. Jimmy Carter understood this as well as anyone. At his inaugural address in January 1971, in what has been referred to as one of the shortest yet most memorable inaugural addresses in the state's history, Carter proclaimed: "No poor, rural, weak, or black person should ever have to bear the additional burden of being deprived of the opportunity of an education, a job, or simple justice."[7] With those words, Carter would begin the process of setting Georgia's history on a new course.

Jimmy Carter's administration remains significant as an important turning point in Georgia history because of his progressivism on race relations. Because his political ambitions went well beyond being governor of Georgia, he understood the importance of compiling a record of achievement that would play well at the national level as well. How he dealt with the issue of race would be crucial to the success of his larger program, and he used his appointment power to bring about social change in the state. He greatly increased the number of women and minorities appointed to major state boards and agencies; in particular, the number of African American state employees increased from 4,850 to 6,684. He appointed blacks to his own staff, and he appointed six blacks and six whites to a Governor's Council on Human Relations to promote racial justice and harmony. In a move clearly designed to signal the dawning of a new day in Georgia, Carter refused to reappoint segregationist Roy V. Harris to the University System Board of Regents and appointed a black man in his place. Carter also proclaimed January 15, 1973, as Martin Luther King Jr. Day, and on the first anniversary of that occasion King's portrait was hung in the state capitol.[8]

During one of their conversations while serving together in the Georgia legislature a few years earlier, Horace Ward had mentioned to Carter that he might prefer a judicial career rather than a legislative one. Carter had not forgotten the conversation, and on May 8, 1974, he appointed Ward to the Fulton County Civil Court, making him the first black trial court judge in Georgia's history.[9] Three years later, on January 25, 1977, Governor George Busbee appointed Ward to the Fulton County Superior Court, where Ward would serve as one of eleven judges in the Atlanta Judicial Circuit.[10] Ward's friendship with Jimmy Carter had certainly helped facilitate his rapid ascent within the judiciary, and owing to a fortuitous set of historical circumstances he was about to rise even higher.

Jimmy Carter's victory in the 1976 presidential election was due in no small measure to the overwhelming support he received from African Americans. Carter enjoyed the support of virtually all of the mainstream civil rights establishment and he acknowledged his debt to African American voters throughout his presidency. "I could not have been standing here today as President," Carter proclaimed in 1980, "had it not been for Martin Luther King Jr. and others like him, who fought for equal rights for blacks and who took the yoke of racial discrimination from around the necks of white people as well."[11] President Carter would seek to repay that debt by helping blacks to achieve a greater measure of representational democracy in the area of judicial appointments.

Although he was the only American president to serve an entire term without appointing a single justice to the U.S. Supreme Court, Carter appointed more judges to the federal district and appeals courts than any previous president, and he appointed more African Americans to government positions (including the federal judiciary) than any previous president.[12] By the end of his presidency, Carter, who appointed thirty-seven African American federal judges, had placed more blacks on the federal bench than all previous presidents combined, an accomplishment all the more noteworthy in light of the fact that some southern U.S. senators and several of his own top advisers opposed his efforts to diversify the judiciary.[13]

In the second year of his presidency, Carter was given the opportunity to fill a record number of newly created federal judgeships, which he saw as "a unique opportunity to begin to redress another disturbing feature of the Federal judiciary: the almost complete absence of women, or other members of minority groups." As he had done elsewhere, Carter urged Georgia's Judicial Nominating Commission to recommend a diversified slate of candidates, one that was representative of the state as a whole. Whatever the commission did, however, would be determined largely by the sentiments of Georgia's two U.S. senators, who at the time were Sam Nunn and former segregationist governor Herman Talmadge.[14]

Horace Ward, at the time serving as a judge on the Fulton County Superior Court, was surprised and pleased to learn that the Judicial Nominating Commission had submitted his name for consideration. Senator Talmadge, who as governor of Georgia in 1950 had vowed to use every means at his disposal to keep Ward out of the University of Georgia law school, was certainly a most likely candidate to derail Ward's nomination. But the political landscape, especially in the South, had changed drastically since 1950, and apparently Senator Talmadge had become attuned to the new political realities. As Ward remembers it:

> Both Nunn and Talmadge had apparently agreed to designate me for one of the openings. As I understood it, I was actually in Talmadge's area of influence, and he could have blocked my nomination on any number of grounds; in fact, he need not have given a reason. But he took the position that he was going to support me. There was some opposition to my candidacy. Some argued that I did not have the background; others said that I had not specialized in some sophisticated areas. Senator Talmadge called me and explained that there was some opposition, but he

told me to hang in there, and assured me that he would support my nomination all the way. It's quite ironic, I guess. He now openly admits that he opposed my efforts to enroll at UGA, but be that as it may, he supported my nomination, and in all candor and fairness to the Senator, I would not have gotten the position had he not supported me.[15]

Despite some initial uncertainty, Ward's nomination eventually made it to the White House, and President Carter promptly nominated him for one of Georgia's district court judgeships. Following Senate confirmation, Ward was sworn in as a judge on the U.S. District Court for the Northern District of Georgia on December 27, 1979, becoming the first African American ever to serve on the federal bench in Georgia. Ward remembers that during their time together in the Georgia legislature Carter once asked him if he might someday be interested in a judgeship; Ward replied in the affirmative, but said he never really expected it to happen. "Not that I ever doubted Carter's sincerity," Ward said; "it was just that I couldn't have known back then that he would someday be President of the United States. I guess you could say that I was in the right place at the right time."[16]

Ward's Oath of Office Ceremony was held in the U.S. District Court in Atlanta, Georgia, on December 27, 1979. Ironically, it was the same courtroom where Ward's lawsuit against the University of Georgia had been argued twenty-three years earlier, almost to the day. Among those present were Ward's former law partner and mentor, Donald L. Hollowell, Coretta Scott King, Reverend Martin Luther King Sr., Judge Elbert P. Tuttle, numerous other judges, and representatives from the National Bar Association and the American Bar Association.

Herman Talmadge's support of Horace Ward's federal judgeship was proof that the civil rights movement had brought about fundamental changes in American society, and nowhere was that more evident than in the realm of southern politics. In addition to having served two terms as Georgia's governor, Talmadge served in the U.S. Senate from 1957 until 1981. In response to the *Brown* decision, Talmadge authored a book in 1955 entitled *You and Segregation,* a blueprint for maintaining segregation in the South. When Talmadge began his term as the junior senator from Georgia in January 1957, he immediately joined the other southern Democrats in their fight against civil rights legislation. Talmadge once said, "I never read a civil rights bill that didn't destroy more constitutional rights than it purported to give any group. The theory behind every civil rights bill that I ever read is to make one particular group . . . a favored group and to discriminate against other Americans."[17] Throughout the 1960s, he and Georgia's senior senator, Richard B. Russell, maintained a united front in their opposition to civil rights causes.

But, in the early 1970s, Herman Talmadge's politics slowly began to change. Ever the politician, Talmadge understood the growing importance of the black vote in the South and perhaps believed that if blacks in Alabama could forgive George Wallace, then maybe blacks in Georgia could forgive him. "I could see that his position was moderating over the years," said Judge Ward. "I remember his being at the Hungry Club, which used to be a major political forum in Atlanta's black community; black leaders met once a week for lunch at the Butler Street YMCA. Talmadge came to speak once, and during the Q & A session, someone asked him to comment on his appearance before this all-black gathering, given his political background. He replied, 'Black people weren't voting in the same numbers back then as they are now.' Everybody burst into laughter. Clearly this was a smart politician who knew what time it was."[18] Journalist and political commentator Bill Shipp agrees: "Herman Talmadge was a pragmatic politician, and it was no coincidence that his political views began to moderate as black voter registration increased. He rode the racial horse as far as he could for as long as he could, but he knew when it was time to dismount."[19]

Ward's appointment to the federal bench was for him a dream come true; but more than that, it was an indication of how far his state had come since his application to UGA's law school nearly thirty years earlier. Ward could now honestly say that he had witnessed the transformation of the South from the Old to the New, and that although he had been victimized by the former, he had lived long enough to become a beneficiary of the latter. The political worlds of Herman Talmadge and Jimmy Carter had converged at just the right moment, and now a black man of humble origins from LaGrange, Georgia, held a lifetime appointment as a district court judge.[20] Ward was fifty-two years old.

Ward's early rulings as judge indicated that he held a profound respect for individual freedoms and that in matters of equal rights and civil liberties he expounded a broad interpretation of the Constitution. One of the first and most significant cases brought before Judge Ward involved the issue of education for mentally retarded children. In 1978, Ginger Oliver and her former husband Doug Caine, both of Savannah, sued the state of Georgia to force school systems to provide year-round schooling for children who were mentally retarded. Their son, Russell, was nine years old at the time and had been diagnosed as severely mentally retarded. His parents argued that their son's condition had worsened after he was transferred from a private school that offered a twelve-month training program to the public school system, which had a nine-month school year. The three-month summer break, they maintained, had caused their son to regress. (Prior to 1978, severely retarded children were not allowed in Savannah's public schools. A federal law that year required public school systems to provide individual learning programs for all handicapped children.)[21]

In the case of *Georgia Association of Retarded Citizens v. McDaniel* (1981), Judge Ward ruled that public schools had to provide an extended school term for retarded children if individual evaluations showed that such programs would be beneficial. "This court concludes," Ward wrote, "that the plaintiffs are entitled to . . . an injunction against the continued application of the 180-day policy. . . . In the instant case, it is clear that a continued application of defendants' policy prohibiting the consideration of or provision for a child's educational needs would work an irreparable harm on the plaintiff class. As long as that policy is in effect, the mentally retarded children . . . will not receive the full individualized consideration to which they are entitled. . . . Neither money damages nor any other legal remedy would compensate for this loss."[22] Arguing that such a requirement would be prohibitively expensive and could cost taxpayers $1 billion if implemented nationwide, the state department of education and the local board of education filed an appeal. In October 1983, the Eleventh U.S. Circuit Court of Appeals upheld Ward's ruling, and in February 1985, the U.S. Supreme Court affirmed Judge Ward's decision.[23] Coming seven years after his parents had initially filed suit, the Supreme Court's affirmation of Judge Ward's decision came too late for Russell Caine, who by then was fifteen years old and living in an institution. But as a result of Ward's decision, educational opportunities for mentally retarded children improved vastly throughout the state.

Two additional cases that came before Judge Ward in 1981 were notable because they involved First Amendment issues. In *American Civil Liberties Union v. Rabun County Chamber of Commerce* (1981), the ACLU and several other non-Christian plaintiffs filed suit, alleging that a lighted Latin cross violated the constitutional guarantee of the separation of church and state. The eighty-five-foot-tall cross had been erected in Black Rock Mountain State Park, a state recreational facility located in Rabun County. When illuminated, the lights from the cross not only covered two camping areas but could be seen for several miles from highways in the area. The Chamber of Commerce maintained that the cross had not been erected for a religious purpose, but for the secular one of promoting tourism. But Judge Ward rejected the defendants' argument, writing that "there was considerable and convincing evidence . . . that the cross was placed on the mountain for religious reasons," not the least of which was the fact that the cross was actually dedicated in a religious service held on Easter Sunday. "The court concludes as a matter of law that the presence of this lighted cross in Black Rock Mountain State Park offends against the Establishment Clause of the First Amendment, and that defendants must remove it." Ward's decision was later affirmed by the Eleventh Circuit Court of Appeals.[24]

In another case later that year, Judge Ward took up the issue of free speech. In *American Booksellers Association v. McAuliffe* (1981), the plaintiffs (consisting of individuals, organizations, distributors, publishers, writers, and various merchants) brought suit against the state legislature of Georgia, alleging that the state's obscenity law was excessively broad and vague. Act 785 of the Georgia Code prohibited the sale or display of certain written materials to children under the age of eighteen if the state deemed those materials to be pornographic or sexually explicit. While acknowledging that he shared state lawmakers' concern for minors, Judge Ward concluded that the law, as it was written, was broad and vague, and violated the First, Fifth, and Fourteenth Amendments of the Constitution. Ward wrote: "Because the Act prohibits materials whose cover or contents contain descriptions or depictions of persons of the opposite sex without clothes, or of 'illicit sex or sexual immorality which is lewd, lascivious, or indecent,' many works of art and literature would have to be removed from display. These materials could include best-seller novels as well as the classic plays and sonnets of Shakespeare and volumes on the history of art." Ward also explained that many of the phrases contained in the act were uncertain and without specific meaning (such as "partially denuded figures") and that there are varying interpretations of what materials would "provoke or arouse lust or passion." Quoting Supreme Court Justice

district court he has maintained a low reversal rate on appeal but generally receives low marks for rendering decisions promptly and is regarded as one of the slowest judges in the Northern District of Georgia. For Ward, it boils down to whether a jurist wants to be known for speed or precision, and he prefers the latter. Currently a member of the American Bar Association, Atlanta Bar Association, Gate City Bar Association, Lawyers' Club of America, National Bar Association, and the State Bar of Georgia, Ward says that his career in law has been rewarding. "I find it to be a rather noble profession," Ward said recently. "It does require a certain judicial temperament, legal ability, and a sense of balance. Those are things you're either born with, or you develop over time; otherwise, you should get another job."[52]

As for the downside of being a judge, Ward believes that the isolation is perhaps the worst part. As a federal judge, he is prohibited by law from commenting on public policy, though he is free to say whether he thinks a certain law is good or bad. He cannot be a member of certain clubs or associations, and he has to watch his associates. Ward's only regret is that his wife, Ruth, did not live long enough to share in his accomplishments. Her departure from his life so many years ago has created an emptiness for him, and many of his later achievements were bittersweet because of her absence. "I was fortunate to have had such a wonderful wife to be such a source of comfort and support and advice to me. She was such a smart person. She would share any success I have had because she helped make it possible." After his wife's death, Ward moved into a condominium in downtown Atlanta, and, never having learned to drive, takes a taxi to work every morning. He never remarried.[53]

Ward took the first step toward retirement in 1994, when he officially went on senior status. But because he still enjoys living the life of a federal judge, and because his health is still good, he is uncertain when he will call it quits for good. Despite his personal setbacks over the years, he has managed to rise to the top of his chosen profession, and he often speaks of his life as his "long journey from LaGrange to Atlanta," ever mindful of those who assisted him along the way. "I do not believe that there will ever be another Justice Thurgood Marshall. There might not be another Donald Hollowell. There certainly can be replacements for Horace Ward. I stand ready to pass the torch to a new generation of lawyers and judges committed to the task of fulfilling the ideal of equal justice for all."[54]

Burying Unhappy Ghosts

> For even as the uglier moments are
> embedded in my consciousness like
> the reality of a snakebite . . . so too are
> the kindnesses, both large and small,
> of people, white people especially,
> whose humanity triumphed over the
> bigotry around them.
> —Charlayne Hunter-Gault

As the University of Georgia prepared to celebrate its bicentennial in 1985 university officials decided to seize the opportunity to begin a reconciliation with its first black undergraduate alumni, both of whom by now had distinguished themselves in their chosen careers. Hamilton Holmes had earned a medical degree from Emory University, the first black person to do so, and had a successful orthopedics practice in Atlanta. Charlayne Hunter-Gault had worked as a journalist for the *New York Times* for ten years before joining PBS's *MacNeil-Lehrer NewsHour,* where she would work for twenty years as an anchor and news correspondent. Both Holmes and Hunter-Gault still felt some bitterness because of the way they had been treated as students, and though twenty-two years had passed, neither of them had ever been officially welcomed back to the university. Holmes had appeared on campus once, in 1977, after being invited by the Committee on Black Cultural Programming to speak at the university's annual observance of Martin Luther King's birthday. In 1983 he became the first black to be appointed to the UGA Foundation Board of Trustees. Hunter-Gault had been back twice—first in 1979 to do a documentary on the evolution of race relations in Georgia since her days as a student, and again in 1981 to join the alumni advisory board of the School of Journalism.

In 1985, the University of Georgia created the Holmes-Hunter Lecture series as a way of paying tribute to its first black students. Each year, the university invites a noted scholar or civil rights activist to address the university community on race relations. Both Holmes and Hunter-Gault were on hand for the first lecture in 1985, which was delivered by civil rights attorney Vernon Jordan, who in 1961 had escorted Holmes and Hunter onto the campus of the University of Georgia. The Holmes-Hunter inaugural lecture in 1985 marked the first time that the two former students had appeared on campus together since their 1963 graduation and, to some extent, it marked the beginning of a long healing process. At the occasion, both Holmes and Hunter were presented with the university's Bicentennial Medallion, and Holmes received the Distinguished Alumni Merit Award and the Blue Key Award.[1] At the occasion a tearful Holmes said, "I have come in the last three years or so to really love this university. I must admit that when I was over here I didn't get much chance to love it."

Making peace with the past had not been easy for either Holmes or Hunter-Gault, and both had endured a degree of personal anguish not unlike that of other civil rights pioneers. Though he had always seemed the more bitter of the two, ironically it was Holmes who eventually became the more loyal alumnus, and it was also he who showed the most emotion at such events, a sharp contrast to the emotionally detached person he was as a student. He later worked with the Alumni Society and also helped recruit African American students. His appearances at the university became more frequent after 1985, and while he was never totally comfortable with his fame, a part of him at least seemed pleased that his one-time notoriety had turned into celebrity. His son, Hamilton Jr. (Chip), earned a marketing degree from UGA in 1990.

Charlayne Hunter-Gault continued on her path toward reconciliation in 1988, when she became the first African American in the university's 203-year history to be invited to give the commencement address. It marked the twenty-fifth anniversary of her and Holmes's graduation, and for her, as she addressed an integrated audience on that sultry day, it was a time of introspection:

For centuries, we shared a world of courtesy and difference established on utter tragedy. As Blacks, we gave to the white world, and that world gave to us. But the gifts were ambiguous, weighted as they were with the force of unequal tradition. You were not ours, but we were yours. Then, slowly, painfully, came the furious dawn of recognition. We saw, half hidden in the blazing noonday sun, the true outline of our burden. . . . No one here today would pretend that the Old South is dead and buried, that the events of the past twenty-five years, even my presence here today, have transformed our peculiar world into one that is beyond recognition. The Confederate flag still flies in places on this campus . . . and it would still be unwise for me to spend too much time in certain municipalities a few hours' drive from here. . . . [But] I do not believe we can function as a secure society if we are not at peace with ourselves. . . .

I first came here, in the words of Stephen Vincent Benet, "a brown girl bearing an idle gift." I stand before you now a woman who has drunk from the waters (and the wines) of the world, not at peace but confident of my capacities and yours, praising the shepherds' and the lawyers' gifts, because we have had our justice after all.[2]

In the audience on that occasion, in addition to her family and some of her former professors, was William A. Bootle, the federal judge who had first ordered the university to admit her and Holmes. Hunter-Gault had called him personally and invited him to attend, because, as she put it, "After all these years, I thought it was time to say thank you."[3]

At the 1992 Holmes-Hunter Lecture, at which the Reverend Jesse Jackson was the guest speaker, Holmes and Hunter-Gault announced the creation of the Holmes-Hunter Scholarship, which would award $1,500 annually to a black student who showed academic promise. In making the announcement, Holmes said, "I would like to think that I would have made it if I had not been one of the first black students here. But I think I have been enriched much more because of that experience." UGA's first black students had reached the pinnacle of their careers, and now they wanted to give something back. As a news correspondent on the *MacNeil-Lehrer NewsHour*, Hunter-Gault had an evening audience of millions, and later, as a correspondent in Africa for National Public Radio, she received numerous awards, including two Peabody Awards for her coverage of apartheid in South Africa. In addition to his orthopedics practice, Holmes now served as senior vice president for medical affairs at Grady Hospital in Atlanta and as associate dean of the Emory School of Medicine. But this was to be their last joint appearance at the University of Georgia. On October 26, 1995, Hamilton Holmes died in Atlanta following quadruple bypass heart surgery. He was fifty-four years old. In 1996 the Georgia State Legislature, by unanimous vote in both houses, renamed the former Hightower Road in Atlanta Hamilton E. Holmes Drive. In 1999, the University of Georgia established the Hamilton E. Holmes Professorship in the Humanities, the first endowed chair ever named for an African American.[4]

On her fiftieth birthday, in 1992, Charlayne Hunter-Gault published her memoirs, *In My Place,* which traces her life from her birth in Due West, South Carolina, in 1942 to her graduation from the University of Georgia in 1963. The book's last chapter is a reprint of the commencement address she delivered at the University of Georgia in 1988. She crafts her narrative around a spatial metaphor, underscoring both the depth of her solitude on UGA's all-white campus and the haunting realization that blacks have always had a clearly defined place in white society, and that stepping out of that place often carried a steep, sometimes deadly, price. The book focuses heavily on her early life, and her discussion of her experiences at the University of Georgia at times appears almost matter-of-fact, as if she is trying to conceal her raw emotions. But when she sat down for an interview in May 2000 there *was* emotion, and it became readily apparent that, at least to some extent, the happy, smiling face that adorns the cover of the book belies her disappointment that the University of Georgia has not completely fulfilled its obligation to blacks: "I think that Hamp had made his peace with UGA. As for me, I thought for a long time that I had; I certainly moved in that direction after making the graduation speech in 1988. And I took a few more steps over the years as I began to make more appearances on the campus. But I don't think I will ever make my peace with that institution until black students and black professors there are as comfortable as whites are and until I'm convinced that they [university officials] have made every effort to ensure that. But from what I can tell, that's not yet happened."[5]

At age fifty-nine and sporting dreadlocks, Charlayne Hunter-Gault possesses the regal bearing of a woman confident in her abilities and certain of her place in history. She does not mind talking about her past, though she is skeptical of those who try to rewrite it to their own advantage, something she witnesses regularly in her new position as CNN's chief correspondent in South Africa. While she is still struggling to come to terms with all that took place during UGA's desegregation crisis, she believes that Holmes finally did. "Hamp had all but buried the unhappy ghosts of the past; he had even forgiven the University, becoming one of its governing officials and biggest boosters. In fact, at the foot of the blanket of flowers that adorned his coffin lay a red and black Georgia Bulldogs cap." Holmes's sudden death from heart failure in 1995 took a heavy emotional toll on Hunter-Gault, and she recalled their last encounter. "I had come to Atlanta for a speaking engagement at Emory. I was having trouble with my foot, and I went to see him on my way out. I was always on Hamp about his weight, and Marilyn [his wife] used to encourage me, since he never paid her any attention. While he was examining my foot, I noticed just how much weight he had put on, and I told him that he needed to start eating right, and start getting some exercise, and he said, 'Yeah, Char, I know I should, and I'll do better.' It wasn't long after that that I got the news that he had died. It was like losing a brother."[6]

While Hunter-Gault readily acknowledges that she and Holmes had their own approaches to their integration experiences, it bothers her that some have tried to magnify those differences. Though they had started out as rivals at Turner High, they had become a team over the years. "Hamp and I were always close and remained so over the years. Whenever I was in Atlanta for anything, Hamp and Marilyn were always in the front row. I remember that on one occasion, after I had finished reading from my book, he told me that *his* book, if he should ever write one, would be different than mine. So I said, 'OK, go write your own book.' And given how important it was to him to prove to whites that he was as good as any of their best, his book no doubt would have told a somewhat different story." A few minutes later, when she thought that Hamilton and Marilyn had left, she headed toward the lobby, where a long line of people were waiting for her to sign their books. When she looked up, to her surprise there stood Hamilton Holmes talking with the crowd and signing everybody's book, the book that Hunter-Gault later referred to as "our book." The two of them really were a team, Hunter-Gault said. "About the best team I ever joined."[7]

On January 9, 2001, on the fortieth anniversary of Holmes's and Hunter's arrival on campus to register as the University of Georgia's first two African American students, the university sponsored a one-day symposium to commemorate the event. Nearly one thousand people filled the university's Hodgson Hall at the Performing Arts Center where the morning session was held. In attendance at this historic gathering was a virtual who's who among the principals who were involved in the integration crisis forty years before. Among them were Ernest Vandiver; Donald Hollowell; Horace Ward; Constance Baker Motley (now a federal judge in New York); several of the journalists who covered UGA's desegregation, including Calvin Trillin; Mary Frances Early; Charlayne Hunter-Gault; her husband, Ronald; and her daughter, Suesan Stovall (from her first marriage to fellow UGA student Walter Stovall); and a large contingent from the family of the late Hamilton Holmes, including his wife, Marilyn, his mother, his children, grandchildren, brothers, and sister. Most of these people had been on UGA's campus at one time or another over the past forty years, but never before had all of them gathered at the same time to observe such a landmark event in the university's history. The only notable absence, except for Holmes, who was deceased, was Judge Bootle, who had been invited but had declined to attend because of his age.

The highlight of the day's festivities came at the end of the afternoon session, when everyone adjourned to the Academic Building for the official unveiling of a plaque in front of the newly renamed Holmes-Hunter Academic Building. Several months earlier the university's Board of Regents had voted unanimously to rename the building where Holmes and Hunter had registered. Saying that she was speaking on her husband's behalf, Marilyn Holmes said that her husband "would have said thank you" to everyone involved in the commemoration. "He also would have laughed out loud," she said, noting the irony in having the building that whites had fought so hard to keep him out of now bearing his name.[8]

Charlayne Hunter-Gault had traveled eighteen hours from Johannesburg, South Africa, to attend the occasion and to deliver the annual Holmes-Hunter Lecture. Looking out at the huge multiracial audience she reflected on the events of the past forty years and spoke eloquently of how her life had been shaped by those experiences, and how she now watches as South Africa struggles with the same racial problems that were a part of this country's not too distant past. Observing the situation in South Africa on a daily basis, she said, "gives wings to memory and transports me—sometimes as in a dream, sometimes a nightmare—back in time. It was called apartheid, but it looked just like Jim Crow."

She concluded her lecture by remembering her friend Hamilton Holmes, who had fulfilled his lifelong ambition to become a healer, and she spoke of her hopes for the building that now bears both their names:

> If anyone had given Hamp and me a crystal ball into which we could have looked to the future forty years hence and seen only 6 percent students of color . . . I think we might have sat down under the Arch and cried. . . .

> I would hope that the kind of education that takes place in and around the building bearing our names will lead to scholarship that results in the kind of knowledge that will enable each and every student, as well as each and every teacher, to see things with what Malcolm X called "new eyes"—eyes that will be able to see the old world as it was, and for how it attempted to deny the aspirations of young black boys and girls like Charlayne Hunter and Hamilton Holmes. Eyes that will be able to see the new world for what it could be—a welcoming place for the dreams of all young people, of all races, of all cultures. A place where it is possible for those dreams to fly on wings of unfettered ambition.[9]

Notes

One. More than a Matter of Segregation

1. See Franklin and Moss, *From Slavery to Freedom;* Bartley and Graham, *Southern Politics and the Second Reconstruction.*

2. *Smith v. Allwright,* 321 U.S. 649 (1944).

3. *Morgan v. Virginia,* 328 U.S. 373 (1946). Justice Jackson did not participate in this case. At President Truman's request, Jackson was in Nuremberg serving as chief prosecutor in the Nazi war-crimes trial.

4. *Shelley v. Kraemer,* 334 U.S. 1 (1948). Only six justices participated in this case, presumably because the other three—Justices Reed, Jackson, and Rutledge—owned or occupied premises covered by restrictive covenants and excused themselves from sitting on the case. See Kluger, *Simple Justice,* 239–55; Tushnet, *Making Civil Rights Law,* 81–115; and Hine, *Black Victory.*

5. In 1926, in *Corrigan v. Buckley,* the Supreme Court held that although restrictive covenants were discriminatory, they were a form of private, not state, action, and therefore legal. The Court's ruling in 1948 did not overturn *Corrigan*—which would have had the effect of nullifying all existing restrictive covenants. Instead, the burden of challenging these covenants now fell on the plaintiffs. Most of the barriers to equal housing were not removed until the passage of the Fair Housing Act of 1968. The *Morgan* ruling in 1946 outlawed segregated interstate travel only on buses and trains; it did not apply to stations and terminals, where "Colored" and "White Only" waiting rooms were still the law in much of the South. A Supreme Court decision in December 1960 made segregated waiting rooms illegal, but southern authorities refused to comply, prompting the 1961 "Freedom Rides" by the Congress of Racial Equality (CORE) and the Student Non-Violent Coordinating Committee (SNCC). Eventually, the Interstate Commerce Commission issued an order banning all forms of segregation in interstate travel. As for voting, the poll tax remained a major barrier until it was abolished for federal elections with the adoption of the Twenty-fourth Amendment in 1964. Most of the remaining obstacles to voting were removed with passage of the Voting Rights Act of 1965.

6. For a more detailed account of Houston's early life and legal training see McNeil, *Groundwork;* see also Tushnet, *Making Civil Rights Law,* 6–9.

7. *Plessy v. Ferguson,* 163 U.S. 537 (1896).

8. For a detailed analysis of the NAACP's legal strategy as it related to school deseg-regation cases, see Tushnet, *The* NAACP's *Legal Strategy.*

9. Transcript of the oral argument, NAACP Papers, Box I-D-94, file: Cases Sup-ported—University of Maryland, Briefs; *Pearson v. Murray,* 169 Md. 478, 182 A. 590 (1936), quoted in Tushnet, *Making Civil Rights Law,* 11–15.

10. Lincoln University in Missouri should not be confused with Lincoln University in Pennsylvania, the black college that Thurgood Marshall attended.

11. *Missouri ex rel. Gaines v. Canada,* 305 U.S. 337 (1938). Although the Supreme Court had reaffirmed its position regarding a state's obligation to all its citizens, not all in the black community were pleased with the *Gaines* ruling because it permitted the state to establish a separate black law school without addressing the issue of equal-ity. The NAACP was preparing a case in which the equality of the facilities would be examined, but the plaintiff, Lloyd Gaines, had suddenly disappeared. After earning a graduate degree in economics from the University of Michigan he had apparently gone to Chicago, but NAACP attorneys were unable to locate him in time for him to appear in court for a pretrial examination. Thus, the NAACP was unable to pursue the case any further. Missouri's legislature eventually appropriated $200,000 to expand graduate education at Lincoln, and its law school—with three faculty members and a librarian, and located in a building with a hotel and a movie theater—opened in the fall of 1939, less than a year after the Supreme Court's decision, with thirty students enrolled. But Gaines was not among them.

12. In late 1945, before Sweatt applied to law school at Texas, Ada Lois Sipuel asked the NAACP to help her gain admission to the University of Oklahoma's law school. Her suit was filed a month before Sweatt's. Her attorneys sought an order admitting her to Oklahoma's all-white law school, although other parts of the complaint suggested that Sipuel would also accept admission to a segregated law school within the state, if there were one. The trial judge dismissed the case, saying that Sipuel could not challenge segregation using the procedure she chose. A year later the state supreme court affirmed that decision, saying that since Sipuel was apparently willing to attend a segregated law school in Oklahoma, her attorneys erred in not demanding that the state create a separate law school for her. On January 12, 1948, the U.S. Supreme Court ruled that Oklahoma had to provide Sipuel with a legal education "as soon as it does for applicants of any other group." The case was then remanded to the state supreme court, which interpreted the U.S. Supreme Court's decision to mean that Oklahoma could fulfill its legal obligation by merely creating a separate law school for Sipuel, which it did two days later. This "law school" consisted of three rooms in the state capitol and was staffed by three local white attorneys. Exasperated by

this stunt, Thurgood Marshall filed a motion in the Supreme Court to have Sipuel admitted to the white law school, but the Court rejected his motion, ruling 7–2 that the NAACP, in the initial suit, had given the state a way out by suggesting that Sipuel would accept a segregated law school, and the state could not now be penalized for having chosen that option. Justices Rutledge and Murphy dissented, with Rutledge writing that Oklahoma had to end its discrimination "at once, not at some later time," and that no decent law school could be created "overnight." Oklahoma continued to operate its black law school for eighteen months, during which time only one student attended. After it closed, Sipuel was admitted to the previously all-white law school in August 1949, from which she graduated in 1951. See Tushnet, *Making Civil Rights Law,* 126–36.

13. Kluger, *Simple Justice,* 268.

14. *Sweatt v. Painter,* 339 U.S. 629 (1950); *McLaurin v. Oklahoma State Regents,* 339 U.S. 637 (1950).

15. Coleman, *A History of Georgia,* 361.

16. For a more detailed discussion of Eugene Talmadge and Georgia politics, see Anderson, *The Wild Man from Sugar Creek,* and Henderson and Roberts, *Georgia Governors.* See also Bartley and Graham, *Southern Politics and the Second Reconstruction.* Eugene Talmadge was elected to his fourth term as governor in 1946 but died that December before taking office, igniting quite a furor over the issue of succession. Since the state's constitution did not specify who should fill the office in the event that the governor-elect could not assume his duties, three different men—none of whom had run in the primary or general election—claimed to be the legitimate successor. Outgoing governor Ellis Arnall announced his intention to remain in office until the matter was resolved. M. E. Thompson, Georgia's newly elected and first ever lieutenant governor (the 1945 state constitution created the position), claimed that he was the obvious successor. Talmadge's supporters, however, backed Eugene's son, Herman. Concerned about Eugene's failing health, Talmadge supporters had begun a write-in campaign for Herman, which they now used to their advantage. Citing a constitutional provision, Speaker of the House Roy V. Harris and six other prominent Talmadge leaders argued that the General Assembly had the duty of choosing the next governor from the two candidates receiving the highest number of write-in votes in the general election. But problems arose in the Talmadge camp when the first ballot count showed Talmadge trailing two other write-in candidates. But at the last minute Telfair County (home to the Talmadges) reported finding some additional "misplaced" votes, enough, as it turns out, to put Herman over the top. Subsequent newspaper investigations revealed that several dead men were among those whose ballots had been cast for Herman. On January 15, 1947, the General Assembly declared Herman

Talmadge governor. A storm of protest erupted across the state, with the national press gleefully reporting on Georgia's "three-governors controversy." Unfazed and undaunted, Talmadge locked Arnall out of his office and ignored Thompson's claim to the governorship. Once Thompson was sworn in as the lieutenant governor, Arnall resigned as governor, thus removing himself from the controversy. Thompson then sued to have himself proclaimed the rightful governor, and Georgia's Supreme Court agreed with him on March 22, 1947, ruling that Thompson should serve as governor until the general election in 1948, at which time the people would choose a new governor to serve out the remainder of the term. For a detailed discussion of the gubernatorial controversy, see Henderson, "The 1946 Gubernatorial Election in Georgia," and Bartley, *Creation of Modern Georgia.* See also Bernd, "White Supremacy and the Disenfranchisement of Blacks," 492–513, and Roche, *Restructured Resistance,* chapter 1.

17. Herman Talmadge is quoted in Robert Sherrill, *Gothic Politics in the Deep South* (New York: Grossman Publisher, 1968), 48.

18. Violence against blacks in Georgia increased dramatically in 1946, which some observers have linked to Herman Talmadge's racist gubernatorial campaign and white backlash against the Supreme Court's ruling in *Smith v. Allwright* (1944), which outlawed the all-white primary. "Inexplicably," wrote historian John Egerton, "Georgia seemed in 1947, as in the preceding year, to have a worse case of racial bloodlust than most of the other states." All but one of the recorded lynchings in the United States in 1946 occurred in Georgia within days of the primary. In Taylor County, a young black veteran, Macio Snipes, who had voted in the 1946 primary, was murdered on his porch by ten white men just three days after the election. (Ironically, Private Snipes had not thought about voting until after hearing of a Ku Klux Klan warning that the first black to vote in Taylor County would be attacked.) One of the most gruesome acts of racial violence in that era occurred in 1946 in Monroe, Georgia, in Walton County, when two black couples—Roger and Dorothy Malcolm and George and Mae Murray Dorsey— were lynched by a white mob in broad daylight. In neither of these lynchings were the guilty parties brought to justice. For an excellent account of the murders in Walton County, see Warren, "The Moore's Ford Lynching of 1946," 266–88. See also Grant, *The Way It Was in the South,* and Egerton, *Speak Now Against the Day.*

19. Georgia's unique county-unit system dated back to the turn of the century. Defenders of the system argued that it protected the state against political machines and from the sinister and subversive elements they identified with the urban electorate, namely blacks, Yankees, members of labor unions, and agents of the Soviet Union. Critics charged, correctly in my view, that the system perpetuated white, rural supremacy because sparsely populated counties had a disproportionate share of the

votes (which operated something like the Electoral College). The Supreme Court's "one man, one vote" ruling in *Baker v. Carr* (1962) eliminated the county-unit system.

20. *Sweatt v. Painter,* 339 U.S. 629 (1950); *McLaurin v. Oklahoma State Regents,* 339 U.S. 637 (1950).

21. Political scientist Earl Black has noted that before the *Brown* decision, race and segregation were rarely key issues in southern gubernatorial races. Herman Talmadge's campaigns in 1948 and 1950 were two exceptions. After *Brown,* however, the nature of southern politics changed dramatically. As Michael Klarman argues, the most immediate consequence of *Brown v. Board of Education* was not to achieve desegregation, but rather to galvanize white resistance to it. Thereafter, many white southern politicians—of which Alabama's George C. Wallace was the best example—defined themselves in terms of their unalterable opposition to school desegregation. For a better discussion of both arguments, see Black, *Southern Governors and Civil Rights,* and Klarman, "How *Brown* Changed Race Relations," 81–118. Talmadge is quoted in Black, *Southern Governors and Civil Rights,* 29.

22. For more on Talmadge's racial views see Herman Talmadge, *You and Segregation* (Birmingham: Vulcan Press, 1955). See also O'Brien, "Georgia's Response to *Brown v. Board of Education.*"

23. Horace T. Ward, interview by author, June 29, 1999.

24. Ibid.

25. Ibid.

26. Biographic information on A. T. Walden can be found in the A. T. Walden Papers Collection, mss 614, Box 25, Folder 10, located at the Atlanta History Center Library/Archives, Atlanta, Georgia.

27. Ibid.

28. Ibid.

29. The correspondence between Ward and Seibert is detailed in the records of Ward's suit against the university. See *Horace T. Ward v. Regents of the University System of Georgia* (cited hereinafter as *Ward v. Regents*), Federal Records Center, East Point, Georgia, December 1956, 212–16. See also Silverman, *"Horace T. Ward."* For a brief summary of the *Ward* case see also Dyer, *The University of Georgia,* 303–13.

30. Silverman, *"Horace T. Ward,"* 9. See also the University of Georgia's student newspaper, the *Red and Black,* June 21, 29, 1951.

31. Ward to Aderhold, August 2, 1951, *Ward v. Regents,* 247.

32. Aderhold to Ward, August 16, 1951, Ward to Aderhold, August 17, 1951, *Ward v. Regents,* 249.

33. Ellis Merton Coulter was a prolific writer and his pro-southern sympathies are

a matter of record. For an example of Coulter's racist scholarship, see E. Merton Coulter, *A Short History of Georgia* (Chapel Hill: University of North Carolina Press, 1933), especially 328–79. After a research trip in 1965 to the Library of Congress in Washington, D.C., he wrote one friend: "Washington is fast becoming an African city—as you know more than half of the population are Negroes. They have taken possession of the city in a greater proportion than their number would indicate. . . . The government service is almost completely overrun by them, from top to bottom, and Congress is now about to hand over to them the government of the city, when the bill is passed which gives Washington self-government, which . . . means Negro government. As lamentable as it is, it will be interesting to watch what happens." Ellis Merton Coulter Papers, MSS 1710, Box 49, Folder 1, located at the University of Georgia Library.

34. Ward, interview.

35. Ibid. At one point during the interview, Ward explained to the committee that the lack of funds had caused him to delay corrective surgery that he did not consider life threatening. As Ward now remembers, the committee seized upon that statement in an attempt to prove that he was being untruthful, since, as the committee put it, he could apparently find money to pay for law school. In the later trial, university officials would use this "inconsistency" against Ward.

36. Ibid.

37. Ibid.

38. Caldwell to Ward, October 18, 1951, *Ward v. Regents,* 266.

39. Regents Minutes, February 13, 1952, 15.

40. "Memorandum to the Law School Faculty," March 19, 1952. James J. Lenoir Papers, private collection (in the author's possession). The author gratefully acknowledges the family of the late James J. Lenoir for making the papers available.

41. *Atlanta Constitution,* December 16, 1952.

42. Regents Minutes, June 11, 1952, 2; January 14, 1953, 3; April 8, 1953, 20–23.

43. James J. Lenoir to J. Alton Hosch, April 30, 1952, Lenoir Papers.

44. James J. Lenoir to Elliott E. Cheatham, January 10, 1953, Lenoir Papers.

45. Walter Gellhorn to Robert A. Leflar, September 15, 1953, Lenoir Papers.

46. Lenoir and Lenoir, "Compulsory Legal Segregation," 211–41.

47. Joseph E. Gibson to James Lenoir, July 15, 1954; Benton Elliott to James Lenoir, July 7, 1954, Lenoir Papers.

48. Lenoir to O. C. Aderhold, August 18, 1953; Aderhold to Lenoir, August 19, 1953, Lenoir Papers.

49. O. C. Aderhold to Harmon W. Caldwell, Omer Clyde Aderhold Papers Collection, MS 2127, Box 53, Folder "School of Law, September 1950–June 30, 1957," located at the University of Georgia Library, Athens.

50. Lenoir and Lenoir, "Compulsory Legal Segregation," 228, 232–33. See also Dyer, *The University of Georgia,* 307. Governor Talmadge's argument that a desegregation ruling by the Supreme Court would result in Georgia's counties having no power to levy taxes for educational purposes, which would of itself destroy the state's public school system, lacked legal merit and was clearly political. The *Brown* decision did not hamper any school district's ability to levy taxes for educational purposes. For a statement of Governor Talmadge's argument, see "Talmadge's Text on School Plan," *Atlanta Constitution,* March 14, 1954, 14.

51. *Ward v. Regents,* 7.

52. Complaint, June 23, 1952, *Ward v. Regents,* Federal Records Center, East Point, Georgia.

53. *Atlanta Constitution,* June 24, 1952, 1.

54. One of the NAACP's major activities in the 1920s and 1930s was lobbying Congress for a federal antilynching law. Under the federal tax laws, the NAACP's lobbying meant that it was not a tax-exempt organization. Concerned that donations would dry up if such contributions were not tax deductible, the NAACP tried in vain to get the Internal Revenue Service to change its position. IRS officials did, however, suggest that the NAACP set up a separate arm for lobbying. Donations to the lobbying component would not be exempt, but donations to the rest of the organization would be. Marshall liked the idea, but decided to switch the proposal around and set up a separate arm for legal and educational activities (donations to which would be tax deductible), since he realized that it would be easier to get large donors to give money for legal and educational causes than for lobbying, which could be supported by membership dues. See Tushnet, *Making Civil Rights Law,* 27, 35.

55. Betty Boyd Mapp, interview by author, September 26, 2000.

56. Mapp, interview. See also the William Madison Boyd Collection located at the Trevor Arnett Library, Special Collections, Atlanta University, Atlanta, Georgia.

57. Mapp, interview.

58. Ibid.

59. Remarks by Benjamin E. Mays at the dedication of the William M. Boyd Elementary School, Atlanta, Georgia, December 3, 1972; Mapp, interview.

60. Ward, interview; *Atlanta Journal,* January 15, 1953; Dyer, *The University of Georgia,* 308–9.

61. Ward, interview.

62. Ward, interview. Ward refuses to speculate on what his decision concerning the surgery would have been had he known the consequences. Hosch's letter to Keeton is located in the Aderhold Papers, MS 2127, Box 10, Folder "School of Law," dated September 30, 1954 (italics added).

63. Ward, interview; Dyer, *The University of Georgia,* 309.

64. D.D. to Harmon Caldwell, June 13, 1951, Chancellor's Papers, Personal Files, Box 24, MS 2909, Hargrett Library, University of Georgia (italics in original). Because private citizens (as opposed to public figures) who wrote to Chancellor Caldwell to express their views on segregation perhaps expected that their correspondence would be kept confidential, it would be inappropriate for me to divulge their identities here. Therefore, I have chosen not to include their names in the text and will refer to them in the notes by their initials only.

65. R.H. to Chancellor Caldwell, June 14, 1951, Chancellor's Papers, Personal Files, Box 24, MS 2909 (italics in original).

66. Caldwell to E.P., June 22, 1951, Chancellor's Papers, Personal Files, Box 24, MS 2909.

Two. "The Color Is Black"

1. Harmon Caldwell to Herman Talmadge, June 17, 1952, Chancellor's Records, Box 56, MS 2909.

2. Regents Minutes, July 12, 1950, 20.

3. *Atlanta Constitution*, September 12, 1952, 12.

4. Regents Minutes, July 12, 1950, 20; November 14, 1951, 19 (italics added).

5. For a brief look at Roy Harris's political life, see Anderson, *The Wild Man from Sugar Creek,* 59, 216–23, 228, 230–32. Harris, referred to by historian Numan V. Bartley as "the most feared man in Georgia politics," successfully organized gubernatorial campaigns for Enrith D. Rivers, Ellis G. Arnall, and Eugene Talmadge and was also a key figure in Herman Talmadge's victories in 1948 and 1950. As Bartley writes, "He had never backed a loser in a state campaign and seemed able to make or break candidates with ease. Harris was devoted to white supremacy and, because he was Talmadge's leading ally, his prejudices carried no small weight, especially since they coincided with sound political strategy and, probably, the governor's personal convictions." See Bartley, *The Rise of Massive Resistance,* 43. For more detailed information on Harris's personal and political life, see the Roy Vincent Harris Papers (1931–1983), Richard B. Russell Library for Political Research and Studies, University of Georgia Libraries, Athens.

6. *Red and Black,* October 8, 1953.

7. Ibid., November 5, 1953.

8. Gene Britton, interview by author, August 12, 1998.

9. *Augusta Courier,* November 23, 1953.

10. *Red and Black,* November 12, 1953; Britton, interview.

11. *Augusta Courier,* November 23, 1953.

12. *Atlanta Constitution,* December 3, 1953.

13. It should be pointed out that the Board of Control was not created as a result of the *Red and Black's* feud with Roy Harris, but in fact was already in existence. Its purpose, however, was to select new staff members for the newspaper every quarter. Its function was modified after the integration controversy.

14. *Atlanta Constitution,* December 3, 1953; *Atlanta Journal,* December 3, 1953.

15. *Gainesville Daily Times,* December 14, 1953; *Cornell Daily Sun,* December 9, 1953; *Miami Hurricane,* December 11, 1953.

16. *Atlanta Constitution,* December 5, 1953; *Augusta Courier,* December 14, 1953.

17. These letters, some of which were addressed to Lundy or Shipp individually, others of which were addressed to both of them, were made available to me by Walter A. Lundy Jr. At the time they were a part of his private papers collection. They have since been donated to the Richard B. Russell Library at the University of Georgia and are filed under the Walter A. Lundy Jr. Papers.

18. Ibid.

19. Ibid.

20. For a good discussion of Ralph McGill and other progressive southern journalists see Kneebone, *Southern Liberal Journalists.*

21. Bill Shipp, interview by author, August 4, 1998.

22. Ibid.

23. Walter A. Lundy Jr., telephone conversation with author, July 13, 1998.

24. Ibid.

25. Britton, interview.

26. Bartley, *The Rise of Massive Resistance,* 54.

27. *Brown v. Board of Education,* 347 U.S. 483 (1954).

28. *Georgia Journal,* May 29, 1954.

29. Ibid.

30. Ibid.

31. See O'Brien, "Georgia's Response to *Brown v. Board of Education,*" 55–66.

32. Interposition, the notion that a state had the authority to interpose its sovereignty between its citizens and the federal government, was not a novel concept. First used in 1798 by Thomas Jefferson and James Madison in response to the Alien and Sedition Acts and again in the 1830s by John C. Calhoun during South Carolina's nullification crisis over protective tariffs, interposition became a popular, if not always effective, strategy among ardent defenders of states' rights. Though used by several southern states during the desegregation crisis, Virginia is generally credited with having revived it during the 1950s. See Gates, *The Making of Massive Resistance;* Muse, *Virginia's Massive Resistance;* and Pratt, *The Color of Their Skin.*

33. Bartley, *The Rise of Massive Resistance*, 54–75.

34. Henderson and Roberts, *Georgia Governors*.

35. Cook, *The Governors of Georgia*, 260–65; Francis M. Wilhoit, *The Politics of Massive Resistance* (New York: Braziller, 1973), 42; Bartley, *The Rise of Massive Resistance*, 68–72; Robert W. Dubay, "Politics, Pigmentation, and Pigskin: The Georgia Tech Sugar Bowl Controversy of 1955," *Atlanta History* 39 (spring 1955): 23–25.

36. For a good discussion of the history of Georgia and Georgia Tech's institutional policies concerning race and sports from 1892 to 1957 (focusing mainly on football), see Martin, "Racial Change and 'Big-Time' College Football," 532–62.

37. Ibid., 552–53.

38. Ibid., 553.

39. Ibid., 553–54. Though perhaps never in favor of Georgia Tech participating in the bowl game, Griffin likely concluded that the prestige of a Tech victory was far more important than Pittsburgh's lone black player. Apparently Griffin later changed his position after several of his segregationist political allies complained.

40. Ibid., 554–56. Sympathetic students at Emory University and Mercer University also staged small protests against Griffin.

41. *Atlanta Constitution*, December 4, 1955; *Technique*, December 6, 1955; *New York Times*, December 3, 4, 1955; "Tempest O'er the Sugar Bowl," *Tech Alumnus* (December 1955), 8–9, quoted in Martin, "Racial Change and 'Big-Time' College Football," 556.

42. Martin, "Racial Change and 'Big-Time' College Football," 556–57.

43. Ibid., 557; Dyer, *The University of Georgia*, 315.

44. Martin, "Racial Change and 'Big-Time' College Football," 534, 558.

45. *Atlanta Journal*, August 15, 1962.

46. O'Brien, "Georgia's Response to *Brown v. Education*," 56.

Three. "A Qualified Negro"

1. *Atlanta Journal*, July 8, 1955.

2. J. Alton Hosch to Harmon Caldwell, July 12, 1955, Caldwell Papers, Box 38, MS 2909; Eugene Cook to Robert Arnold, July 14, 1955, Caldwell Papers, Box 32.

3. Bolster, "Civil Rights Movements," 132, 180, 183; Murphy, "The South Counterattacks," 371–90.

4. *Atlanta Constitution*, August 29, 1974.

5. Ibid.; *Atlanta Journal*, April 3, 1960.

6. *Atlanta Journal*, September 14, 1955, January 4, 10, 1956.

7. *Atlanta Journal*, February 20, April 7, July 6, 9, and 10, 1956; *Red and Black*, December 6, 13, 1956.

8. *Ward v. Regents.*

9. For a good discussion of her involvement with the NAACP, see Motley, *Equal Justice Under Law.*

10. Hollowell and Lehfeldt, *The Sacred Call,* 143.

11. Motley, *Equal Justice Under Law,* 81.

12. Both Julian Bond and Lonnie King figured prominently in Atlanta's sit-in movement in 1960. To some of the younger black activists, as Clarence N. Stone writes, "the older generation was hopelessly compromised by their financial and other ties to Atlanta's white civic elite—an elite that made deposits in black financial institutions, advertised in the black newspaper (the [conservative] *Atlanta Daily World*), donated to black colleges and social agencies, and helped to make business opportunities available. A. T. Walden and the Atlanta Negro Voters League came under especially sharp criticism as Uncle Toms, who had 'done little but feather their own nests'" (Stone, *Regime Politics,* 53). Walden's death in 1965 is generally considered to mark the passing of the old era in Atlanta's black politics. For more insight into Walden's involvement with other civil rights activists (and younger activists' perception of him), see Julian Bond's and Lonnie King's reflections in Raines, *My Soul Is Rested,* 65, 86, 91. For a good discussion of racial politics in Atlanta, see Stone, *Regime Politics.*

13. *Ward v. Regents,* 115–20.

14. Ibid., 99–101.

15. Ibid., 196.

16. Ibid., 26–28.

17. Ibid., 109–11.

18. Ibid., 30–33, 454–60.

19. Ibid., 147–50.

20. Ibid., 376–413.

21. Regents Minutes, February 13, 1952, 15.

22. *Ward v. Regents,* 413–41.

23. Ibid., 205–8.

24. Ibid., 198.

25. Ward, interview.

26. *Atlanta Constitution,* December 19, 1956.

27. *Ward v. Regents,* 288–93.

28. Ibid., 270.

29. Plaintiff's Amendment to Complaint, January 3, 1957, *Ward v. Regents.*

30. Ward, interview.

31. Ibid.

32. Mays, *Born to Rebel,* 206.

33. *Red and Black*, January 11, 1957. The reference here is to the violence that followed Autherine Lucy's attempt to desegregate the University of Alabama in 1956.

34. *Ward v. Regents*, 191 F. Supp. 419 (1957), 492, 494–495 (italics added).

35. Mays, *Born to Rebel*, 207.

36. Comments by Donald L. Hollowell, "Civil Rights in Small Places," a symposium held at the University of Georgia, April 15–16, 1996.

37. Shipp, interview. As for Shipp blaming Governor Talmadge for arranging Ward's induction into the army, he's alluding to a comment Talmadge is alleged to have made in response to a reporter who questioned whether Talmadge had used his political influence to arrange Ward's draft. As legend has it, Talmadge rather matter-of-factly replied: "I am not a member of the Draft Board." Talmadge has since admitted to having used the full power of his office to keep Ward out of law school, but he has never admitted to any direct involvement in Ward's draft. Still, suspicion lingers, if for no other reason than, as a lifelong segregationist, he clearly had the will, and as Georgia's governor, he had the way.

38. See Klarman, "How *Brown* Changed Race Relations," 81–118.

39. Jeff Roche, *Restructured Resistance*, 47, 50.

40. Ward, interview.

41. Ibid.

42. Roche, 37–38.

Four. "Journey to the Horizons"

1. Over the past twenty or so years there has been a virtual explosion of scholarship on various aspects of the civil rights movement. Some have been organizational histories, some have been biographies of the era's most notable figures, some have been local studies, and still others have been general histories of the movement. The best studies of the Student Non-Violent Coordinating Committee (SNCC) remain Carson's *In Struggle*, Forman's *The Making of Black Revolutionaries*, and Zinn's SNCC. For an examination of the Southern Christian Leadership Conference (SCLC), see Fairclough's *To Redeem the Soul of America*. For biographies of Martin Luther King Jr., see generally Bennett, *What Manner of Man*; Garrow, *Bearing the Cross*; Lewis, *King*; and Ward and Badger, *The Making of Martin Luther King, Jr.* (New York: New York University Press, 1996). For excellent studies of local movements see Chafe, *Civilities and Civil Rights*; Dittmer, *Local People*; Eskew, *But for Birmingham*; Norrell, *Reaping the Whirlwind*; and Payne, *I've Got the Light of Freedom*. For studies of public policy, voting rights, and school desegregation, see Carter, *The Politics of Rage*; Clark, *The Schoolhouse Door*; Douglas, *Reading, Writing, and Race*; Graham, *The Civil Rights Era*; Kluger, *Simple Justice*; Lawson, *Running for Freedom*; Orfield

et al., *Dismantling Desegregation;* Pratt, *The Color of Their Skin;* and Tushnet, *Making Civil Rights Law.* For general histories of the civil rights era, see Branch, *Parting the Waters;* Carson, *The Eyes on the Prize Civil Rights Reader;* Hampton and Fayer, *Voices of Freedom;* Harding, *There Is a River;* Marable, *Race, Reform, and Rebellion;* Morris, *The Origins of the Civil Rights Movement;* and Robinson and Sullivan, *New Directions in Civil Rights Studies.* For memoirs of the movement, see Lewis with D'Orso, *Walking with the Wind;* Young, *An Easy Burden;* and Manis, *A Fire You Can't Put Out.*

2. Charles Pyles, "S. Ernest Vandiver and the Politics of Change," in Henderson and Roberts, *Georgia Governors*, 143–56.

3. Henderson, *Ernest Vandiver*, 82–83.

4. In the years following the crisis at Central High School in Little Rock, Arkansas, countless other schools across the South closed their doors in defiance of *Brown.* During the next two years, the federal courts decided *Cooper v. Aaron, Aaron v. Cooper, United States v. Faubus,* and *James v. Almond,* all of which weakened the massive resistance strategy.

5. Vandiver realized that his most important promise to Georgia voters was his pledge to preserve segregation in the schools. The degree of that commitment, however, was the subject of some intense discussions between Vandiver and his top advisers. Some of them, such as his brother-in-law Robert L. "Bobby" Russell Jr. and Peter Zach Geer Jr., urged Vandiver to promise that there would be no integration during his administration. Others, such as Griffin B. Bell and Henry G. Neal, counseled the governor to promise only that he would use every legal means to maintain segregation. But because of Bodenhamer's charges, Vandiver opted for the stronger position, which he later conceded was a mistake, especially given the inevitability of desegregation. Bodenhamer's campaign eventually came under a blistering attack from the media for making false statements about Vandiver's record, whereas Vandiver's campaign was praised for having taken the high road. For a thorough discussion of this issue, see Henderson, *Ernest Vandiver*, 77–82. See also Pyles, "S. Ernest Vandiver," in Henderson and Roberts, *Georgia Governors*, 148.

6. Hunter-Gault, *In My Place*, 124.

7. Ibid., 125.

8. *Hunt v. Arnold*, 172 F. Supp. 847 (N.D. Ga. 1959). The first suit that the NAACP Legal Defense Fund brought in Georgia after the *Brown* decision was against the Georgia State College of Business Administration in 1956. Three black women in Atlanta volunteered to be plaintiffs in the case. After the suit was filed, state investigators went on a witch-hunt to find something in the plaintiffs' backgrounds that would disqualify them from admission on grounds other than race. It was later discovered that

one of the plaintiffs, Barbara Hunt, had given birth to a daughter on March 3, 1953, eight months before she got married on November 7. Another plaintiff, Myra Payne Elliott Dinsmore Holland, was married on May 1, 1954, and had given birth to a son three months later on August 4. Such actions, the state contended, were not evidence of good moral character. Confident that Judge Boyd Sloan would dismiss the suit, state officials were stunned when the judge ruled against Georgia State's alumni certificate requirement. Although Judge Sloan held that institutions could make determinations concerning the moral fitness of prospective students, he rejected the notion that the endorsement regulation guaranteed that only students of good character would be admitted to Georgia's colleges and universities. Barbara Hunt and Myra Holland were humiliated and embarrassed by the disclosures and the suggestion they were morally unfit and neither woman pursued her application. Although the judge did rule that Iris Mae Welch was qualified for admission, he did not order that she be admitted. After his ruling, the state legislature passed a law that stipulated that no one over the age of twenty-one could begin undergraduate study at any of Georgia's colleges or universities, and no one over the age of twenty-five could begin graduate school. This new law effectively disqualified Iris Mae Welch. State officials believed that since black applicants tended to be older, this new law was a good way of reducing the number of eligible plaintiffs. When the bill became law, it contained enough loopholes to accommodate white servicemen, veterans, and others whom the Board of Regents might see fit to exempt from the rule.

9. See Motley, *Equal Justice Under Law*, 141; and Dyer, *The University of Georgia*, 319–20.

10. Henderson, *Ernest Vandiver*, 95.

11. Ibid., 95–96.

12. Trillin, *An Education in Georgia*, 12. Calvin Trillin was a reporter for *Time* magazine in 1961 who covered the trial extensively. He developed a personal interest in Holmes and Hunter, and they befriended him as well; consequently, he would spend a lot of time with them in Athens over the next several months. Before being published as a book, his stories on UGA's desegregation were published by the *New Yorker*. Based largely on interviews with many of the participants, Trillin's book is a compelling personal narrative. The book was reissued in 1991 with a foreword by Charlayne Hunter-Gault.

13. The Holmeses were joined by a fourth man, Charles T. Bell. For a good discussion of their efforts to desegregate Atlanta's golf courses, see Ambrose with Bargeron and Oliver, "Negroes Cannot Play Here."

14. Trillin, *An Education in Georgia*, 18.

15. Hunter-Gault, *In My Place,* 5–106.

16. Trillin, *An Education in Georgia,* 4.

17. Hunter-Gault, *In My Place,* 127–28.

18. *Atlanta Constitution,* July 11, 1959; *Atlanta Journal,* July 25, 1959; Dyer, *The University of Georgia,* 323.

19. Dyer, *The University of Georgia,* 324.

20. Ibid., 325.

21. Ibid., 325–26.

22. Herbert Holmes, interview by author, May 27, 2001.

23. "Plaintiffs' Brief," *Holmes v. Danner,* 191 F. Supp. 394 (M.D. Ga. 1960).

24. Ward, interview.

25. *Athens Banner-Herald,* September 14, 1960.

26. Trillin, *An Education in Georgia,* 23; Dyer, *The University of Georgia,* 327.

27. Hunter-Gault, *In My Place,* 150–51.

28. Ward, interview.

29. Dyer, *The University of Georgia,* 327.

30. Hunter-Gault, *In My Place,* 158.

31. Ibid., 158–59.

32. Hunter-Gault, *In My Place,* 157; Trillin, *An Education in Georgia,* 38–41.

33. Hunter-Gault, *In My Place,* 162–63.

34. For a discussion of Negrophobia among white southerners, see George M. Fredrickson, *The Black Image in the White Mind: The Debate on Afro-American Character and Destiny, 1817–1914* (New York: Harper, 1971), especially chapter nine.

35. Dyer, *The University of Georgia,* 328.

36. Trillin, *An Education in Georgia,* 40.

37. Ward, interview.

38. Trillin, *An Education in Georgia,* 41; Hunter-Gault, *In My Place,* 162.

39. *Holmes v. Danner,* 191 F. Supp. 394 (M.D. Ga. 1961), 402–10.

40. Herbert Holmes, interview; Isabella Holmes, interview by author, May 27, 2001.

41. Gary Holmes, interview by author, May 27, 2001.

42. *Atlanta Constitution,* January 7, 1961; *Athens Banner-Herald,* January 10, 1961; *Red and Black,* January 10, 1961.

43. Donald Hollowell, telephone conversation with author, March 2, 2000; Hollowell and Lehfeldt, *The Sacred Call,* 9.

44. Dyer, *The University of Georgia,* 329.

45. Pete McCommons, interview by author, April 25, 2000.

46. William Tate Papers, "Integration Crisis, January 1961, Student Petitions, Meetings, Notices, etc.," University of Georgia Library.

47. Dyer, *The University of Georgia*, 329–30; *Red and Black*, January 9, 1961.

48. Earl T. Leonard Jr., interview by author, May 9, 2001.

49. Hollowell and Lehfeldt, *The Sacred Call*, 9–10.

50. Hunter-Gault, *In My Place*, 171–72.

51. Ibid., 172–74.

52. Ibid., 175–76.

53. For a good discussion of Tuttle, see Bass, *Unlikely Heroes*, 23, 25.

54. William A. Bootle, interview by author, March 21, 2001.

55. Hunter-Gault, *In My Place*, 175.

56. Hollowell and Lehfeldt, *The Sacred Call*, 14.

57. Pyles, "S. Ernest Vandiver," in Henderson and Roberts, *Georgia Governors*, 149.

58. Archibald Killian, interview by author, December 12, 2000.

59. Hunter-Gault, *In My Place*, 177–79.

60. Ibid., 179–80; see also Charlayne Hunter-Gault's foreword in the 1991 edition of Trillin's *An Education in Georgia.* Hunter-Gault recalls that while some reporters seemed genuinely interested in detailing her and Holmes's experiences, others were more interested in sensationalism, even to the extent of helping to create it. The best example of this is the now infamous incident involving CBS reporter Robert Shackney or his cameraman (according to Hunter-Gault, there has always been some dispute over which one it was, but it was definitely a CBS employee), who had arrived late to a demonstration that had taken place just as Hunter walked by. Not to be outdone by the other networks, which had already caught the incident on film, the CBS crew allegedly organized a group of students to reenact the incident long after Hunter had left. See Hunter-Gault, *In My Place*, 179; *Red and Black,* January 10, 1961.

61. Ibid., 180–81; *Atlanta Constitution*, January 11, 1961; *Red and Black,* January 5, 1961; *Columbus Ledger,* January 11, 1961.

62. Archibald Killian, interview.

63. Ibid.

64. S. Ernest Vandiver, interview by author, April 19, 2000. See also the *Atlanta Journal, Atlanta Constitution,* and *Athens Banner-Herald,* January 11–15, 1961.

65. J. A. Williams to Hamilton Holmes, January 12, 1961, Papers of Hamilton Holmes, Box 1, Folder 1 (Correspondence), Martin Luther King, Jr., Center for Nonviolent Social Change.

66. *Athens Banner-Herald,* January 13, 1961.

67. Tate Papers, "Integration at the University of Georgia, 1961–63," Folder 1, labeled "Crack Pot" Mail, January 1961, (00–016.1), University of Georgia Library.

68. Tate Papers, Folder 3, "Letters-A, Integration Crisis."

69. *Atlanta Journal and Constitution,* January 15, 1961. For a more detailed discussion of Ku Klux Klan involvement in the riot, see Cohen, "G-Men in Georgia," 524–29.

70. Trillin, *An Education in Georgia,* 59.

71. *New York Times,* January 12, 1961; "Shame in Georgia," *Time,* January 20, 1961, 44; *Atlanta Journal,* January 12, 1961; *Atlanta Constitution,* January 12, 1961; *Newsweek,* January 23, 1961, 50–51.

72. Part of the folklore surrounding the basketball game was that Georgia lost a closely contested game in the last few seconds, which is not exactly true. In fact, one of Georgia Tech's players scored a basket in the last few seconds of regulation that actually tied the game, sending it into overtime. That basket did generate some controversy because of an apparent lack of synchronization between the buzzer and the official game clock (the buzzer sounded about two seconds after the clock indicated that the game was over, but the officials allowed the basket to be counted). Bulldog fans were understandably angry at the officials, but Georgia's nine-point loss to Georgia Tech in overtime (89–80) was not that close. If anything, it was the questionable officiating, rather than the closeness of the final score, that may have angered Bulldog fans—but hardly to the point of sparking a major campus riot, since none of the violence was directed at the referees.

73. Trillin, *An Education in Georgia,* 52.

74. Hunter-Gault, *In My Place,* 182–91.

75. Cohen, "G-Men in Georgia," 508–38. Acknowledging the FBI's unforgivable reputation regarding its civil rights involvement (or the lack thereof), Cohen points out that the FBI's investigation of the University of Georgia riot was significant because in some ways it contradicted what we have come to know about the organization—and its leader, J. Edgar Hoover—during the civil rights era. According to Cohen, FBI agents in Athens made "an immediate impression on UGA students," and "The FBI's presence signaled at least the possibility that segregationist rioting (past or future) might yield federal prosecution . . . This had a chilling effect on segregationist organizing, which helped to prevent any renewal of mob violence at UGA when the federal court reinstated Hunter and Holmes." The student riot leaders, who "did not yet know that for them the FBI was more friend than foe," were clearly intimidated by the agents' presence. It is important to note (as Cohen does) that J. Edgar Hoover played no direct role in the decision to launch an investigation into the UGA riot. That decision came from the Justice Department's Civil Rights Division and Attorney General Robert F.

Kennedy. According to Harold R. Tyler Jr., the assistant attorney general who headed the Civil Rights Division, Hoover "was otherwise occupied on that day" when the UGA investigation was launched. Cohen was able to obtain the FBI files on its investigation of the UGA riot, which he has since made available to the author. See Cohen, "G-Men in Georgia," 514–18.

76. *Atlanta Journal and Constitution,* January 15, 1961; *Atlanta Constitution,* January 12, 1961.

77. *Atlanta Journal and Constitution,* January 15, 1961.

78. "FBI Files on the Desegregation of the University of Georgia," Field Office File No. 72–39, 113–15.

79. Cohen, "G-Men in Georgia," 521–22; *Atlanta Journal,* January 16, 1960.

80. Charlayne Hunter-Gault, interview by author, May 29, 2000, Atlanta, Georgia.

81. See Clark, *The Schoolhouse Door.*

82. Constance Baker Motley, interview by author, May 8, 2001. According to Judge Motley, "Judge Grooms told us in his chambers not to send Autherine Lucy back because the Eisenhower Administration had advised that they were not going to send any federal troops to protect her. In other words, if we sent her back, there was a chance that she might be killed. So we abandoned the case, explained it to her, and she agreed. It wasn't until the crisis in Little Rock that Eishenhower decided to send in troops. Autherine Lucy really didn't say anything. We, her attorneys, filed an affidavit pointing out that we thought that the Board of Trustees was in collusion with those who were rioting on the campus, and that in their silence it appeared as if they were siding with the rioters."

83. Bill Shipp, *Murder at Broad River Bridge: The Slaying of Lemuel Penn by Members of the Ku Klux Klan* (Atlanta: Peachtree Publishers Limited, 1981), 4, 13.

84. Ibid., 22–23, 28, 29, 71, 76. According to an FBI informant, the Klan in Athens (Clarke County Klavern No. 244) claimed to have four hundred dues-paying members, as well as a sizeable number of "silent" members, such as those who voted for acquittal in the state trial. More than fourteen years after the first trial, an attorney connected with the case recalled that the defense was certain of victory, no matter what evidence was presented: "The jury had been checked out. Two-thirds of them were either members of the Klan or known to be sympathetic to the Klan" (Shipp, *Murder,* 72). A list of jurors was passed among defense attorneys. A dot beside a juror's name indicated he was either a member of the KKK or pro-Klan.

85. Ibid., 72.

86. For an excellent account of University of Georgia students' attitudes toward the desegregation of the university, see Cohen, " 'Two, Four, Six, Eight,' " 616–45. Cohen makes the astute observation that even the best studies of desegregation on south-

ern college campuses tend to be top-down political and legal histories, which focus upon the tactical maneuverings of politicians, university administrators, and attorneys rather than on the racial attitudes of the white students themselves, who, in fact, had more direct impact upon the lives and experiences of those first black students to attend all-white universities.

87. Ibid., 624, 626–27.

88. Ibid., 638–39.

89. Ibid., 622–23 n. 13, 624, 627–28. It is important to note that all but one of the essayists were southerners, and most were Georgians, which generally reflected the profile of the larger student body. Also, as Cohen notes, at the time that the students penned these essays, they expected Professor Brahana (who the students knew was more progressive on racial matters) to read them, which might have been sufficient reason for the students to tone down their racism. But if they were concerned that their opinions might adversely affect their grades, their essays certainly do not reflect it. Only a few of the students did *not* sign their essays, but the signed essays rather than the unsigned were the most ardently segregationist. For whatever reason, Professor Brahana never read most of the essays. Instead, he deposited them in the university library and labeled them "results of an appropriate peaceful demonstration" of student opinion. The essays were uncovered years later by Professor Robert Cohen, then a faculty member in the university's School of Education.

90. Vandiver, interview.

91. For a good sampling of some editorial cartoons that denounced the UGA riot, see *Cleveland Plain Dealer,* January 13, 1961; *Louisville Courier and Journal,* January 11, 13, 1961; *Baltimore Sun,* January 13, 1961; *Los Angeles Times,* January 13, 1961; *Chicago Defender,* January 12, 1961; and *Macon Telegraph,* January 13, 1961. Negative coverage of the riot appeared in several magazines, including *Time, Life,* and *New Republic.* For a more detailed listing, see Cohen, "G-Men in Georgia," 523 n. 24.

92. Cohen, "G-Men in Georgia," 530–31.

93. McCommons, interview.

94. Ray Moore, interview by author, October 9, 2000.

95. Ibid.

96. Hunter-Gault, interview.

97. Vandiver, interview. Robert Cohen asserts in "G-Men in Georgia" that previous chroniclers of UGA's desegregation (especially Calvin Trillin in *An Education in Georgia* and Thomas Dyer in *The University of Georgia*) underestimated the violent nature of the mob. While I concur wholeheartedly with Cohen's assessment, it is important to point out that Cohen's observations are based on FBI interviews with members of the Athens police force, which were a part of the information Cohen requested un-

der the Freedom of Information Act. That information also revealed that the Athens police apparently took seriously their role as defenders of the peace, which in many ways runs counter to the traditional image of white law enforcement officers involved in civil rights protests. In Cohen's account, the Athens police are seen as protectors of Charlayne Hunter (Holmes was off campus) rather than coconspirators with local segregationists. The FBI files certainly support this conclusion, although Cohen himself writes that "Athens police may have exaggerated the dangers of the riot scene" (531). And given that their interviews were conducted by FBI agents, police might also have had a good reason to put a more positive spin on their role in the crisis. Cohen writes, "The contrast between the response of the Athens police and the state patrol to the riot could not have been more stark. While the [Athens] police made advance preparations for the riot and spent hours battling a violent mob, state patrol officers lounged around in their nearby office, drinking coffee and smoking cigarettes" (533).

98. For a more detailed discussion of this controversy, see Henderson, *Ernest Vandiver,* 137–38.

99. *Atlanta Constitution,* September 24, 1980; see also Henderson, *Ernest Vandiver,* 138. For Mayor Ralph Snow's criticism of the Georgia State Patrol, see *Athens Banner-Herald,* January 12, 1961. For Governor Vandiver's denial of the mayor's allegations, see *Augusta Chronicle,* January 13, 1961.

100. The *Atlanta Constitution* (on January 13, 1961) reported that everyone present at the meeting held at the Chapel signed the resolution, when in fact it was later estimated that 95 percent of those present had signed. An actual list of those who signed the document is located in the Walter Danner Papers, file no. 97–1166, "Faculty Petition" (Original), located at the University of Georgia Library. Horace Montgomery later wrote an essay about the faculty resolution, titled "Origins of the University of Georgia Faculty Resolutions of January 12, 1961," which was published in *The Negro History Bulletin,* April 1962, 157–58.

101. Horace Montgomery, interview by author, April 12, 2000.

102. Ibid.

103. *Red and Black,* January 19, 1961.

104. The text of Judge Bootle's ruling can be found in the *Atlanta Constitution,* January 14, 1961.

105. Vandiver, interview.

106. Following a federal order to desegregate Atlanta's public schools in 1959, the state legislature created the Sibley Commission (named after John A. Sibley, an influential Atlanta banker who chaired the committee) to gauge community sentiment. The committee—consisting solely of white males who were among the state's

most prominent businessmen, politicians, and educators—held hearings in each of the state's ten congressional districts, listening to some 1,800 witnesses, 1,600 of whom were white. By a three-to-two majority, the witnesses, who claimed to represent more than 115,000 Georgians, favored maintaining segregated schools even if it meant abandoning public education. On April 28, 1960, the committee issued its report. Eleven members, including Sibley, condemned the *Brown* decision as "utterly unsound" but conceded the inevitability of desegregation and urged the state to abandon massive resistance. Eight other members called for continued defiance. Both groups favored local option and private school–tuition grants so that no white student would be forced to attend an integrated school. Court-ordered desegregation of Atlanta's public schools began in the fall of 1961. See Henderson, *Ernest Vandiver,* 114–19. For a detailed discussion of the Sibley Commission, see Roche, *Restructured Resistance.*

107. Trillin, *An Education in Georgia,* 12.

108. S. Ernest Vandiver, "Vandiver Takes the Middle Road," in Henderson and Roberts, *Georgia Governors,* 157–66.

109. Hunter-Gault, *In My Place,* 190.

110. Ibid., 194.

111. Ibid., 172.

Five. Tolerated, but Not Integrated

1. For a good brief examination of the civil rights movement, see Williams, *Eyes on the Prize,* the companion volume to the PBS television series.

2. Thomas Brahana, interview by author, September 21, 2000.

3. Hunter-Gault, *In My Place,* 195.

4. Trillin, *An Education in Georgia,* 55–56. In a recent interview, Hunter-Gault told me that she still has every letter she received during those years, which she keeps in a trunk in the basement of her New York apartment. Not long ago, the apartment was flooded, and some of the letters got wet, but they dried out with no permanent damage. As a result of that scare, Hunter-Gault says she is now considering donating the letters to a repository.

5. Hunter-Gault, 196–99. In Horace Ward's trial, Chancellor Harmon Caldwell had testified that some white students felt discriminated against because the state offered tuition grants for black students to study out of state. Of course, what Caldwell refused to admit was that these same black students were forbidden by law from attending Georgia's white institutions.

6. Hunter-Gault, interview.

7. Hunter-Gault, *In My Place,* 206–7.

8. Joan Zitzelman, interview by author, March 20, 2001.

9. Caroline Ridlehuber, interview by author, March 19, 2001.

10. Larry Jones, editor of the *Red and Black,* took exception to some of Holmes's remarks in a speech given in Savannah, in which Holmes, in response to a question, said that he had made no friends while at the university. In criticizing Holmes's comments, Jones wrote, "Holmes entered the University forcibly, as an alien. He attended as an alien. And when he graduates this June (with honors, I understand) he will still be an alien. The treatment he has received; the friendless atmosphere he has encountered: he could have expected no more and he has received no less . . . He made his choice when he entered Georgia two years ago." The story appears in the *Red and Black,* March 21, 1963.

11. Hunter-Gault, *In My Place,* 213–14; Trillin, *An Education in Georgia,* 120–21; Cohen, "Two, Four, Six, Eight," 643–45. Two other fraternities that Trillin mentions as being "dependably hostile" were the Sigma Nus and the Alpha Tau Omegas (130).

12. Hunter-Gault, *In My Place,* 222–24.

13. Ibid., 222–23.

14. Trillin, *An Education in Georgia,* 67.

15. Ibid., 169–70.

16. Hunter-Gault, interview.

17. Mary Frances Early, interview by author, April 24, 2000.

18. Ibid.

19. Ibid.

20. Ibid.

21. Ibid.

22. Herbert Holmes, interview.

23. Trillin, *An Education in Georgia,* 83, 88–89.

24. Hunter-Gault, *In My Place,* 238.

25. Ibid., 76–78.

26. Shipp, interview; Trillin, *An Education in Georgia,* 136–37.

27. Harold A. Black, telephone interview with author, May 9, 2000.

28. Trillin, *An Education in Georgia,* 136–38. By the fall of 1962, Holmes, Hunter, and Early had been joined by five other black students: Mattie Jo Arnold, Harold Black, Mary Blackwell, Alice Henderson, and Kerry Rushin.

29. Black, interview.

30. Ibid.

31. Ibid; see also Trillin, *An Education in Georgia,* 139–44.

32. Black, interview. During his time in Reed Hall, Black developed close relation-

ships with a few of his white dorm mates. On one occasion, some of them invited him to go swimming with them, and he accepted. As he recalls it now,

> The first time I dove in the University of Georgia swimming pool, this guy runs out and says, "Everybody out of the pool." So everybody got out. When we walked by the pool later on the way to dinner, we discovered that they had drained the pool. At that point I told my friends that we were going to swim in that pool every single day. And so the next day I went back, and no sooner had we gotten in the water, this guy runs out again and says, "Everybody out of the pool." At that point I called Dean Tate, and Dean Tate asked to speak to the guy. Now, I don't know what Dean Tate said to him, but he turned bright red, and we had no trouble swimming in the university pool after that. Well, fast forward about twenty years. In 1979, I was sworn in as one of the directors of the National Credit Union Administration, and I was appointed by President Carter. Well, before I could be sworn in I had to be briefed by the staff before the Senate confirmation hearing. And so, I'm sitting in this office waiting for the staff to come in to brief me on some issues. And this guy walks in [Leonard Skiles, the Deputy General Counsel of the National Credit Union Administration], and he looked at me, and says, "You know, I was the student working in the aquatic center, and I was the one who drained the pool." Now, that's my small world story. Today, I count Len Skiles as one of my closest friends.

33. Rubye J. Potts, interview by author, July 18, 2000.

34. Ibid.

35. Homer R. Wilson, interview by author, April 4, 2001.

36. Hunter-Gault, 242.

37. Trillin, *An Education in Georgia*, 175–78.

38. Donald Hollowell, interview by author, March 2, 2000. For a fuller discussion of the Preston Cobb case, see Hollowell and Lehfeldt, *The Sacred Call*, 145–50.

39. Hunter-Gault, interview.

40. Ward, interview.

Six. "Wouldn't Take Nothing for My Journey Now"

1. Ward, interview.

2. Ibid.

3. *Bell v. Georgia Dental Association*, 231 F. Supp. 299 (N.D. Ga. 1964).

4. Ward, interview.

5. Ibid. Ward's efforts to abolish the death penalty in Georgia were unsuccessful, but his resolution did lead to the creation of a committee to study the death penalty;

consequently, the state reduced (from twenty-four to five) the number of crimes for which a defendant could be executed. Ward's proposal to create a human rights commission did not pass the senate, but such a commission was created after he had left the senate. Ward's efforts at reapportionment in the House of Representatives bore fruit in the 1965 session of the General Assembly when a significant number of house districts were created on a single-member basis, which enhanced the electoral opportunities for African Americans. During his time in the state senate, Ward served on the following committees: Judiciary, Rules, County and Urban Affairs, Business Trade and Commerce, and Penal and Correction Affairs.

6. Ward, interview.

7. Gary M. Fink, "Jimmy Carter and the Politics of Transition," in Henderson and Roberts, *Georgia Governors,* 233.

8. Ibid., 240, 242–43.

9. At the time of Ward's appointment, the civil court consisted of five judges and had broad civil jurisdiction but only limited criminal jurisdiction. A judge on the civil court could be called upon to handle a variety of lawsuits between private litigants in most areas of civil law, with the exception of equity, domestic relations, land titles, and personal injury. On January 2, 1977, the civil and criminal courts were combined into what came to be known as the State Court of Fulton County.

10. The superior court is the main trial court in Georgia and is a court of general jurisdiction that covers all areas of state cases. A superior court judge is called upon to try felony criminal cases, all types of civil cases (including tort actions, domestic relations, and equity cases), and many other special or extraordinary claims for relief, such as injunctions and appeals from lower courts and state agencies.

11. Merrill, "Jimmy Carter," 1–2.

12. When Carter was elected president in 1976, only 16 out of 525 federal judges were black. Franklin D. Roosevelt appointed the first black person, William Hastie, to the federal bench in 1937. In the years following Roosevelt's appointment of Hastie, President Truman appointed one black federal judge, Eisenhower appointed none, Kennedy appointed five, Johnson appointed eight, Nixon appointed six, and Ford appointed three. Of those, only four were named to the circuit courts: one by Truman, one by Kennedy, and two by Johnson. In the Fifth Circuit Court of Appeals, which contained most of the Deep South states, there had never been an African American judge prior to the Carter administration. When Carter's record of judicial appointments is compared to that of his two immediate predecessors, the differences are glaring. Twenty-eight of Carter's 202 district court appointees (13.9 percent) were black; 3 of Ford's 52 appointees (5.8 percent) were black; and 5 of Nixon's 179 appointees (2.8 percent) were black. At the court of appeals level, 9 of Carter's 56 appointees

(16.1 percent) were black; none of Ford's 12 appointees (0 percent) were black; and none of Nixon's 45 appointees (0 percent) were black. For an excellent discussion of Carter's African American judicial appointments, see Merrill, "Jimmy Carter."

13. Some of the whites that Carter appointed to top cabinet positions, such as Attorney General Griffin Bell, were not sympathetic to the African American community. Some of Carter's black judicial appointments were made over Bell's objections. See Merrill, "Jimmy Carter," especially 29–66.

14. Statement by the President, October 20, 1978, quoted in Merrill, "Jimmy Carter," 41. On October 8, 1978, Congress passed the Omnibus Judgeship Act, which created 152 new federal judgeships; 35 of the judgeships would be in the circuit courts, and 117 of them would be in the district courts. This act, representing the single largest increase ever in the size of the federal judiciary, was designed to relieve the massive backlog of federal court cases.

15. Ward, interview.

16. Ibid.

17. Talmadge Collection, Russell Library, 1960 Subseries, Box 296 (Speeches).

18. Ward, interview.

19. Shipp, interview.

20. Of the ten new federal judges appointed in Georgia, seven were white men, two were white women, and one—Ward—was black. Not only did President Carter have a respectable record in appointing African Americans to the federal bench, but his appointees in general (black and white) tended to be more sympathetic to African American plaintiffs in civil rights cases. Also, Carter's willingness to appoint black activist judges like Nathaniel Jones and A. Leon Higginbotham Jr. was yet another distinguishing feature of his nominations. But for a variety of reasons, no blacks were appointed to the First, Fourth, Seventh, or Tenth Circuits, and only in two circuits, the Second and the Ninth, did Carter appoint more than one black judge. As has already been noted, Carter's goal of achieving greater diversity on the federal bench was sometimes frustrated by un-Reconstructed U.S. senators. See Merrill, "Jimmy Carter," 86–87.

In what he refers to as "the retreat from pluralism within the federal judiciary," noted jurist A. Leon Higginbotham Jr. points out that there was an intentional reduction of the number of African American judges on the federal courts in the post-Carter years. During that twelve-year period from 1980 to 1992, only 2 of 115 appointees to the U.S. Courts of Appeals were black. (One of those was Clarence Thomas, who was appointed by Reagan to the U.S. Court of Appeals for the District of Columbia and who would later be appointed to the U.S. Supreme Court by George Bush in 1991.) More than fifty judges were appointed to the federal courts of the Sixth Circuit, a region comprising the states of Michigan, Ohio, Kentucky, and Tennessee, and not one was black. Four African American judges in the Southern District of New York went on senior status and all were replaced by white judges. When comparing President Clinton's record on judicial appointments to that of Presidents Reagan and Bush, Higginbotham observes that in the *first three years* of Clinton's presidency, thirty-six blacks were appointed to the federal judiciary. By contrast, during the *entire twelve years* of the Reagan-Bush era, only eighteen blacks were appointed. See Higginbotham, *Shades of Freedom,* viii–ix.

21. *Savannah Morning News,* February 20, 1985.

22. *Georgia Association of Retarded Citizens v. McDaniel,* 511 F. Supp. 1263 (N.D. Ga. 1981), 1285–86.

23. Ibid., 716 F.2d 1565 (5th Cir. 1983); 721 F.2d 822 (5th Cir. 1983); 104 S.Ct. 3581 (1984); 740 F.2d 902 (5th Cir. 1984); 105 S.Ct. 1228 (1985).

24. *American Civil Liberties Union v. Rabun County Chamber of Commerce,* 510 F. Supp. 886 (N.D. Ga. 1981), 698 F.2d 1098 (11th Cir. 1983), 889, 892.

25. *American Booksellers Association v. McAuliffe,* 533 F. Supp. 50 (N.D. Ga. 1981), 54, 57–58.

26. *Kemp v. Ervin,* 651 F. Supp. 495 (N.D. Ga. 1986).

27. Ibid. See also *Athens Daily News/Banner-Herald,* February 28, 1999.

28. *Kemp v. Ervin.*

29. Ibid.; *Atlanta Constitution,* April 25, 1986.

30. *Athens Banner-Herald,* February 13, 1986.

31. *Atlanta Journal,* February 28, 1986.

32. *Athens Daily News/Banner-Herald,* February 28, 1999.

33. *Atlanta Constitution,* February 14, 1986.

34. *Atlanta Constitution,* February 25, 1986.

35. Ward, interview.

36. *Kemp v. Ervin,* 500, 505. See also *Atlanta Constitution,* April 23, 1986.

37. *Kemp v. Ervin,* 509.

38. In order to become a senior judge, one must be at least sixty-five years old with at least fifteen years of service (if one is at least sixty-six, he or she needs only fourteen years of service, etc.). In some instances, the designation does not mean very much, other than that the president can appoint a successor. A senior judge can work at whatever pace he or she wishes and has the luxury of being able to decline certain cases, though he or she cannot select them. Judge Ward now estimates his workload at roughly 30 percent.

39. The full text of Ward's speech may be found in "Ceremony Commemorating Senior Status and Portrait Presentation for The Honorable Horace T. Ward, Senior

Judge, United States District Court," Northern District of Georgia, Atlanta, May 16, 1994.

40. Ward, interview.

41. The conference grew out of discussions between Professors William S. McFeely, John C. Inscoe, and Robert A. Pratt, all members of UGA's history faculty. Several others, including Professor Robert Cohen of UGA's School of Education, eventually joined the committee. It was Professor Cohen who drafted the letter to UGA President Knapp asking him to extend the personal invitation to Judge Ward.

42. Comments by Charles B. Knapp, "Civil Rights in Small Places," conference held at the Georgia Center for Continuing Education, University of Georgia, April 15–16, 1996. The entire conference was videotaped, and copies of all tapes are in the author's possession. The videotapes of the conference were made available courtesy of Professor John C. Inscoe, History Department, University of Georgia.

43. Comments by Horace T. Ward, "Civil Rights in Small Places."

44. Ward, interview.

45. Henderson, *Ernest Vandiver,* 131–32.

46. Vandiver, interview.

47. Hollowell, interview.

48. Ibid..

49. Ibid..

50. Ward, interview; *Atlanta Constitution,* May 2, 1986.

51. Ward, interview.

52. *Atlanta Constitution,* May 2, 1986; Ward, interview.

53. Ward, interview; Margaret Shannon, "Justice at Last for Horace Ward," *Atlanta Journal and Constitution Magazine,* March 13, 1977.

54. Ward, interview; Comments by Ward, Commemorating Senior Status and Portrait Presentation, May 16, 1994.

Epilogue. Burying Unhappy Ghosts

1. *Columns,* the University of Georgia newsletter, November 15, 1999.

2. Hunter-Gault, *In My Place,* 253, 254, 256.

3. Ibid., 247–48.

4. *Columns,* November 15, 1999.

5. Hunter-Gault, interview.

6. Ibid. See also "Integrated Paths," *Georgia Magazine,* March 1996, 48.

7. Ibid.

8. Comments by Marilyn Holmes at the Commemoration of the Fortieth Anniversary of the Desegregation of the University of Georgia, January 9, 2001.

9. Comments delivered by Charlayne Hunter-Gault, Holmes-Hunter Lecture, given at the Observance of the Fortieth Anniversary of the Desegregation of the University of Georgia.

Bibliography

Papers and Archival Collections

Omer Clyde Aderhold Papers, University of Georgia Library, Athens, Ga.

William Madison Boyd Collection, Trevor Arnett Library, Special Collections, Atlanta University, Atlanta, Ga.

Harmon Caldwell Papers, University of Georgia Library.

Ellis Merton Coulter Papers, University of Georgia Library.

Walter N. Danner Papers, University of Georgia Library.

Files of the Federal Bureau of Investigation, "Files on the Desegregation of the University of Georgia," Field Office File No. 72–39, United States Department of Justice, Washington, D.C.

Georgia Government Documentation Project Interviews, Pullen Library, Georgia State University, Atlanta, Ga.

Roy Vincent Harris Papers, Richard B. Russell Library, University of Georgia.

Hamilton E. Holmes Papers, Martin Luther King Jr. Center for Non-Violent Social Change, Atlanta, Ga.

James J. Lenoir Papers, private collection (in the author's possession).

Living Atlanta Series and Interviews, Atlanta History Center/Archives.

Walter A. Lundy Jr. Papers, Richard B. Russell Library, University of Georgia.

NAACP Papers, Library of Congress, Washington, D.C.

Herman E. Talmadge Papers, Richard B. Russell Library, University of Georgia.

William Tate Papers, University of Georgia Library.

A. T. Walden Papers, Atlanta History Center/Archives.

Court Cases

American Booksellers Association v. McAuliffe, 533 F. Supp. 50 (N.D. Ga. 1981).

American Civil Liberties Union v. Rabun County Chamber of Commerce, 510 F. Supp. 886 (N.D. Ga. 1981).

Bell v. Georgia Dental Association, 231 F. Supp. 299 (N.D. Ga. 1964).

Brown v. Board of Education, 347 U.S. 483 (1954).

Brown v. Board of Education II, 349 U.S. 294 (1955).

Corrigan v. Buckley, 271 U.S. 323 (1926).

Georgia Association of Retarded Citizens v. McDaniel, 511 F. Supp. 1263 (N.D. Ga. 1981).

Holmes v. Danner, 191 F. Supp. 394 (M.D. Ga. 1961).

Hunt v. Arnold, 172 F. Supp. 847 (N.D. Ga. 1959).

Kemp v. Ervin, 651 F. Supp. 495 (N.D. Ga. 1986).

McLaurin v. Oklahoma State Regents, 339 U.S. 637 (1950).

Missouri ex rel. Gaines v. Canada, 305 U.S. 337 (1938).

Morgan v. Virginia, 328 U.S. 373 (1946).

Pearson v. Murray, 169 Md. 478, 182 A. 590 (1936).

Plessy v. Ferguson, 163 U.S. 537 (1896).

Shelley v. Kraemer, 334 U.S. 1 (1948).

Smith v. Allwright, 321 U.S. 649 (1944).

Sweatt v. Painter, 339 U.S. 629 (1950).

Horace T. Ward v. Regents of the University System of Georgia, Federal Records Center, East Point, Georgia, December 1956.

Newspapers and Periodicals

Athens Banner-Herald, 1950–2001; *Atlanta Daily World,* 1956–63; *Atlanta Inquirer,* 1961–63; *Atlanta Journal and Constitution,* 1950–2001; *Augusta Chronicle,* 1953; *Augusta Courier,* 1952–61; *Baltimore Sun,* 1960–63; *Chicago Defender,* 1954–61; *Christian Science Monitor,* 1961–63; *Cleveland Plain Dealer,* 1961; *Columbus Ledger,* 1954–61; *Cornell Daily Sun,* 1953; *Gainesville Daily Times,* 1953–54; *Life,* 1961; *Los Angeles Times,* 1961; *Louisville Courier and Journal,* 1961; *Macon Telegraph,* 1954–62; *Miami Hurricane,* 1953; *New Republic,* 1961; *Newsweek,* 1961–63; *New York Times,* 1961–63; *Red and Black* (student newspaper of the University of Georgia), 1950–2001; *Saturday Evening Post,* 1963; *Savannah Morning News,* 1961–63; *Time,* 1961–63; *Washington Post,* 1961–63.

Author's Interviews

Milner Ball, Athens, Georgia, August 23, 2000; Leslie K. Bates, Athens, Georgia, July 15, 1998; J. Ralph Beaird, Athens, Georgia, August 17, 2000; Robert Benham, Atlanta, Georgia, September 8, 2000; Harold Black, telephone conversation, May 9, 2000; William A. Bootle, Macon, Georgia, March 21, 2001; Thomas Brahana, Athens, Georgia, September 21, 2000; Gene Britton, Athens, Georgia, August 12, 1998; Chester C. Davenport Jr., telephone conversation, August 17, 2000; Ken Dious, Athens, Georgia, August 17, 2000; Thomas Dyer, Athens, Georgia, December 8, 2000; Mary Frances

Early, Athens, Georgia, April 18, 2000; T. David Fletcher, Athens, Georgia, May 4, 2001; Thurmon Garner, Athens, Georgia, October 13, 2000; Hugh Gloster, telephone conversation, September 20, 2000; Richard Graham, Athens, Georgia, September 19, 2000; Donald Hollowell, telephone conversation, March 2, 2000; Gary Holmes, Atlanta, Georgia, May 27, 2001; Hamilton Holmes Jr., Athens, Georgia, January 8, 2001; Herbert Holmes, Atlanta, Georgia, May 27, 2001; Isabella Holmes, Atlanta, Georgia, May 27, 2001; Marilyn Holmes, Athens, Georgia, January 9, 2001; Charlayne Hunter-Gault, Atlanta, Georgia, May 29, 2000; Randall Johnson, telephone conversation, August 14, 2000; Giles Kennedy, Athens, Georgia, August 15, 2000; Alfred Killian, Athens, Georgia, December 12, 2000; Archibald Killian, Athens, Georgia, December 12, 2000; Charles B. Knapp, Athens, Georgia, May 30, 1997; Earl T. Leonard Jr., Atlanta, Georgia, May 9, 2001; Calvin Logue, Athens, Georgia, October 13, 2000; Walter A. Lundy, telephone conversation, July 13, 1998; Betty Mapp, telephone conversation, September 26, 2000; Pete McCommons, Athens, Georgia, April 25, 2000; Adrienne McFall, Athens, Georgia, August 15, 2000; Horace Montgomery, Athens, Georgia, April 12, 2000; Ray Moore, Athens, Georgia, October 9, 2000; John H. Morrow Jr., Athens, Georgia, October 19, 2000; Constance Baker Motley, telephone conversation, May 8, 2001; Rubye Potts, Athens, Georgia, January 10, 2001; Caroline Ridlehuber, Athens, Georgia, March 19, 2001; Gregory Roseboro, Athens, Georgia, August 15, 2000; Bill Shipp, Atlanta, Georgia, August 4, 1998; Edward D. Spurgeon, telephone conversation, August 23, 2000; S. Ernest Vandiver, Lavonia, Georgia, April 19, 2000; Horace T. Ward, Atlanta, Georgia, June 29, 1999; Homer Wilson, Athens, Georgia, April 4, 2001; Joan Zitzelman, Athens, Georgia, March 20, 2001.

Books and Articles

Ambrose, Andy, with Brooke Bargeron and Alexis Oliver. "'Negroes Cannot Play Here': The Desegregation of Atlanta's Golf Courses," *Atlanta History* 63, no. 1 (1999): 21–32.

Anderson, William. *The Wild Man from Sugar Creek: The Political Career of Eugene Talmadge.* Baton Rouge: Louisiana State University Press, 1975.

Baldwin, James. *Nobody Knows My Name: More Notes of a Native Son.* London: Penguin, 1964 and 1991.

Banner-Haley, Charles T. *The Fruits of Integration: Black Middle-Class Ideology and Culture, 1960–1990.* Jackson: University Press of Mississippi, 1994.

Bartley, Numan V. *The Creation of Modern Georgia.* Athens: University of Georgia Press, 1983.

———. *The Rise of Massive Resistance: Race and Politics in the South during the 1950s.* Baton Rouge: Louisiana State University Press, 1969.

Bartley, Numan V., and Hugh D. Graham. *Southern Politics and the Second Recon-struction*. Baltimore: Johns Hopkins University Press, 1975.

Bass, Jack. *Unlikely Heroes: The Dramatic Story of the Southern Judges of the Fifth Circuit Who Translated the Supreme Court's Brown Decision into a Revolution for Equality*. New York: Simon and Schuster, 1981.

Bass, Jack, and Walter Devries. *The Transformation of Southern Politics: Social Change and Political Consequences since 1945*. New York: Basic Books, 1976.

Bennett, Lerone, Jr. *What Manner of Man: A Biography of Martin Luther King, Jr.* Chicago: Johnson Publishing Company, 1968.

Bernd, Joseph L. "White Supremacy and the Disfranchisement of Blacks in Georgia, 1946." *Georgia Historical Quarterly* 66, no. 4 (winter 1982): 492–513.

Black, Earl. *Southern Governors and Civil Rights*. Cambridge, Mass.: Harvard University Press, 1976.

Bolster, Paul D. "Civil Rights Movements in Twentieth Century Georgia." Ph.D. diss., University of Georgia, 1972.

Boney, F. N. *A Pictorial History of the University of Georgia*. 2nd ed. Athens: University of Georgia Press, 2000.

Branch, Taylor. *Parting the Waters: America in the King Years, 1954–63*. New York: Simon and Schuster, 1988.

Carson, Clayborne. *In Struggle: SNCC and the Black Awakening of the 1960s*. Cambridge: Harvard University Press, 1981.

———. *The Eyes on the Prize Civil Rights Reader*. New York: Penguin Books, 1991.

Carter, Dan T. *The Politics of Rage: George Wallace, the Origins of the New Conservatism, and the Transformation of American Politics*. New York: Simon and Schuster, 1995.

Chafe, William H. *Civilities and Civil Rights: Greensboro, North Carolina, and the Black Struggle for Freedom*. New York: Oxford University Press, 1980.

Clark, E. Culpepper. *The Schoolhouse Door: Segregation's Last Stand at the University of Alabama*. New York: Oxford University Press, 1995.

Cobb, James C. *Georgia Odyssey*. Athens: University of Georgia Press, 1997.

Cohen, Robert. "G-Men in Georgia: The FBI and the Segregationist Riot at the University of Georgia, 1961," *Georgia Historical Quarterly* 83, no. 3 (fall 1999): 508–38.

———. "'Two, Four, Six, Eight, We Don't Want to Integrate': White Student Attitudes Toward the University of Georgia's Desegregation," *Georgia Historical Quarterly* 80, no. 3 (fall 1996): 616–45.

Coleman, Kenneth, ed. *A History of Georgia*. Athens: University of Georgia Press, 1977.

Cook, J. F. *The Governors of Georgia, 1754–1995.* Macon, Ga.: Mercer University Press, 1995.

Dittmer, John. *Local People: The Struggle for Civil Rights in Mississippi.* Urbana: University of Illinois Press, 1994.

Douglas, Davison M. *Reading, Writing, and Race: The Desegregation of the Charlotte Schools.* Chapel Hill: University of North Carolina Press, 1995.

Dudziak, Mary. "Desegregation as a Cold War Imperative," *Stanford Law Review* 41 (November 1988): 61–120.

Dyer, Thomas G. *The University of Georgia: A Bicentennial History, 1785–1985.* Athens: University of Georgia Press, 1985.

Eagles, Charles W., "Toward New Histories of the Civil Rights Era," *The Journal of Southern History* 66, no. 4 (November 2000): 815–48.

Egerton, John. *Speak Now Against the Day: The Generation Before the Civil Rights Movement in the South.* New York: Alfred A. Knopf, 1994.

Eskew, Glenn T. *But for Birmingham: The Local and National Movements in the Civil Rights Struggle.* Chapel Hill: University of North Carolina Press, 1997.

Fairclough, Adam. *To Redeem the Soul of America: The Southern Christian Leadership Conference and Martin Luther King, Jr.* Athens: University of Georgia Press, 1987.

Forman, James. *The Making of Black Revolutionaries: A Personal Account.* New York: Macmillan, 1972.

Franklin, John Hope, and Alfred A. Moss Jr. *From Slavery to Freedom: A History of Negro Americans,* 6th ed. New York: Alfred A. Knopf, 1988.

Garrow, David. *Bearing the Cross: Martin Luther King, Jr., and the Southern Christian Leadership Conference.* New York: Morrow, 1986.

Gates, Robbins L. *The Making of Massive Resistance: Virginia's Politics of Public School Desegregation, 1954–56.* Chapel Hill: University of North Carolina Press, 1962.

Graham, Hugh D. *The Civil Rights Era: Origins and Development of National Policy.* New York: Oxford University Press, 1990.

Grant, Donald L. *The Way It Was in the South: The Black Experience in Georgia.* New York: Birch Lane Press, 1993.

Hampton, Henry, and Steve Fayer. *Voices of Freedom: An Oral History of the Civil Rights Movement from the 1950s through the 1980s.* New York: Bantam Books, 1990.

Harding, Vincent. *There Is a River: The Black Struggle for Freedom in America.* New York: Vintage Books, 1991.

Harmon, David. "Beneath the Image: The Civil Rights Movement and Race Relations in Atlanta, Georgia, 1946–81." Ph.D. diss., Emory University, 1992.

Henderson, Harold P. *Ernest Vandiver: Governor of Georgia.* Athens: University of Georgia Press, 2000.

———. "The 1946 Gubernatorial Election in Georgia." Master's thesis, Georgia Southern College, 1967.

Henderson, Harold P., and Gary L. Roberts, eds. *Georgia Governors in an Age of Change: From Ellis Arnall to George Busbee.* Athens: University of Georgia Press, 1988.

Higginbotham, A. Leon, Jr. *Shades of Freedom: Racial Politics and Presumptions of the American Legal Process.* New York: Oxford University Press, 1996.

Hine, Darlene Clark. *Black Victory: The Rise and Fall of the White Primary in Texas.* Millwood, N.Y.: KTO Press, 1979.

Hollowell, Louise T., and Martin C. Lehfeldt. *The Sacred Call: A Tribute to Donald L. Hollowell, Civil Rights Champion.* Winter Park, Fla.: Four-G Publishers, 1997.

Hunter-Gault, Charlayne. *In My Place.* New York: Vintage Books, 1992.

Inscoe, John C., ed. *Georgia in Black and White: Explorations in the Race Relations of a Southern State, 1865–1950.* Athens: University of Georgia Press, 1994.

Kellar, William Henry. *Make Haste Slowly: Moderates, Conservatives, and School Desegregation in Houston.* College Station: Texas A&M University Press, 1999.

Klarman, Michael. "How *Brown* Changed Race Relations: The Backlash Thesis," *Journal of American History* 81, no. 1 (1994): 81–118.

Kluger, Richard. *Simple Justice: The History of* Brown v. Board of Education *and Black America's Struggle for Equality.* New York: Alfred A. Knopf, 1975.

Kneebone, John T. *Southern Liberal Journalists and the Issue of Race, 1920–1944.* Chapel Hill: University of North Carolina Press, 1985.

Lawson, Stephen F. *Running for Freedom: Civil Rights and Black Politics in America Since 1941.* 2nd ed. New York: McGraw-Hill, 1997.

Lenoir, James J., and Lora Deere Lenoir, "Compulsory Legal Segregation in the Public Schools, with Special Reference to Georgia," *Mercer Law Review* 5, no. 2 (spring 1954): 211–41.

Lewis, David Levering. *King: A Critical Biography.* New York: Praeger Publishers, 1970.

Lewis, John, with Michael D'Orso. *Walking with the Wind: A Memoir of the Movement.* New York: Simon and Schuster, 1998.

Manis, Andrew. *A Fire You Can't Put Out: The Civil Rights Life of Birmingham's Reverend Fred Shuttlesworth.* Tuscaloosa: University of Alabama Press, 1999.

Marable, Manning. *Race, Reform, and Rebellion: The Second Reconstruction in Black America, 1945–1990.* Revised second edition. Jackson: University Press of Mississippi, 1989.

Martin, Charles H. "Racial Change and 'Big-Time' College Football in Georgia: The Age of Segregation, 1892–1957," *Georgia Historical Quarterly* 80, no. 3 (fall 1996): 532–62.

Martin, Waldo E. Brown v. Board of Education: *A Brief History with Documents.* Boston: St. Martin's, 1998.

Mays, Benjamin E. *Born to Rebel: An Autobiography.* Athens: University of Georgia Press, 1971.

McCoy, Carl Levert. "A Historical Sketch of Black Augusta, Georgia, from Emancipation to the *Brown* Decision: 1865–1954." Master's thesis, University of Georgia, 1984.

McGrath, Susan. "Great Expectations: The History of School Desegregation in Atlanta and Boston, 1954–1990." Ph.D. diss., Emory University, 1992.

McNeil, Genna Rae. *Groundwork: Charles Hamilton Houston and the Struggle for Civil Rights.* Philadelphia: University of Pennsylvania Press, 1983.

Merrill, Jonathan Neal. "Jimmy Carter, Race Relations and the Judicial Selection Process." Master's thesis, University of Georgia, 1992.

Morris, Aldon D. *The Origins of the Civil Rights Movement: Black Communities Organizing for Change.* New York: The Free Press, 1984.

Motley, Constance Baker. *Equal Justice Under Law: An Autobiography.* New York: Farrar, Straus, and Giroux, 1998.

Murphy, Walter F. "The South Counterattacks: The Anti-NAACP Laws," *Western Political Quarterly* 12 (1959): 371–90.

Muse, Benjamin. *Virginia's Massive Resistance.* Bloomington: Indiana University Press, 1961.

Norrell, Robert J. *Reaping the Whirlwind: The Civil Rights Movement in Tuskegee.* New York: Knopf, 1985.

O'Brien, Thomas V. "Georgia's Response to Brown v. Board of Education: The Rise and Fall of Massive Resistance, 1949–1961." Ph.D. diss., Emory University, 1992.

O'Reilly, Kenneth. *"Racial Matters": The FBI's Secret File on Black America, 1960–1972.* New York: Free Press, 1989.

Orfield, Gary, Susan E. Eaton, and the Harvard Project on School Desegregation. *Dismantling Desegregation: The Quiet Reversal of* Brown v. Board of Education. New York: The New Press, 1996.

Patterson, James T. Brown v. Board of Education: *A Civil Rights Milestone and Its Troubled Legacy.* New York: Oxford University Press, 2001.

Patton, Randall. "Southern Liberals and the Emergence of a New South, 1938–1950." Ph.D. diss., University of Georgia, 1990.

Payne, Charles M. *I've Got the Light of Freedom: The Organizing Tradition and the Mississippi Freedom Struggle.* Berkeley: University of California Press, 1995.

Pratt, Robert A. *The Color of Their Skin: Education and Race in Richmond, Virginia, 1954–89.* Charlottesville: University Press of Virginia, 1992.

Raines, Howell. *My Soul Is Rested: The Story of the Civil Rights Movement in the Deep South.* New York: Viking Penguin, 1977.

Reed, Linda. *Simple Decency and Common Sense: The Southern Conference Movement, 1938–1963.* Bloomington: Indiana University Press, 1991.

Robinson, Armstead, and Patricia Sullivan. *New Directions in Civil Rights Studies.* Charlottesville: University Press of Virginia, 1991.

Roche, Jeff. *Restructured Resistance: The Sibley Commission and the Politics of Desegregation in Georgia.* Athens: University of Georgia Press, 1998.

Shipp, Bill. *Murder at Broad River Bridge: The Slaying of Lemuel Penn by Members of the Ku Klux Klan.* Atlanta: Peachtree Publishers Limited, 1981.

Silverman, Peter H. "*Horace T. Ward v. Board of Regents of the University System of Georgia:* A Study in Segregation and Desegregation." Master's thesis, Emory University, 1970.

Sitkoff, Harvard. *The Struggle for Black Equality, 1954–1992.* New York: Hill and Wang, 1993.

Stone, Clarence N. *Regime Politics: Governing Atlanta, 1946–1988.* Lawrence: University Press of Kansas, 1989.

Suggs, Henry Lewis. *P. B. Young, Newspaperman: Race, Politics, and Journalism in the New South, 1910–1962.* Charlottesville: University Press of Virginia, 1988.

Thurmond, Michael L. *A Story Untold: Black Men and Women in Athens History.* Athens, Ga.: Clarke County School District, 1978.

Trillin, Calvin. *An Education in Georgia: Charlayne Hunter, Hamilton Holmes, and the Integration of the University of Georgia.* Athens: University of Georgia Press, 1963.

Tuck, Stephen. *Beyond Atlanta: The Struggle for Racial Equality in Georgia, 1940–1980.* Athens: University of Georgia Press, 2001.

Tushnet, Mark V. *Making Civil Rights Law: Thurgood Marshall and the Supreme Court, 1936–1961.* New York: Oxford University Press, 1994.

———. *The NAACP's Legal Strategy against Segregated Education, 1925–1950.* Chapel Hill: University of North Carolina Press, 1987.

Wallenstein, Peter. "Black Southerners and Non-Black Universities: Desegregating Higher Education, 1935–1967." *History of Higher Education Annual* 19 (1999): 121–48.

Ward, Brian, and Tony Badger. *The Making of Martin Luther King, Jr., and the Civil Rights Movement.* New York: New York University Press, 1996.

Warren, Wallace H. "The Best People in Town Won't Talk: The Moore's Ford Lynching of 1946 and Its Cover-Up," in John C. Inscoe, ed., *Georgia in Black and White: Explorations in the Race Relations of a Southern State, 1865–1950.* Athens: University of Georgia Press, 1994.

Weisbrot, Robert. *Freedom Bound: A History of America's Civil Rights Movement.* New York: Norton, 1990.

Williams, Juan. *Eyes on the Prize: America's Civil Rights Years, 1954–1965.* New York: Penguin, 1988.

Young, Andrew. *An Easy Burden: The Civil Rights Movement and the Transformation of America.* New York: Harper Collins, 1996.

Zinn, Howard. *SNCC: The New Abolitionists.* Boston: Beacon Press, 1965.

Index